"She went to war and...
spellbinding tale"

★ ★ ★

GAETA, Italy—Sailors, dressed in their white uniforms, asked to shake Army Maj. Rhonda L. Cornum's hand, get her autograph and pose with her for snapshots.

"I'm sure you've heard it a million times," said Petty Officer 3rd Class Donald C. Rogers, "but your story was an inspiration."

European *Stars and Stripes*

Cornum's story filled me with strong pride. She and the servicemen and women bonded, not as two individual sexes, but as part of our military strength. They worked together for one common goal of unity—which should involve all Americans.

The book is worth reading, and when you've finished, don't be ashamed of the tears in your eyes. Be proud.

Tulsa World

[*She Went to War*] is easy reading, fast-paced and gives a unique point of view of war from the female perspective. It also gives an insight into the Middle East culture that few Westerners might ever see.

The Friday Review of Defense Literature

[Cornum's] fears and concerns are recounted, but she doesn't whine or complain. Her determination to serve is pervasive. Problems and difficulties were seen as challenges.

She Went to War may be pegged as a woman POW's story, and that is unfortunate. It is a biography of a doctor, pilot, military officer, spouse and parent who went to war and, in this instance, is a women.

Leatherneck

This book is as fast-paced and dramatic as a good adventure novel. It's an exciting, well told, war story that I found difficult to put down. More than that it is a personal look at a woman—a wife and mother—who became a hero and set a mark for women in the military. Major Cornum tells us a riveting story about death and torture—her family—being a flight surgeon—being a prisoner—and women in the military and in combat.

The Book Corner, **USA Radio Network**

Well paced and well-rounded...not only an interesting addition to the Gulf War literature, but also a significant piece of testimony on whether women should be in combat.

Fairfield, California, *Daily Republic*

Cornum describes her experiences while she and her comrades waited for the fighting to start. Her story is filled with interesting anecdotes about living conditions in the desert, the hardship of family separation, and the pre-combat anxiety that she noted throughout the battalion.

Cornum's recollections and observations tell much about her character and beliefs. In this age of cynicism, one cannot help but note her patriotism and loyalty to the Army.

BookPage

A gem of a memoir. From its first sentence it is vivid and concrete...a taut and finely rendered narrative.

The Washington Post

★ ★ ★

SHE WENT TO WAR

THE RHONDA CORNUM STORY

Rhonda Cornum
as told to
Peter Copeland

PRESIDIO
PRESS

BALLANTINE BOOKS • NEW YORK

The views expressed in this book are those of the author and do not reflect the official policy or position of the Department of the Army, Department of Defense, or the U. S. Government.

A Presidio Press Book
Published by The Random House Publishing Group

www.ballantinebooks.com

Library of Congress Cataloging-in-Publication Data

Cornum, Rhonda,
     She went to war: the Rhonda Cornum story / Rhonda Cornum as told
to Peter Copeland.
          p.   cm.
     ISBN 0-89141-507-6
     1. Cornum, Rhonda. 2. Persian Gulf War, 1991—Personal narratives, American. 3. Persian Gulf War, 1991—Participation, Female. 4. Persion Gulf War, 1991—Medical care—United States. 5. Persian Gulf War, 1991—Prisoners and prisons, Iraqi. 6. Prisoners of war—United States—Biography. 7. Prisoners of war—Iraq—Biography. 8. United States. Army—Flight surgeons—Biography.
I. Copeland, Peter. H. Title.
DS79.74.C69 1992
956.705'3—dc20

Topography by Prolmage

Cover photo © *Army Times* / Rich Mason
Printed in the United States of Amerca

First Ballantine Books edition: May 2003

This book is dedicated to the real heroes, who gave their lives trying to rescue a fellow aviator:

Sgt. Roger P. Brilinski

Sfc. William T. Butts

CW4 Philip H. Garvey

CW3 Robert G. Godfrey

Sgt. Patbouvier E. Ortiz

Preface

I t wasn't easy to convince Rhonda Cornum to tell her story. She seemed surprised anyone was even interested, and at first she laughed off the idea. Rhonda was more concerned with letting her wounds heal and getting back to jogging and riding horses. The war was behind her already, she insisted, and it was time to look forward. She finally agreed to read a few of my stories, and said later she was pleased to see I had spent time with American soldiers in the desert, and that I had a sense of humor. After much cajoling, she agreed to let me write the book. But she set up some conditions: the story had to be true, and it couldn't embarrass her or the U.S. Army. My only condition was that the book be absolutely accurate, that if she couldn't remember something, we would omit it rather than invent it.

We spent many days together trying to piece together what had happened and deciding how to tell the story. A few times we exasperated each other (and our patient spouses). I feel privileged to have been allowed inside her world, and I only wish everyone had the opportunity to meet her.

I first met Rhonda through Bill Burleigh of Scripps Howard, and I am grateful. He and Dan Thomasson have always supported me. My friend George Hager helped with careful editing and kind encouragement. I also owe a debt to all the men and women in uniform who over the past few years have helped me understand what they do and why. My deepest thanks, however, are to my toughest editor and most loyal friend, my wife Maru.

Peter Copeland

1

We were flying fast and low, so low that the pilot of our helicopter had to pull up to fly over the convoy of American trucks streaming through Iraq. I was sitting on the floor in the back of the Black Hawk, leaning against my medical gear and a stretcher we had cut down so it would fit inside the helicopter. I could see endless columns of American tanks and trucks full of water, ammo and fuel driving across the hard-packed, rocky sand. We were flying close enough to the ground that I could clearly see the faces of the soldiers below as they waved back at us. It was another chilly gray afternoon, February 27, 1991, the fourth day of the ground war against Iraq.

I had wakened that morning at about 6 A.M. in a tent so small that our cots overlapped. Rucksacks, medical bags, food, weapons and supplies were crammed into every inch of space and were covered with a fine dust of sand that made everything look frosted. We were fortunate to have a tent, though, since some of our soldiers were sleeping on the ground with nothing to protect them except a tarp thrown over the tail boom of their helicopter. The air was cold outside my sleeping bag, and I could see my breath in the faint light. We were moving north again, and I didn't know when I'd have another chance to take a bath, so I kicked my three medics out of the tent. As it turned out, it would be my last bath for some time. I grabbed two metal buckets and filled them with cold water from a tanker truck that followed our battalion. We carried the buckets to wash soldiers in case they were sprayed with deadly chemical agents, but they also were handy for heating water for baths. I walked carefully back into our tent, trying to keep the water from sloshing over the top of the buckets and onto the floor, and set one of the buckets on top of the kerosene stove.

When steam finally rose off the water into the chilly morning air, I set the bucket on the ground and got out of my clothes. When we first arrived in Saudi Arabia in August we scurried for shade to escape the broiling sun, but now the days were cold, damp, and steel gray. Naked and shivering in the middle of the tent, I curled up my toes and stepped inside the bucket. I'm only five feet, five inches tall and weigh 110 pounds, so I'm probably one of the few people in the entire U.S. Army who can actually bathe in a bucket. I even shaved my legs. It wasn't like I was going out to dinner that night, but I felt refreshed, cleaner. I guess it was the same for some of the guys who shaved every day of the war; it just made us feel better.

After I had sponged off my body as best I could, I set the other bucket at the foot of the cot and stretched out on my back to lower my head into the water. I used the kind of shampoo with conditioner in it because we never had enough water to rinse twice. There really was never enough water for anything, and the desert easily overwhelmed our attempts to keep clean. When I was more or less clean, or had at least moved the dirt around, I dried my light brown hair with a towel and brushed it straight. At home I prefer to wear my hair down on my shoulders, but for work I braid it into a ponytail, twist it around my finger, and pin it up under my helmet.

I dressed in clean underwear and a flight suit, which is a green jumpsuit that zips up the front. The uniform makes my eyes look even more green. I pulled on thick green knee socks and combat boots, scuffed and dusty after six months in the desert. The layered look was popular during those bone-chilling desert mornings: first I put on my flight jacket, then the bullet-proof flak jacket. Next I fastened my gas mask around my left hip, with one strap around the left thigh. I carried a semi-automatic 9mm Beretta pistol in a shoulder holster under my left arm so I could draw the weapon with my right hand. Last came the survival vest, which had an emergency radio in case we were shot down.

I hadn't worn my wedding ring since we arrived in Saudi Arabia, because I'd seen too many soldiers lose their fingers when their rings became caught in heavy machinery. Instead, I kept the ring with my dog tag on a chain around my neck. My husband, Kory, and I had designed and ordered matching rings when we were married eight years before. The ring was a diamond-shaped cluster of gold strands, sort of a bird's nest, with a diamond in the center.

Like me, Kory is a flight surgeon, but he's in the air force. As flight surgeons, we're doctors who have pilots for patients. The biggest difference between us is that I fly helicopters and was attached to an army Apache helicopter battalion for the war, and Kory is in a squadron of air force F-15 fighter jets. He'd told me years before that if he ever crashed at sea and they couldn't find his wedding ring, that I should have the doctors X-ray his stomach. He was going to try to swallow the ring before he went down so it wouldn't come off when his finger shrank in the cold ocean water.

Clean and dressed, I left the tent for the TOC (Tactical Operations Center) to find out exactly what we were doing that morning and when we would be leaving. As always, there was hot coffee in the TOC, which made the whole day seem better. For breakfast I ate peanut butter on crackers. The coffee tasted good. When we were married, I had stopped drinking it because Kory hates coffee breath and coffee-flavored kisses. But when I went to Saudi Arabia, he said he understood what it's like in the field, and how coffee is a key ingredient in army life, so he wouldn't mind if I started drinking it again. He was sent to the Middle East about a week after I was, but he was living at an air force base seven hundred miles away, so I kept drinking my coffee.

We were moving north and east again, deeper into Iraq, and I packed a rucksack with my essential gear to carry on the helicopter. Everything else would come later, in the massive convoy of trucks that followed us to war. My rucksack held three days' worth of MREs, which stands for Meals, Ready-to-Eat. Those are the individual field rations that come packed in heavy brown plastic pouches. By that time I'd learned to like them all. Well, most of them, anyway. I'll never eat the sticky cherry nut cakes—they're disgusting—and the oatmeal cookies come in little, sharp-edged blocks that could be used to hone a knife. The soldiers joke that "Meals, Ready-to-Eat" is really three lies in one, and that MRE actually stands for Meals Rejected by Ethiopia.

We took down the tent and packed it with the other equipment. I helped the medics get organized and launched two of them in our 2½-ton truck, known in the army as a deuce-and-a-half. Another medic would ride in a second truck. By this time in the war, traveling was the most dangerous thing that we did, and we had lost more soldiers to motor vehicle accidents than to enemy fire. I was riding in a helicopter, and we would meet later at a new position in Iraq that was closer to the Kuwaiti border.

The medics drove off, and I trudged across the sand to another tent where the coffee always was hot. The ground was grayish sand peppered with small stones as far as I could see, which was not that far. There was no horizon: the light was so flat that in the distance I could barely tell where the ground ended and the sky began. This desolate, barren place couldn't have been more different from our sunny farm in Florida with its rich green fields and little creek—but I couldn't think about home now. The weather was getting colder as we went farther north into Iraq. At least it wasn't raining again.

There was a ridge in front of our helicopter battalion, and when I climbed to the high ground there, I could see some of the other battalions. There was movement and activity everywhere, people packing and preparing to leave. The allied planes had been pounding the Iraqis for forty days and nights before we invaded Iraq, and when we flew in, many of the Iraqi soldiers were ready to surrender. So far, the war was going better than we had expected, and our intelligence estimated the fighting would end some time during the next twenty-four to forty-eight hours. We were part of the largest helicopter assault in history, but the fighting might be over before we even got into a major battle.

Everyone was anxious to move out quickly that morning and do something significant before the fighting ended. No one I knew wanted to go home without seeing action. We had been moving north quickly, however, and had seen little opposition. None of us wanted to kill Iraqis, and we were just as happy to blow up tanks and trucks with no people in them, but that was why most of us were in the military: to go to war. During the past two weeks, I had logged a lot of combat hours flying search-and-rescue helicopters and had helped capture a group of Iraqi prisoners, but real war—as compared to the way I had imagined it—seemed relatively easy for us. I hadn't slept much since the ground war began, but a steady flow of adrenaline—and strong army coffee—kept me going. All of my energy was focused on one thing: keep the pilots healthy enough to fly and destroy the enemy. No more forms to fill out, no more paper to push. Fly and fight. I loved it.

After my last cup of coffee, I walked out of the tent and bumped into CW3 Robert Gary Godfrey, a stocky thirty-two-year-old helicopter pilot. He would be the pilot in my helicopter later that day. We had gotten to know each other pretty well by that time. We always joked around and punched each other in the arm, but on this particular morning he grabbed me and gave me a big hug. I thought that was kind of odd. We were friends, but it had always been an "I-can-be-more-obnoxious-than-you" kind of friendship. Now, however, emotions were raw and close to the surface. This was no time to take friends for granted. I hugged Godfrey back, but I didn't really think about that hug until later.

It was probably 10 A.M. by the time all the trucks in the convoy were on their way. The next step was to make sure the Apaches and scout helicopters could get off the ground and move toward our next destination. Finally I climbed aboard our UH-60 Black Hawk helicopter, which is the utility and assault helicopter designed to replace the old "Huey" of Vietnam fame, and took off for our next destination: a very small abandoned airfield from which we would launch our next attacks. There we hovered in a line of helicopters for about an hour waiting for gas at the division's Forward Arming and Refueling Point (FARP). When we had a full load of fuel, we were ordered to pick up some soldiers we had just dropped off at another location. Now they wanted us to drop them somewhere else.

Our helicopter was part of the shuttle service for the rest of our 2-229th Attack Helicopter Battalion, which was attached to the 101st Airborne Division (Air Assault). During attack missions my normal job as the battalion flight surgeon was to fly behind the Apache attack helicopters. If an Apache was shot down, we'd be close enough to rescue the two pilots before they were captured, and I'd provide emergency medical care until we could evacuate them. At that point some of the aircraft had been hit but none shot down. There were no missions that morning, however, so we became a taxi service. There were eight people to be shuttled this time, and they had maps and gear and weapons. We had taken the back seats out of our helicopter and left them in Saudi to make more room, but it still was a tight fit with seven of us in the crew and eight new passengers.

We were sitting on ammo boxes and rucksacks, and someone was sitting on my lap. Godfrey was at the controls with another pilot, CW4 Philip H. Garvey. Before volunteering for Desert Shield, Garvey and Godfrey were instructor pilots at Fort Rucker, Alabama, where I worked in the Aeromedical Research Laboratory and cared for pilots. I knew them to be two of the best Black Hawk pilots around. I tend to be a backseat driver—in a car or a helicopter—but with those two I could relax and admire their skill. I've flown hundreds of times, but I still feel a delicious thrill in the pit of my stomach every time all that metal and power lifts into the sky. I watched the pilots go through the pre-flight checks and run up the engine.

Sitting in the back of the helicopter, I was wearing a flight helmet with a headset to listen to the radio. Just before takeoff I heard a call for "Bengal one-five," which was Garvey's call sign. Mine was "Bengal zero-zero," commonly known in the battalion as "Bengal Balls." I recognized the voice on the radio: it was Capt. Dave Maxwell, the assistant S-3, one of the officers in charge of operations for the battalion.

"Bengal one-five, do you have Doc Cornum on board?" I thought maybe somebody had been hurt.

"Bengal one-five, roger," one of the pilots answered.

"Do you have her stuff on board?"

"Yeah," the pilot said. Then I knew somebody had been hurt.

"Do you have gas?"

"We just left the FARP."

Maxwell explained that an air force F-16 pilot, Capt. Bill Andrews, had been shot down in Iraq. We were the closest helicopter unit that had a chance of rescuing him. The air force has Special Operations units that were assigned to rescuing downed pilots during Operation Desert Storm, and they must have known about Andrews, but apparently they weren't in the area. It was clear that if we didn't reach him soon he'd be captured. Andrews was in radio contact with one of our airborne command posts and said he had a broken leg and might have other injuries; that's why they wanted a doctor.

Our pilots asked if we should first deliver the eight passengers to their destination, but Maxwell said this was an emergency. Dump the passengers and go. Now. The soldiers scrambled to grab their gear and jump to the ground. The wind was picking up, and it whipped sand across our faces. The pilots were talking with Maxwell about the exact coordinates where Andrews was located and how to get there. Those were things I didn't need to know, so I tuned out the radio transmissions and began the mental checklist of exactly what we needed and how we'd do this mission.

A lean young soldier from our unit, Sgt. Troy Dunlap, was watching the frantic effort to unload the helicopter and prepare to fly. He was shouting above the rotors, aching to get on board. Dunlap found out we were going on a combat search-and-rescue mission, and he didn't want to miss it. Like the rest of us, he'd flown on many missions since the war began, but he seemed to miss the ones where we captured prisoners or cleared bunkers or did the things that soldiers like Sergeant Dunlap are trained to do. He's a Pathfinder, a tough infantryman specially trained for helicopter missions.

A fellow Pathfinder already on board waved for Dunlap to join us, but one of the pilots said leave him—the rotors were already turning for takeoff. The other pilot said let him come, so we leaned over and pulled Dunlap into the aircraft. I understood how Dunlap felt: this was the real thing, combat search and rescue. There was no mission that we trained for that was more important, more exciting, or more dangerous. My heart beat faster, and my stomach tightened. This was it. We were doing it for real.

The crew included two pilots, two crew chiefs who worked the door guns, the three Pathfinders, and me. The senior Pathfinder on board was Sgt. Patbouvier Ortiz, 27, who was monitoring the radio. Dunlap and the third Pathfinder wore regular Kevlar helmets without radio headsets. Unless we had something to say to the pilots, we stayed off the radio to keep the channel clear. Sergeant Ortiz and I were yelling over the noise of the rotors to plan the rescue. We knew the Iraqis would be scouring the desert for Andrews, and with a broken leg he couldn't go far. Some of us had to get off the helicopter, the Pathfinders had to secure the area from attack, and the other crew members would carry Andrews back to the helicopter. Someone had to carry the stretcher and the medical bag. We had plenty of IV fluid and a Hare Traction Splint for his leg. I was concerned that if he had internal injuries, such as a fractured pelvis, he'd be bleeding heavily. So I was prepared for everything from a minor fracture that I could splint when we got him on the helicopter, to having to resuscitate him pretty heavily on the ground.

I planned to jump off with one of the Pathfinders to see if Andrews's leg was so bad that we'd need to splint it on the ground before we put him on a stretcher, or whether I could wait to work on him in the aircraft. I knew he was conscious because he was in radio contact, but we still had to move fast to get him on board. We couldn't leave him in the desert long, and the entire crew was vulnerable while we were on the ground. If we started taking fire on the ground, our Black Hawk would leave us there while the Apaches—the heavily armed attack helicopters—suppressed the enemy fire. The Pathfinders, who took their job very seriously and always went armed to the teeth with grenades and machine guns, would try to hold off any attack. I'd work on Andrews until the Black Hawk could return.

I hoped that Andrews had parachuted away from his F-16, and landed in an empty part of the desert. (Kory and his air force buddies who fly the bigger F-15s call the deadly little F-16s "lawn darts," partly because of how they look but also because of how they crash.) The Iraqis probably were heading for the wreckage, and we were liable to land right in the middle of a nest of enemy soldiers who had just proven their skill at shooting down American aircraft.

Listening on the radio, I could tell we had two AH-64 Apache attack helicopters flying with us for protection. They were armed with Hellfire missiles, Hydra 70 rockets, and 30mm chain guns in the nose. In the Black Hawk, we just had two small machine guns mounted in the side doors. The Apache, the most sophisticated helicopter in the world, looks like a big metal dragonfly bristling with sensors and antennae and hung with missiles and rockets. They can be flown with special optical equipment that allows the pilots to see at night while looking through a monocle connected to an infrared camera outside the aircraft. It can be terribly disorienting to learn to fly, and back home at Fort Rucker I was doing research on how to improve the pilots' ability to operate the optical systems.

I recognized the voices of the Apache drivers—they all were my patients back home and most of them were my friends. I was glad to hear that one of them was Lance McElhiney, arguably the best Apache pilot in the army and certainly my best friend in the world. He could be wild and crazy at times, but when he flew, all that energy and wildness was channeled into manipulating the helicopter, turning a very complicated piece of machinery into a lethal weapons system. His confidence, at the controls and in everything, was contagious. When my fourteen-year-old daughter, Regan, had worried about me going to war, my husband told her, "Don't worry, Lance will be there and he won't let anything happen to Mother." That was good enough for Regan.

Overhead an air force Airborne Warning and Control System (AWACS) radar plane, call sign "Bulldog," was going to direct us toward the downed pilot. The AWACS, one of the unarmed jets packed with radar and radio equipment that had been orchestrating the air war for six weeks, would fly orbits high above Saudi Arabia, staying in contact with Andrews on the ground and us in the air. We needed directions because the weather was getting worse, and the blowing sand made it hard to see. Thick black smoke and choking soot from burning oil wells in nearby Kuwait had darkened the sky early. The pilots debated whether to use their night vision goggles, even though it wasn't yet four in the afternoon.

I heard the Black Hawk's turbine engine whine and the rotor picked up speed. The helicopter vibrated and jumped off the ground, creating a dust bowl of sand beneath us. We slipped effortlessly across the desert, just above the ground. We always flew very low because it made us a smaller target. Some of our helicopters had already taken fire, and the pilots were cautious. Now we were heading deeper into enemy territory. For the first fifteen minutes both Apaches, loaded with fuel and "Hellfire heavy," were behind us. Then Lance moved out in front, and the other attack helicopter stayed behind. We were protected in the middle between the two gunships, hurtling over the desert at close to 130 knots.

I remember crossing over a convoy and seeing American vehicles with inverted Vs painted on the sides and tops. Some of the vehicles were flying pieces of orange and yellow cloth to indicate they were friendly forces. We waved to the troops bundled up in their bulky chemical gear, and they waved back at us. The air was filled with smoke and soot from oil fires. The door gunners were keeping close watch on the ground below, their hands firmly on the two 7.62mm machine guns that pointed out the side doors.

About forty-five seconds after we passed over the last American vehicle, and without any warning, green tracers began streaking up at us from the ground, while I heard the crack-crack of weapons firing. The empty desert below us erupted with fire and white flashes of light. It was as if we were a lawn mower that had run over a beehive, and the bees were coming up to sting. Sergeant Ortiz, the lead Pathfinder, took my head and slammed it to the floor, and in a second all three Pathfinders instinctively were half lying on me with their weapons ready. I almost laughed at their reaction: it would have been a good way to cover me in a foxhole, but we were in a helicopter. I'm sure their hearts were in the right place, but the rounds were coming up at us from the ground, so I was actually shielding them. The Pathfinders were very protective of me because that was their mission: protect the doctor and the patient. We didn't have the patient yet, so they worried about protecting me.

The two door gunners—SSgt. Daniel Stamaris and Sfc. William T. Butts—were fighting back and spraying machine-gun fire at the ground.

I heard the sharp pop-pop-pop and clank of metal, and smelled acrid burning gunpowder inside the helicopter. The shell casings were jumping out of our smoking black door guns like brass popcorn, and one hit me in the face. It felt hot against my skin. One of the pilots shouted over the radio, "We're taking fire." Looking back, I'm sure he was informing the AWACS plane about what was happening, but at that moment, pressed to the floor under the weight of the Pathfinders, all I could think was, No kidding.

We heard the rattling Iraqi antiaircraft guns following us across the sky, and the rounds began tearing through the metal tail boom and the fuselage and rocking the aircraft. I clutched the floor in front of me, not knowing if a bullet would come ripping up through the helicopter and into my body. It would only take one round, and we were flying through a wall of lead, as if we had been caught in a sudden cloud-burst of bullets. The pilots tried to get away by breaking sharply to the left. The army would call it an "evasive maneuver," but we call it "yanking and banking." The helicopter was still just a few feet off the ground, but I never saw any Iraqis, only their tracers and the muzzle flashes.

I felt something big hit the aircraft and I knew it wasn't doing well. The engine strained and the fuselage shook and shimmied. Then Garvey yelled, "We're going in!" I was trying to make myself smaller on the floor during the shooting. The firefight probably lasted only twelve seconds, but there was a big adrenaline rush that made my brain work faster so time seemed slower. I remember having time to hold on, knowing we were going to crash. I was thinking, I wonder if this is it, is this the end? What will it be like? I don't even remember being scared; it was more like curiosity. I took hold of something on the door frame and felt the aircraft shuddering. We were still banked to the left when the left nose hit the sand, flattening, and then twenty thousand pounds of aircraft went end over end in a ball of flying metal and gear and spinning rotors. Everything went black.

I was lying on my back with a big piece of the wreck on my chest pinning me to the ground. It seemed like it was completely dark already, but it couldn't have been because it was still afternoon. The air was chilly, but I didn't feel cold. My head was lying to the left, my arms were at my sides and I was very comfortable, very peaceful. I had no desire to move. Nothing hurt as I lay motionless. The gray sky above me was empty and quiet. In fact it was absolutely still. There was no more shooting, no rotor sounds, no yelling or scratchy radio traffic; there was nothing. It was just still, and my first thought was that maybe I was dead and this was an out-of-body experience. I could see, or rather I could feel, this scene on the desert floor: a big piece of the fuselage and me pinned under it

I was relaxed, calm, nestled in the sand, until I glanced farther to the left toward an embankment and saw a yellow flame. The fear was like a spark beneath me: Fire. Fuel lines. Explosion coming. I wasn't totally convinced that I was alive, but if I was, there was no way I was going to die in a post-crash fire. That was the only thing that motivated me to try to move; otherwise I could have stayed there forever. I didn't think to call out for help. I was on my own, alone. The pile of broken metal was so quiet that I was sure I was the only survivor. And if the enemy was nearby, I didn't want to call out and alert him that I was alive.

I had to get out by myself, but I couldn't move my arms, presumably because they were pinned. I took stock of what I could use to escape from under the fuselage. The only part of my body that still worked reasonably well was my left leg. I pulled the good leg toward me and straightened it again to push the sand away. I pushed and pushed to clear the sand from underneath my right leg. Luckily we had crashed on sand and not on rocks, so the ground was soft. I dug and scraped at the sand until there was a shallow hole underneath me that freed my legs from the fuselage. With my body in the slight hole, I could move my right leg a little, but my knee hurt badly. I didn't mind, though, because if it hurt, I figured it was still connected, and it was another sign that I was alive.

The flames flickered in the corner of my eyes. Keep digging. All I could think about was, I have to get out from under the helicopter. I dug the heel of my left boot deeper into the ground and pushed away more sand. When I was clear enough to move, I tried to turn over and crawl out, but I couldn't turn or crawl. My arms were no longer stuck under the fuselage, but they wouldn't respond. I couldn't move them at all. I'm hurt worse than I thought, I realized. Things are broken. Still, there was no pain, just numbness as the shock of the crash froze the nerves.

I was wiggling around on my left side trying to get out and away from the helicopter when I looked up and saw four or five Iraqi soldiers standing over me. They were wearing good uniforms and helmets and carrying AK-47s, the Soviet-made assault rifle. They had a professional way about them, and I recognized them as members of the

Republican Guard. One of them, without saying anything, reached down and grabbed my right arm. He pulled hard to get me up, and the pain shot through me and came out my mouth in a piercing scream. It wasn't even the pain that got to me as much as the sound: a crunching noise or the sound of grinding teeth, a sound not so much that I heard but felt. My arm was broken between the shoulder and the elbow, but it wasn't a displaced fracture. At least not until the Iraqi pulled apart the pieces of bone.

The men were talking among themselves in Arabic. I couldn't understand the words, but it seemed they were trying to decide what to do with me. A couple of them swarmed over me like ants, taking off my pistol, my survival vest with the radio, my flak jacket, and my helmet. I stood still, looking at the ground. When they took off my green helmet, my hair came tumbling down. That's when they realized I was female. There was a flurry of comment about it, and they talked louder and faster for a minute, but I couldn't understand them. I stared straight ahead, standing with my weight on my left leg since my right leg hurt when I tried to stand on it. I was just a few feet from the wreckage. The helicopter had disintegrated and pieces were thrown everywhere, but I didn't see any fire. The flames I'd seen must have been from a nearby campfire or from oil wells burning in the distance. Or maybe I just imagined them.

One of the Iraqis grabbed my arm again and tried to drag me forward. I yelled sharply in pain, and he dropped my arm. The arm flopped in front of me like a piece of meat, completely out of my control. Then he grabbed a bunch of my hair, and pulled me along with him across the sand. I had no choice but to follow, trying to keep my balance. It sounds like caveman behavior, but actually it was far better than trying to take me by the arm. I realized that not one arm, but both of them, were broken between the elbows and shoulders, and they were swinging uselessly beside me like sticks tied to my shoulders with string. They reminded me of horses I had seen with their legs broken so badly that only the skin was holding on the hooves, like rocks in a sock. I stumbled along in the sand, trying not to fall but unsure of my right knee. It felt like a busted hinge on a broken door, and I thought it might collapse under me. If I fell, I couldn't protect myself, and I'd hurt my arms even more.

What if my arms weren't just broken? Oh God, what if they're severed? What if they're being held on by my flight suit? No, they hurt too much.

They must be attached. Thank goodness for the pain. I imagined there were open fractures beneath the thick sleeves of the flight suit and I was losing blood. I felt weak and nauseous, which must have been caused by a lack of blood, but I couldn't see any serious open wounds. There was blood on one hand from a cut and I knew there was blood above my eye, but not enough to make me feel so dizzy. I still wasn't sure how badly I was injured.

The sky was growing darker. The Iraqis didn't have flashlights, but they obviously knew where we were going. I wasn't going fast enough, and one of them kicked me in the butt, making me lurch forward and almost knocking me down. I stumbled but didn't cry out or yell. Keep control. Don't succumb. I recovered my balance and kept walking, my eyes straight ahead. The soldiers were excited about having a prisoner, and they were saying things to me in guttural Arabic, a language I'd always considered pretty. But now their shouted words and harsh invectives didn't sound pretty at all.

I wasn't afraid at that point. There had been times in the past when I'd thought about being captured and tried to imagine what it would be like, but there wasn't really any way to prepare for the experience. Actually, I'd always thought it more likely that I'd be killed rather than captured. I'm not overly pessimistic; it's just that usually air force or navy pilots eject from their high-flying jets, parachute to the ground, and are captured. In the army we don't even wear parachutes in a helicopter because we fly so low. If you managed to somehow eject, you'd be decapitated by the rotor, so in the army we "ride in" the wrecks. If you crash in a fast-moving helicopter, there is little chance of surviving to be captured by the enemy.

Crew members frequently survive in slower-moving accidents, however, and I remember talking to my army pilots about this before the war. They weren't afraid of death; they were afraid of landing behind enemy lines or having engine trouble that led to being captured. All the pilots had heard stories about what the Iraqis would do to the "infidels" if they caught us, stories of torture and abuse. Back where we lived in Saudi before the start of the ground war, we'd seen the Iraqi pictures of captured American pilots. They'd been forced to make videos denouncing the war. We'd also heard about the special abuse reserved for the women of Kuwait. Some Iraqi soldiers had behaved like animals, raping and sexually torturing Arab and foreign women living there.

Back home before the war, Kory and I had talked about something bad happening to one of us, but we always thought he was in more danger because he flew jets. From his base in Florida, he often flew F-15s far out over the ocean, and he could have been lost at sea in a mid-air collision or if something happened to the aircraft. The likelihood of me being captured or killed doing research at the Aeromedical Laboratory at Fort Rucker was pretty low. I had thought occasionally about dying, especially when we deployed to Saudi Arabia and were preparing for war. I did that on purpose, though; it was part of my psychological survival plan. In any dangerous situation, I always try to imagine the worst thing that could happen to me. Then whatever does happen has to be better, or at least no worse.

I'd talked about dying in my final letters to my family, just before February 24, when we launched the air assault north and west of Kuwait to cut off the Republican Guard. We only half-jokingly called the mission the "Air Assault to Hell," and we knew it could be dangerous. I wanted my family to know that I went to war because the battalion wanted me to go, and I wanted to be with them. I wrote my grandparents that I was proud of what I was doing, and that if anything happened to me, they should remember that I chose to be here. I told my sister that if something bad happened, she should make sure my parents didn't do anything embarrassing. My worst fear was that they would shame me or the army, that they would be hysterical, try to sue the government, or say I shouldn't have been in combat because I was a doctor or a woman or just because I was their daughter. All I hoped was that my parents would take their folded American flag gracefully after the funeral, say "Thank you," and quietly hang it on the wall somewhere. As things turned out, they didn't exactly follow my plan.

I'd been writing to my daughter, Regan, every day since the air war began on January 17, but once the ground campaign began, I wanted to send her a special letter. She was only fourteen, but I wanted her to understand what I was doing and why. During all those months in Saudi Arabia, not having her with me was the only hole in my life. Regan was born when I was still in college, and we had grown up together. She already was bigger than I am, and was a pretty good fullback on her soccer team at school. She was at that stage in life where she felt she had to choose between wearing makeup and playing sports with the boys, and for now, she was leaning toward sports. I was so proud of her, and my love for her was beyond any words I could find to put on paper.

The Iraqis led me toward a hole that opened in the earth like the shadowed entrance to a coal mine. In the fading light of the darkening evening I could see sandbag stairs leading down into an underground bunker. This network of bunkers was the reason we had not seen any Iraqi soldiers from the helicopter. They had been completely protected when firing at us as we flew overhead. The passageway was fairly wide, but there were soldiers lining both sides of the stairs. Two guards went ahead of me and two followed behind, pushing me step by step through the gauntlet of soldiers. They jeered and shouted at me, but no one tried to touch me as I slowly negotiated the stairs with a bad leg and two broken arms. I didn't know what the men were saying, but it was clear they weren't happy to see me. I had the feeling they were gloating because they had just shot us down, and we had crashed right on top of their bunkers.

The bunker was very well made, about fourteen steps underground. If they had wanted to the Iraqis could have stayed there defending it forever. There was a kerosene lantern below, and as my eyes adjusted to the faint light, I could see that the walls had been scraped out of the earth with a backhoe. It smelled of dirt and men and sweat. I didn't see any other members of my crew, and I assumed I was the only survivor. At the bottom of the stairs, there was a junior Iraqi officer, probably a lieutenant, sitting at a wooden table, staring at me and the procession of jeering soldiers. He questioned one of my guards and then said to me in heavily accented English, "Who are you?"

"Major Rhonda Cornum."

I was not going to keep my name secret, since it was printed on the name tag on my flight suit. I noticed that my dog tag chain was partially out of my flight suit, and I remembered my wedding ring threaded on the chain. I thought about trying to swallow the ring, remembering what Kory and I had talked about, but I couldn't move my arms at all.

The lieutenant ignored me, and talked to his men. One of them loosely tied my hands in front of me with a thin piece of rope. They searched me again and took my journal and the little camera I kept in the right leg pocket of my flight suit. I felt bad because the camera actually belonged to my daughter, who had let me borrow it to take to Saudi Arabia. I had some good pictures of our unit taking Iraqi prisoners on that roll, so it was probably a good thing they didn't have anywhere to process the prints.

The lieutenant barked an order at his men. I didn't understand, but they started to move me toward the stairs. The guards pushed me up the sandbag stairs again, past the same group of soldiers who had nothing better to do than jeer at me. I had to walk slowly because my knee wasn't working well as I left the warmth and yellow lantern light of the bunker and stepped back into the cold air and flat gray light above ground.

It was then that I saw Sergeant Dunlap, the young Pathfinder who had desperately wanted to get on the helicopter. He was in the center of a circle of ten Iraqi soldiers, kneeling down in the sand, looking at the ground in front of him. His hands were tied behind his back. My hands were tied in front, which was a good thing, really, because it kept my arms from flopping. I didn't know Dunlap well at all; we had spoken maybe fifty words since coming over to Saudi, mostly of the "Good morning" or "Yes, ma'am" variety. He'd never been one of my patients; he must never have gotten sick.

I'd known some of the other crew members on board well, such as Sergeant Ortiz. We had gone on many missions together, and just before we deployed to Iraq, I'd done a physical on him so he could apply to flight school. Godfrey had given me that big hug just this morning. There were no jokes between us then, none of the usual wisecracks, just a genuine hug. Godfrey, Ortiz, and the others must be dead.

I'd never even seen Dunlap without his helmet. Now I saw his close-cropped haircut, scraggly blond mustache, and big eyes wide with fear. He looked strange without his helmet, vulnerable. I was relieved to find another American, and it didn't matter if I knew him well. Right then he felt like a friend. I felt responsible for him, even though I was in no condition to be responsible for anybody.

Dunlap and I didn't try to say anything, but the Iraqis kept yelling, "No talking!" One of the guards led me into the circle of men and pushed me alongside Dunlap. The guard put his hand heavily on my shoulder and tried to shove me to the ground. I resisted for a moment because I was afraid I would fall on my bad knee, but then I carefully went down on my left knee and balanced precariously. Dunlap glanced over at me and gave me a little smile. I nudged him, as much as I could nudge him with my arms broken, and I said something stupid, something motherly: "It's going to be okay." He smiled weakly. Dunlap was almost young enough to be my son. He was twenty; I was thirty-six. I was a doctor and an officer; he was an enlisted man. I couldn't really do much for him, but I felt responsible and I wanted to make him feel better. "No talking!" one of the Iraqis yelled in English.

There were two soldiers standing behind us, both with rifles pointed at our uncovered heads. I could feel the cold metal barrel poking me in the back of the neck. The Iraqis were having an animated discussion, and it seemed they were trying to decide what to do with us. This was the first time I was truly afraid. It was then that I realized we would be killed.

The war had been going badly for them, and many of their comrades had died. Some had been buried in bunkers just like these when American B-52 strikes turned the underground shelters into sandy tombs. The American enemy had been elusive, distant, airborne. The Americans dropped their bombs from high above, never within range of Iraqi small arms, and flew back to the safety of Saudi Arabia. Now these men had a chance for revenge. The soldiers who had found us could have saved themselves the trouble and killed us at the crash site, but they'd waited for instructions from their commander. The lieutenant must have ordered them to kill us.

My head was lowered, and my hair had fallen in my face. I couldn't see out of my left eye; it was smashed shut and my hair was stuck to it with matted blood. My right eye swept back and forth across the ground in front of me, and I saw pebbles on the ground, small rocks with jagged edges. The air was cool around us. One of the guards spoke a few words of English and he seemed to say, "Kill them! Kill them!" I waited for the click of metal and the explosion. The moment seemed to last forever. My pain had vanished with the fear. My last thought was, At least it won't hurt.

Without warning, a strong hand grabbed me by the hair and jerked me to my feet. Another soldier roughly pulled up Dunlap. The ring of shouting Iraqis parted, and they marched Dunlap across the sand to a small civilian pickup truck, with me following. What are they doing? Maybe we're not going to be killed. At least for now. It seemed the Iraqis couldn't decide what to do with us, and the discussion continued. I followed quietly; there was nothing else to do. We were prisoners, but maybe we were being allowed to live.

I was badly injured, but I knew I'd heal eventually. The crash had been so devastating that I should have died then, and I regarded every minute I was alive as a gift. The Iraqis could have killed us easily when they found us at the crash site, but they chose not to. Then in the circle of men, a slight pressure on a single trigger would have been enough to kill us, but we had been spared. It was just enough good luck for me to grab on to and hold. I vowed to survive.

The soldiers pushed Dunlap into the truck first. I walked to the back and put my left leg up on the bumper, trying to ease myself into the truck. But someone pushed me up from behind and hurled me into the truck. I couldn't catch myself, and I rattled down on my shoulder and let out a raw scream of pain. Dunlap tried to catch me and strained against the bonds that held his arms; I could see the anguish in his dirt-streaked face. Two guards got in and sat down next to us. I managed to sit up in the bed of the truck and straighten my bad leg. It was horribly frustrating to not be able to control my own body. Everything I had done in my life until then had been active. I didn't make a living sitting around; I made a living doing things. Now I was helpless.

As the truck lurched along, I concentrated on keeping my arms forward and slowly walking my fingers together until I could hook them in my lap. If I could do that, then my arms were still attached, and I had some control. It meant I had circulation to the arms and that the nerves had not been severed. Well, maybe this problem is fixable after all, I thought. With every bump on the pitted road, I was tossed around in the bed of the truck, banging my knee and arms and wincing in pain. It was excruciating if my arms swung lose, so I kept my fingers locked together in front of me. I bit my tongue and vowed not to scream. Dunlap was watching me, and without saying anything because the two guards in back didn't allow us to talk, he put his strong legs on top of mine so I wouldn't bounce. I smiled a thank you.

As long as I didn't move anything, my arms didn't hurt. The brain is very good at knocking out pain when it's not useful. I was withdrawn, pulled inside of myself, concentrating on staying conscious because it would have been so easy to have just given up and relaxed, drifting off into sleep. Stay awake. Remain an active participant. Stay with Dunlap. Mostly, I didn't want to be unconscious with the Iraqis. I felt them staring at me, their dark eyes raking over my body. I didn't know if I was afraid of what they might do to me, or if I wanted to present an image of strength, but it was very important to concentrate on being conscious. I didn't have much energy left to expend on anything else.

2

I almost missed the call for Operation Desert Shield because I was at the feed store near our house. Home for us is an eighty-acre farm with a little creek outside of a small town called DeFuniak Springs in northwestern Florida. We have forty acres of the best pasture in Walton County, forty acres of woods, a creek running through the whole farm, and a small pond that swells into a lake during flood season. It's as close as we could find to somewhere between my work at Fort Rucker in Alabama and Kory's work at Eglin Air Force Base in Florida. Our nearest neighbor is a mile away, but for company we have five horses, a dog that's mostly arctic wolf, and five cats. The fields were deep green that summer, the creek was low, and the days were hot and sticky.

When Saddam Hussein invaded Kuwait on August 2, 1990, the news spread quickly through the military, and all of us wondered what, if anything, the United States would do in response. It was hard to imagine at the time that the United States was ready to go to war thousands of miles from our shores, but President Bush was talking tough and Saddam was a proven menace. If there were going to be a U.S. military response, most people I knew in the military wanted to be part of it. But none of us knew who would be going. The day after the invasion, I was speaking at a special operations safety conference in Texas. Beepers were going off, and people spent most of the conference talking on the telephones in the hallway, trying to figure out what was happening.

Six days after the invasion, I was still traveling, now on my way home from Fort Hood, Texas. I was sitting in a bar in the Dallas–Fort Worth Airport with Moshe Cohen, the first (and still only) Apache squadron commander in the Israeli Air Force, and like the rest of the world, we were glued to CNN. Because of the war, Moshe was leaving his training at Fort Hood early to get back to Israel. He is something of an Israeli war hero, and we talked about what it's like to go to war. Since he had more experience than I did, I mostly listened. One thing that stuck in my mind was his insistence that if I went to war as a doctor, I had to stick close to the pilots during combat. "It's even more important than in training," he told me. "Don't leave them out there alone." On the flight home I wondered what was in store for me and Kory and our friends, most of whom were operational pilots in the army and the air force.

I arrived home late that night, and at our little farm, nothing had changed. There were lots of rumors about units deploying, Kory said, but nothing definite. He went to work as usual the next morning, and I drove into town to buy feed for our horses. The phone was ringing when I drove back into the yard. It was Kory calling to tell me that Lt. Col. Bill Bryan, commander of the 2-229th Attack Helicopter Battalion, was calling everywhere—the research lab, our house, and finally Kory's office—trying to locate me. I wasn't sure what Bryan wanted, but I felt my heart beat a little faster. I wasn't the assigned flight surgeon for that unit, but I knew most of the pilots and I'd visited them at least monthly when they did seven months of Apache training at Fort Hood. Lieutenant Colonel Bryan had taken command only a month before, and I knew him fairly well. He had finished the Apache course early in the spring, and I knew all the Apache students.

The battalion normally has fewer than three hundred soldiers, nineteen Apache attack helicopters, three Black Hawk utility helicopters and thirteen OH-58s, little two-seaters we call "Sky Scooters." I knew the battalion was likely to be tapped for Saudi, mostly because the Apaches are designed to kill tanks, and Saddam Hussein had a lot of tanks. Lieutenant Colonel Bryan had called Kory on an unsecure telephone line, so he couldn't say what was happening, but Kory seemed to know something anyway. I was excited and wanted to know what was up, but now Kory and I were on an open line, and Kory kept saying, "Just call Lieutenant Colonel Bryan."

His phone was always busy, and it took forever to get through to Lieutenant Colonel Bryan. In between my attempts to call him, my secretary called from the lab to say Lieutenant Colonel Bryan was looking for me. Finally I got him on the phone. All he asked was, "Do you want to go?" It wasn't, "Do you want to go to Saudi Arabia?" or, "Do you want to go to the Persian Gulf?" Just, "Do you want to go?" I knew what he meant. Without even thinking or weighing the pros and cons, I said, "Yes!"

My decision to go to war had been made long before, probably when I chose to go to the military medical school instead of a civilian school. There were plenty of reasons for wanting to go to Saudi Arabia: as the battalion flight surgeon, I'd be a staff officer under Lieutenant Colonel Bryan and in charge of the medics. My job would be to care for the 300 people in the battalion and to design and execute a plan for treating our casualties in a war. I thought I could do a good job as a doctor, as an officer, and I honestly believed that more people would come back alive if I went. If a commander such as Lieutenant Colonel Bryan thought his unit would do better with me there, that was a great compliment.

I didn't think to ask Kory. He knew me well enough to know that I would go. He would have gone in a heartbeat. That's part of the reason we're so happily married—we feel the same way about the big things: duty, honor, country, and loyalty. When Kory came home from work that night, I told him the news. He was excited for me and hoped to go himself. His squadron of F-15 fighters had been alerted, but then was taken off alert. That was the situation throughout the military: no one knew who was going or when.

Regan was spending the summer with her father in North Dakota. I called her father, my first husband, and he said that "with world events the way they were" maybe it would be better if Regan stayed with him for a while longer. We were trying to be vague because, again, it was an open telephone line, but I told him that if I was going anywhere, then I definitely wanted to see Regan before I left and to send her home. When she arrived at the house a few days later, I told her I was going to Saudi Arabia. She wasn't at all surprised; she had been watching television and expected as much from her mother. Regan was only fourteen, but she was a very patriotic girl and had been following the news about the Middle East. She would have thought that I was a wimp if I stayed home. Everyone, even my own daughter, expected me to go to Saudi Arabia, and I would have found some way to get there, even if I hadn't been asked.

Getting ready meant doing laundry so I would have clean uniforms, swimming one last time in our pool, and taking care of one hundred details around the house and at work. We didn't know when we were leaving, or how long we would be gone, but we expected to depart within a week. The next day I went to Fort Rucker to process through, get my shots, check my will, and make sure my pay checks were being directly deposited in the bank. The research lab where I worked was not very excited about me going, but the commander understood my need to go with the unit. I met the three medics already assigned to the battalion and two additional hospital medics who had volunteered to go as well. I made a wish list of the things we would need in the desert. Colleagues who had served in Vietnam told me to take all the medical equipment and supplies I could think of, because once we got there it would be hard to find anything. I was fortunate that the hospital commander had been a flight surgeon in Vietnam and understood the need to support us. Not every unit had that kind of help.

Driving home that night from Fort Rucker, the reality finally hit me. Getting ready for the deployment had been busy and exciting up to that point, but now I realized what I was about to do. I was going to war. I might be killed in Saudi Arabia. I might never again see Kory or Regan, my farm, the horses. I guess I was scared, but everybody thought I was too macho to be scared. I was overwhelmed by the enormity of the responsibility I felt to go, and I knew it probably would be the only time in my life that I would be called upon to go to war. My biggest fear was of failure, and I thought it was important to do well.

I had been on an adrenaline high since Lieutenant Colonel Bryan called, and as I processed out, people at the lab kept asking, "Are you scared?" I said no because I didn't recognize it for a long time, and because it wouldn't do any good to tell them how I felt. Everyone expected me to be tough, and I thought, basically, that I *was* tough. But that night driving in the darkness, I clutched the wheel of my 1981 Volkswagen and did not feel very tough. I stared straight ahead into the night and bawled my eyes out, all the way home. It must have been good for me, and it was the last time I would cry until I returned to America seven months later.

I moved into the bachelor officers' quarters at Fort Rucker, since our house was more than an hour from the post, and everyone in the battalion was supposed to be ready to leave for Saudi on a moment's notice. Kory and Regan drove up to the base every evening, and we had dinner together and spent the night. We woke up at four each morning, said goodbye as if it were the last time, and they raced back to Florida so Kory could drop Regan at school and get to work on time. Then by afternoon, I would learn we didn't have airlift yet, and we weren't going to Saudi Arabia that day. Kory and Regan would drive back for dinner and spend the night again.

It was draining emotionally, and I felt more tired from the strain than I did from my actual work. There was not much for me to do once we had packed our gear and all the medical equipment I could find. We just sat and waited for orders. Finally, on the morning of August 22, I said goodbye to my family in the parking lot once more, and this time it really was the last time. That night when we loaded onto the bus, I was glad Kory and Regan were not there, because the parking lot was filled with too many soldiers, kids and wives and sweethearts, all crying and hugging, and it was awful. My thoughts were already seven thousand miles away in Saudi Arabia.

When we left Fort Rucker, I carried one pair of blue jeans, a t-shirt, sneakers, and a few pairs of shorts so I could run. I had all my military gear, including three flight suits and two sets of desert BDUs, which are the fatigues with the chocolate-chip camouflage pattern. I had the flight surgeon's handbook, a few books on treating and teaching trauma, a case of Diet Coke, and some toiletries. I taped a picture of Regan and Kory to the inside cover of my journal.

The way I imagined our arrival in Saudi Arabia, we would be fighting as soon as we got off the airplane. It was exciting, and I would be lying if I said I wasn't pumped up, but mostly I felt responsible for the emotional and physical well-being of all those people who expected me to know how to care for them. The younger soldiers looked to me because I was senior and had been in the army a long time. I was feeling confident, and I knew it was important to project confidence.

One advantage of being a doctor trained in the military was that I wasn't so afraid of chemical warfare, which was the big fear when we first sent people to Saudi. As far as causes of casualties were concerned, I was more afraid of the heat. The chemical suits we use provide good protection from chemicals, but they're so bulky and hot to wear that soldiers would have died from heat stroke, not chemicals, if we'd had to wear them in August. One of the projects I researched as the chief of the Crew Life Support Branch of the lab was pilot performance wearing the suits in various climates. I knew exactly what was going to happen: people were going to cook. It's terribly inconvenient to wear the suits, but if people are well trained, few will die in a chemical attack.

They might die because they're wearing all that clumsy gear and can't see and fly into a telephone pole or a sand dune, but they won't die from chemicals. The soldiers were afraid because it was something they didn't practice frequently, and they didn't understand how chemical agents or the antidotes worked. While they trained occasionally with the chemical suits, they had never seen the chemicals actually used in the field. The news media exaggerated the threat, which scared everyone even more.

We drove to Fort Benning in Georgia and spent the night before flying to Westover, Massachusetts, the next day. Then the airplane broke down, so we had time to give ourselves a going away party. We went to the officers' club, and I danced with Rucie Moore, one of the Apache pilots, and a few of the enlisted guys bought me tequila shooters. There was plenty to drink, and some people were too sick to fly the next day. That was one of the contingencies I had planned for, and I gave them a little Phenergan, which is an antinausea medication that also helped them sleep.

We flew seven and a half hours to Torrejon Air Base in Spain and spent the night sitting in a hangar. I sent postcards to Kory, Regan, and my mother. There was a bulletin board in the hangar filled with the new Middle East addresses of the people who had already passed through on the way to Saudi Arabia. It gave me some idea of just how big this deployment was going to be, and I found several familiar names, including a friend from medical school. We left Spain in large groups early on August 25, and I arrived in Saudi Arabia at 1:30 P.M. that day.

When I stepped off the plane in Dhahran, the Saudi city on the Persian Gulf, it was more desolate and hot than I thought any place could be. As we climbed off the plane, we thought maybe we were standing in the jet blast, but the blustery hot air seemed to be following us around the tarmac. Then we realized it wasn't exhaust at all, but hot wind from the desert. Mostly the heat was dry as a blast furnace, but when the wind shifted, the humidity from the Persian Gulf covered everything in a smothering blanket of moist air. The air was thick and cottony, something palpable, a presence you couldn't take for granted.

We moved off the ramp to an open air hangar and dropped our gear. The battalion was coming over on twenty different flights, and the first arrivals told us where to get food and water. No one knew where we were going from Dhahran, but first we had to put the helicopters back together, having taken them apart for shipment on the transport planes. The sun was so hot that it burned your hand just to touch one of the helicopters during the day. So for the first forty-eight hours, we did almost nothing during daylight except try to adjust to the heat, and we decided to reassemble the aircraft at night. The heat was still bad, and the flight line simmered from being baked all day, but the scorching sun was gone for a few hours, replaced by huge floodlights.

Giant C-5 and the smaller C-141 transport planes were landing every few minutes, all day and all night, unloading tons of gear, vehicles, and more and more soldiers, who quickly overwhelmed the facilities at the Saudi airport and air base. The Saudis ignored us and tried to pretend we weren't there—that was when the two countries were still testing the limits of our cooperation—but the British Aerospace employees who worked at the base kindly let us use their bathrooms and borrow a fire hose for showers.

When we got the first UH-60 Black Hawk flying, Lieutenant Colonel Bryan, Capt. George Hodge, the executive officer of the battalion, and I flew to King Fahd International Airport, a sprawling, still-unfinished complex under construction forty-five miles from Dhahran. That was to be our home for the next four months. Lieutenant Colonel Bryan and I had a very good relationship, and he was a terrific boss for me; he was confident I knew what to do and how to do it, and I tried hard to make sure his confidence was justified.

The Black Hawk circled for a few minutes above the air base at Dhahran, and we saw the beautiful, emerald water of the Persian Gulf and the immaculate royal palace surrounded by high walls on the coast. Just seconds after leaving the busy, fairly modern cities of Dammam and Al-Khubar, we were flying over empty desert. No roads, no houses, no fences, just gleaming white sand punctuated by an occasional palm tree or bush. I saw my first camels that day: big, gangly beasts walking lazily across the sand. The Saudi cities seemed to rise out of the sand, giving an illusion of protection from the environment. The Saudi men we saw wore comfortable white robes, but the women were covered from head to toe in oppressive black robes. The soldiers called them BMOs—Black Moving Objects.

Even flying fast and high above the desert, the air was no cooler than on the ground. The hot wind pushed its way through the open helicopter, stinging us with sand and making me slightly woozy. Nothing could have prepared us for these conditions, not the desert at the National Training Center in California or even the training grounds in Yuma, Arizona.

After a few minutes in the air, we spotted the one empty road that led to an enormous complex of new buildings and some of the longest runways I'd ever seen. On top of the cement parking garage was a huge, gleaming mosque and a gold dome topped by a beautiful golden crescent. I noticed a few A-10 tank-killer planes on one side of the runway and a battalion of Apache helicopters, but little else. There were no guards that we could see, and no one greeted us when we landed. We wandered into the half-finished terminal, where tools and building supplies were spilled everywhere, and found staff members from the 101st Aviation Brigade. Together we began to prepare for the arrival of the battalion.

The mosque on the third floor of the parking garage was off limits to us as non-believers. Technically it was illegal in Saudi Arabia to practice any religion except Islam. Not long after we arrived, however, the chaplains began to hold weekly services for all the major religions in the military. Our services were always well attended by the many foreign workers—from Korea, the Philippines, Pakistan, and around the world—who lived and worked in Saudi Arabia but weren't allowed to practice their religions.

Construction continued on the airport, and it was crawling with foreign engineers, contractors, and laborers. The Saudis insisted that nothing unusual was happening in their country and tried to pretend it was business as usual. It seemed to us that they didn't want to recognize that Saddam's tanks were just a few hours to the north, and that war could break out any day, any hour. The only road from occupied Kuwait to the main Saudi oil fields passed by this airport, and Saddam's men would have had to fight their way through us. Still, the legions of foreigners hired by the Saudis poured cement and worked to finish the airport. So what if the airport was being occupied by several U.S. Air Force wings and the entire 101st Air Assault Division?

We returned to Dhahran to meet the rest of the battalion as they trickled in during the next week. The first thing I told them was to drink at least ten bottles of water a day to get used to the heat and dryness. The First Tactical Fighter Wing from Langley Air Force Base had arrived in Dhahran with an Air Transportable Hospital, which is a well equipped medical facility housed in a puffy, air-conditioned tent that looks like the inside of a vacuum cleaner bag. The hospital staff shared facilities and supplies with us. This was the first, but not the only, time I was glad I had attended the military medical school. Not only had we been trained to function under these austere conditions, but I found classmates from school, people who had played rugby with Kory, and doctors who had been residents when I was a student. The "old boy" network was very valuable.

By the end of August, we had moved the entire battalion to King Fahd airport and settled into the second floor of the parking garage. The building gave us some shelter from the sun, but the concrete absorbed the heat all day and then radiated it back all night. So despite the cooler temperatures at night, it was never very cool inside the building. To combat this, at night we spread our sleeping bags on the sidewalks and slept under the stars.

Inside the building, the empty, dusty floors were marked off with white lines dividing the garage into parking spaces. Officers who ranked major and higher each got to live in a private parking space. Not exactly private, but at least an entire space to ourselves. Captains and lower ranks were assigned two people per space. Initially there were hundreds, and then thousands of people living there. We were issued green canvas cots, and we rigged shelves out of water boxes, boards, and bricks. Later we constructed tables, chairs, and shelves from packing crates and other material scrounged from dumps on the airfield.

Since I was a major, I had my own parking space, with the commander on one side of me and the S-2, or intelligence officer, on the other. I was the only woman in sight because I was the only female officer in the battalion. We did have five enlisted women in the battalion—one was a medic and the others worked in maintenance, the motor pool, and the headquarters company—but they lived down the aisle with the other enlisted soldiers. A woman officer from another unit living in the garage suggested we establish a separate place for all the women to live, maybe in the basement of this mammoth structure. She asked me if I'd talk to the executive officer in the Aviation Brigade of the 101st Airborne Division (Air Assault), which is the unit we were attached to. I said I certainly would talk with him, but I didn't tell her what I'd say.

She wanted to segregate the women, but when I met with the executive officer, Lt. Col. Richard Gill, I argued that putting the women in a separate area was a terrible idea. The commanders wanted to enhance unit integrity and cohesiveness, so segregating people according to sex was obviously not the way to do it. If anyone was worried about the safety of the women, they certainly would have been less safe living by themselves in the basement than upstairs surrounded by people they knew. (I say "they" because I wasn't going anywhere.) So from all standpoints I could see, other than one lady's modesty, that was a bad idea, and we remained mixed in with the men for the duration.

Most of the time in the army, especially during peacetime, women are treated the same as men. I'm used to being surrounded by men, and the majority of my friends are men. Like most people, I make friends with the people I work with, and in the army and the air force, I work mostly with men. There was a question raised about me going to Saudi Arabia, however. Back at Fort Rucker, Maj. Gen. Rudolph Ostovich III, who was the head of army aviation, told Lieutenant Colonel Bryan to take anyone he wanted for the deployment. Bryan said he wanted me to be the flight surgeon, and the general said that was fine. But someone at a lower level decided there ought to be an official opinion about taking a female flight surgeon, to guard against questions in the future. Women were serving in many army jobs at that point, but we were still prohibited from serving in combat jobs, especially in the infantry and flying attack helicopters like the Apache. A call was placed to the Department of the Army in Washington. I was told that the response from on high was: "We are going to war. Surely we have something bigger to worry about than the sex of the doctor. Just be happy they have one." I was very proud to be in the army that day.

During the first few days at King Fahd airport, I visited all the other flight surgeons. One of them turned out to be my best friend from medical school, Peter Demitry, an air force flight surgeon who flew A-10 tank killers. He was the one who had introduced me to Kory. The three of us were classmates at medical school from 1982 through 1986, and Peter and Kory convinced me that since I had a Ph.D. in biochemistry, I ought to be their private tutor. Peter was a better pupil, but I fell in love with Kory, and we were married before the end of the first year.

Finding Peter in the desert was a lucky break for me, personally and professionally. Now I had someone to talk with, someone who knew about my life and my family. I also had a professional ally. Peter loaned our battalion supplies we didn't have and accepted my word that we would replace them. Later on, we even taught him to fly helicopters.

We were friends, and we were at a relatively low level of command, so we could cooperate informally, even if the air force and the army aren't supposed to get along very well.

The medics and I set up our aid station in a tent inside a maintenance hangar decorated with a sign that read, "We Treat the Best." Another sign inside the tent advised our patients, "Suffering Is Stupid, but Whining Is Worse." That's one of my philosophies of life: it's stupid to be miserable if you don't have to be, but having made yourself as comfortable as possible, then don't complain, because it doesn't do any good. We had sick call in the mornings, and people came to the aid station for rashes, broken bones, and upper respiratory infections caused by breathing dust and being exposed to new viruses we didn't have at home. There was sinusitis, dehydration, stomach pains, diarrhea, constipation, and muscle aches. The serious cases were evacuated to hospitals in the rear.

I did some minor procedures, such as taking a bit of shrapnel out of Gary Godfrey's leg. Godfrey, one of the pilots flying the day we were shot down, had been shot in civilian life several years before and still had shrapnel that occasionally migrated to the surface. During the quiet days before the war in December, I even did six vasectomies at the air force Air Transportable Hospital in Dhahran. We were bored.

We manned the aid station twenty-four hours a day, but I practice medicine by walking around. I'd stop in at various offices or wander by a tent to see how people were feeling. I'd learned that pilots are especially reluctant to complain to a doctor because they don't want to risk being grounded for a medical problem. Most of the pilots knew me and were confident that I'd only ground them if they had a problem that threatened flight safety.

The living conditions took their toll on the health of the soldiers, and one time after coming back from an exercise in the desert, we had a near-epidemic of stomach problems. All the pilots in one company had fevers of 104 degrees, vomiting, and diarrhea. We teased them about what they must have been doing in the desert, but it was extra-bad for them because we lived a quarter of a mile from the outhouses.

The outhouses themselves were a medical problem. I hadn't even been at King Fahd a week when I went back to see Lieutenant Colonel Gill. "We're not gonna have anybody left to die from the bullets because everyone's gonna get dysentery from these conditions," I warned him. There were no hand-washing facilities at the latrines, and our soldiers might have been brave, but they sometimes were lazy. We had a long line of latrines—four-seater outhouses made of plywood—along what we called "Shithouse Row." The top part of each latrine was screen, so the user's head and chest were visible to passersby, a design that clearly emphasized ventilation over privacy. There were dozens of latrines, but the soldiers would only use the closest one, and they kept urinating in the bucket even when the stuff was running out the other side. And, of course, the seats were always wet. Every evening in the brigade staff meeting, I had to brief the commander on the latrine situation. It got so bad we had to post guards to keep people from using the full ones.

Another job I assumed was resident birth control officer. I made sure we had different kinds of birth control pills, because it seemed other people had not thought about that. I dispensed a lot of condoms, but for all I knew the soldiers were putting them on the ends of their rifles to keep out the sand. I didn't ask if people were sexually active, or where they found the privacy in the parking garage to have sex, because it wasn't my business. But it was unrealistic to think that so many people with nothing to do for six months would all be celibate. They certainly would not all have been celibate if we had stayed in the United States. I figured my job was to make sure no one got pregnant, and no one did. Because we had such a captive population, I only saw one case of venereal disease, which is fewer than I'd ever seen on a deployment. As it turned out, this soldier had been on leave in the United States until two days before he came to see me, so there was no question that he got it back home.

Besides the usual diseases and minor surgery, we had our share of accidents in the field, just like we did back home at Fort Rucker or on training exercises. The army has a lot of very large, fast-moving equipment that is dangerous to operate even when it's not deployed against the enemy. We had an enormous concentration of firepower in Saudi Arabia, and every soldier was armed. One of our soldiers, probably nervous while on night patrol along the flight line, shot himself in the calf with an M-16 rifle and destroyed a big chunk of the bone and leg muscle. We had a scout helicopter wreck that was not too serious, and a Black Hawk helicopter crash that injured five men very badly. They all had broken legs and broken bones in their backs, one had dislocated hips, and another was hit so hard in the chest that he ruptured his aorta.

I was fortunate to be experienced doing trauma, and I like to do it. As a medical student, I had done six weeks of general surgery at Brooke Army Medical Center in San Antonio, and we treated knife wounds, gunshots, and motor vehicle accidents. At Fort Rucker, I had done parachute accidents and helicopter wrecks, and I had seen broken pelvises and amputated limbs. I like trauma work because it requires being able to make a decision and having the self-confidence to act on the decision. You can't stop and think and look around and read or ask someone else. You have to be able to do it.

Technical skill is also required. In a way it's like flying. Watching someone fly or watching someone operate, a professional can tell if the performance is art or a ham-fisted piece of work. There is a certain amount of pride about getting an IV in the first time or making a wound line up when you sew a deep cut. It's fun to do. The accidents in Saudi helped my medics and me to keep our trauma skills sharp, skills we would need if we went to war.

The soldiers kept us pretty busy, but often their problems weren't the kind that could be treated with bandages or medicine. The military is an entire population of pre-screened, healthy people, and so if the soldiers had problems they were likely to be emotional rather than physical, particularly in times like this when we were sitting around waiting to do something. The severest emotional strain for all of us in the desert, and for our families back home, was caused by the uncertainty: we didn't know how long we would be there, what was going to happen, or whether we would fight. Some soldiers suffered from boredom, some were scared, some were lonely, and everyone missed their families. This wasn't like World War II or other conflicts when most of the soldiers were young, single men excited to get away from home. We had many married soldiers with children, and if you asked them what was the toughest thing about living in Saudi Arabia, they wouldn't say it was the heat or the sand or army food or even the lack of alcohol—it was missing their families. Life for the single soldiers wasn't any easier, since there were no movie theaters, bars, or discos, and almost no way to meet local people. I doubt there were many war brides brought home from Saudi Arabia.

There was the usual griping about the conditions in Saudi, and soldiers wondered why the air force and Special Forces people at our base lived better than we did, but most of the unhappiness was caused not by life in the desert but by what had been left at home. Conversations with soldiers often included exchanges of carefully preserved photographs, family portraits of neatly groomed young couples and little girls in ruffled dresses and boys in their Sunday best. Mail call was a highlight of each day, and a lack of letters from home caused great worry. There was always a young soldier away from home for the first time who hadn't received a letter in a month. He didn't know if it was because his wife wasn't writing or because we weren't getting mail. I sympathized with the complaints about the mail, because I wrote Kory one letter that took forty-three days to find him. And we were both in Saudi Arabia.

I'd been in Saudi for twenty days before I finally was able to talk with Kory by phone. I didn't even know that he'd been deployed until someone from our battalion saw him in Spain on the way to Saudi. Kory's unit had been called up right after I left. He organized a community effort to take care of things at home. The Blackwoods took the checkbook to handle the finances, and promised to collect the mail. The Marlows, our closest neighbors, took care of the farm and the animals, which meant feeding the horses twice a day for seven months. The Armstrongs agreed to maintain the pool, which became a headache because of a major malfunction. Kory said he was based in Tabuk on the Saudi border with Jordan. Now at least we were in the same country, although he still was living seven hundred miles from me. We were fortunate to be flight surgeons and have jobs that made it possible to see each other occasionally. We were authorized to show up at any air base and hop on the frequent military flights around the theater. There were plenty of errands to run, so we could combine work with seeing each other. I went to see him twice, and he visited our battalion five times. Most of the American soldiers weren't that lucky, although there were two other couples in our battalion who did see each other.

It was hard not seeing Kory every night, but I knew he was glad to be serving in Saudi Arabia. Our military friends who suffered most during the war were the ones who had to stay home. Kory knew exactly how I was living and had an honest idea of the danger. That made him worry less about me than if he had stayed home. The worst possible scenario would have been me in the desert and Kory at home, wishing he were there, too.

Regan was the one left behind. Kory had sent her to live with her dad in North Dakota. I wasn't able to call her until Thanksgiving, and that was frustrating. I wrote to her at least once a week, though, and every day when the war began. Regan was busy with school and sports, and seemed to understand what we were doing. Her friends were impressed that Kory and I were in Saudi Arabia. Everyone at home seemed to be following the buildup closely, and Regan was no exception.

Many of my colleagues suffered from sharp pangs of loneliness and the emptiness of being so far from home. It was hardest for those who had spouses who weren't in the military and didn't understand why we had to be there. Some spouses, parents, and children found it hard to imagine that this was something we wanted to do. The news reports focused on the rough conditions, the sand and the sun, not on the excitement of being deployed. I know soldiers who felt guilty because they were having fun, while their families at home worried so much. My strategy was to put my thoughts of family into the "home drawer" and lock it up until I saw them again. This might not necessarily be a healthy way of dealing with my feelings, but it certainly was efficient. There was too much to do, and the mission was too important, to worry about something that couldn't be helped.

While many people complained about boredom, I myself was seldom bored. To tell the truth, most of the time before the war actually began, my life in Saudi Arabia was very relaxing. Back at Fort Rucker, my phone rang a hundred times a day, and I was forever chasing little yellow stickers that said call so-and-so or do this and do that. Being deployed in the desert was a relatively pleasant experience. There was a clear focus and an important task; my job was to take care of people, and if I did that I had succeeded.

I used my free time to get to know my medics better, and I was able to teach them a little more about medicine. They always called me "Doc" or "Major Cornum," and I referred to them by their ranks, unless they asked me to call them by their first names. At thirty-six, I was the oldest in the medical group and the only officer. When I could, I got them out of the parking garage and King Fahd to go swimming or visit the nearby towns of Dammam and Al-Khubar. The only army hospitals available were in Dhahran, so we generally had a good reason to go somewhere. One of the British Aerospace employees we'd met, Kris Brown, opened his home to members of the battalion when we came into town. It meant a lot to have a bathtub, a television, and a chance to get away from five thousand soldiers spilling out of a sun-baked parking garage, even for a few hours.

The weather during our first four months in Saudi was so hot that

I liked to get up at 5 A.M. and run four or five miles; the sun was too
hot for exercise later in the day. Since this was an isolated American
base with no Saudis, I was allowed to wear shorts and a t-shirt for running.
In other places, the American women weren't allowed to show their
legs, and we were expected to be sensitive to the Saudi beliefs that
women should be segregated from men and covered in public. Usually I wore my uniform, which covered my arms and legs, when I went
into town. After running, I washed in the homemade showers built from
sheets of plywood. I would step inside the individual stall, stand on a
wooden pallet, and reach up to pull on a chain, which released a cas-
cade of water from a water tank installed above the stall. Unless the
water was warm from the sun or heaters, a shower was an invigorating
experience.

I normally dressed in either a flight suit or fatigues and a floppy
hat. We carried our gas masks, in truth not so much because we thought
we'd need them, but because they would get lost otherwise. I wore
my 9mm Beretta in a shoulder holster. My grandfather taught me to
shoot long before I went into the army, and Kory and I used to shoot
at home. I could hit a beer can or an armadillo with my pistol, and I
was pretty certain I could hit an Iraqi. We always carried our sidearms,
but we didn't have to wear our uniforms on Sundays because Lieutenant Colonel Bryan gave us the day off.

We took days off very seriously as the weeks turned into months
with no end in sight, and life at King Fahd took on some of the char-
acteristics of the peacetime military. The paperwork and the mundane
aspects of life at Fort Rucker were catching up with us, but the fun
things like bars and restaurants never made it. It wasn't long before
we had all the problems of being in garrison without any of the ad-
vantages. We had all the paper pushing and bureaucratic procedures,
but we still took cold showers outside.

Lieutenant Colonel Bryan made life as enjoyable as he could. We
didn't have much free time, but for fun we set up a TV room with a
popcorn machine inside the parking garage. We tried hard to make it
a pleasant place to go, and we scrounged scraps of wood and sheets
of plywood to build tables, chairs, cabinets, and a desk. We had a bar
with a cooler, and we pitched in so there would always be cold soft
drinks for everyone. We built a little booth so people who got tapes
from home could watch them without entertaining the entire battalion, and we had another room with benches where we showed mov-

ies for all the soldiers. I played more games of ping-pong in those months than I had played in my entire previous life, I learned to play Spades, and we had endless volleyball games.

After our first field training exercise, we were able to provide live entertainment for the troops: camel spider fights. The "Flying Tigers" was the nickname of our battalion, and we found a big, ugly, hairy camel spider in the desert and called it "Kid Bengal." We were so desperate for something to break the routine that we put up signs announcing the fights and scoured the desert to find opponents for the Kid, usually other spiders, scorpions, and once a large lizard.

My favorite times were training missions, and we were sent out approximately once a month for ten days to practice setting up base camps and forward bases, and to practice deep attacks and screening missions. When the Apaches went on a mission, a Black Hawk was assigned as the search-and-rescue aircraft, and one of the medics or I would be on board in case of an accident. We were always much happier when we deployed in the desert and escaped from the increasingly regimented life at King Fahd.

Christmas was difficult. It's always a difficult holiday, and there is a lot of depression in civilian life, but Christmas, 1990, in Saudi Arabia was worse than usual. We had the January 15 deadline for Saddam to leave Kuwait, and that was good because it meant we were going to resolve things one way or another, but it also meant that some of the senior leadership got nervous about small details. For example, we were ordered to take down our furniture and the dividers that separated our stalls in the parking garage, supposedly because it didn't look sufficiently military.

We had decorated the garage with wreaths and trees and cards from home, but we were ordered to take them down, too. That was the day before Christmas. I thought that if people felt better with all that stuff, they should have been able to keep it. If our airplanes flew at above 90 percent readiness every day, and we could hit the target when we went out, why did it matter if our cots weren't lined up in a row and we had Christmas lights strung in the parking garage? We knew we were going to move forward soon, and eventually we would have to pack our things and send them home, but I remember the day I saw a group of young soldiers who did long-range reconnaissance—tough guys who did exercises all day and were always motivated—sadly taking down their decorations. All they had were a few Christmas cards hanging from string. They were so sad to box them up just before Christmas that it depressed me just to watch them. Anyway, what was so military about living in a parking garage?

During all those days of training, preparing, and waiting for something to happen, I never doubted that we would go to war. I wasn't sure when it would start, but I didn't think Iraq would leave Kuwait without a fight, and equally importantly, I didn't think the Bush administration would move half a million Americans to Saudi Arabia just to move them back after having done nothing. I'd never claimed to be an expert on world affairs, but a peaceful solution didn't seem very likely to me. In truth, I'd never been very interested in world affairs. The war changed me, though, and being a participant in history and world events made me appreciate how they could alter my life.

I got some valuable insights corresponding with my Apache pilot friend from Israel, a country where people know firsthand about fighting in the desert. It was hard to correspond with Moshe, because the Saudis didn't allow letters to be mailed to or from Israel, which they didn't even recognize as a country and referred to as the "Zionist Entity." So I sent the letters home and had them forwarded. Moshe assured me that a fight was coming because two big armies wouldn't "stand toe to toe in the sand and just talk." That made a lot of sense to me.

Even though we knew the war was coming, our daily lives weren't particularly tense or scary. Reporters were always digging for angst or existential dread or wondering if we were scared. They soon tired of getting the same answer from all the soldiers: we're just here to do a job and then go home. That wasn't a very dramatic or introspective attitude, but that's how many of us felt. There was one tense moment in November when our intelligence reported that the Iraqis might be coming south. The day the warning came, the base was buzzing with rumors about being scrambled. I ran back to get dressed, and when we came up wearing flak jackets and carrying our gear, the entire parking garage went silent. We quickly loaded the helicopters and ran them up, but it was a false alarm.

By November, I was so sure of war that I wrote this poem and sent it to my grandparents:

> There's gonna be war soon in the Kingdom.
> It's only a matter now of time.
> There will be death, there will be glory.
> I hope the end is worth the price.

We are your sons, we are your daughters.
We are your husbands and your wives.
We are your friends, we are your lovers,
And need you more now in our lives.

Mostly we're parents of the children,
There's probably one in every school,
Who doesn't remember where his dad is,
Whose mom's not there each afternoon.

Sir, we are proud to be your soldiers.
No, we are not afraid to die.
All we ask sir is your promise,
We'll be allowed to win this time.

We knew by the end of December that our mission would be a major helicopter assault deep into Iraq to cut off the Republican Guard. Instead of going straight north into Kuwait and the bulk of the Iraqi defenses, which is what Saddam expected, we were going north and west through Iraq. We would go around the main defenses and hit the enemy from the flank. This was the maneuver that General Schwarzkopf later called the "Hail Mary play." At that point, I thought the ground campaign was going to be ugly, and we were told to prepare for up to 25 percent of the combat units to be wounded or killed. One out of every four of the people I was caring for would be wounded or killed, one of out of every four people I considered my friends would be hurt or dead before I went home. Those were hard numbers to turn over in my head, and it made me even more dedicated to making sure the medical side was as ready as it could be.

The possibility of war was a constant theme in our late night conversations, and I remember staying up one night, drinking a little smuggled liquor and talking with my friends Eric Pacheco and Bill Roberts, both Apache pilots. We were in the little room I had built in the parking garage from scraps of wood and packing crates. I had bought a little piece of carpet downtown, and the room was relatively comfy. I used it for an office, clinic, living room, and bedroom. I was wearing my blue sweatsuit that night, and I remember Eric had on a pair of wild, baggy work-out pants from his home state of Hawaii. Of course, we called him the "Big Kahuna." The guys were sitting on a stretcher that rested on two boxes and served as a couch when I didn't have a patient. If I had a very sick patient, I would have him sleep on the stretcher while I stayed nearby on the floor.

Eric has curly black hair, and is short and well built. I had just helped him find a new girlfriend from across the airfield, an air force physician's assistant named Tina, and he was in love. Eric was the standardization instructor pilot for the battalion, which made him the resident expert on the Apache. I'd flown with him back home and in Saudi, and he's a great pilot. He's young, but he was taught by my friend Lance, who said Eric was the best he had ever trained. While Eric looks to me like an attack helicopter pilot, Bill looks more like an accountant. He doesn't swagger when he walks, like some of the other pilots. He talked about his wife that night, and how much he missed her.

"Well, Doc, what do you think?" Eric asked me.

"I don't know," I said. "It's looking pretty real, isn't it?"

"I just don't know what it's going to be like," Bill said.

None of us had ever been in combat, and we kept coming back to the uncertainty. All of us were anxious, of course, but it seemed it would be easier to fight the war than to sit there endlessly thinking and talking about it. We talked about our fear, and I said I wasn't too afraid of death. Dying was the worst thing that could possibly happen to me, and it did not seem so horrible. I'd done a lot in thirty-six years and had led a great life. Being killed doing an honorable thing like defending my country wasn't the worst end I could envision.

I wasn't afraid that I would panic in combat or fail to do my job; I knew I could do it. By then my medics and I had treated enough victims of car wrecks, airplane crashes, and gunshots that I felt good about our medical skills. We had scrounged supplies and equipment from around the theater, even things we didn't have at Fort Rucker. Kory brought us some extra stretchers he didn't need. We borrowed big catheters from one unit and chest tubes from another. We needed the tubes to inflate collapsed lungs. I didn't have any packaged blood because most healthy young people will live a while without extra blood, as long as they have some kind of liquid volume. So IV fluid was vital to keep the remaining red blood cells circulating.

Eric and Bill talked about the possibility of being shot down in combat, and I told them, "Don't worry about that because I'll be there to pick you up."

"It could happen to you, too, Doc," Eric warned.

"But I can't live my life afraid of that," I said. "We'd never fly at all. Come on, Eric! Look at some of the crazy stuff we've done."

The battalion finally moved out of King Fahd at 6 A.M. on January 10, seven days before the start of the air war. Everything we couldn't take with us, such as my jeans and sneakers and things I didn't want to carry, we packed and left in the basement of the parking garage. We set up a new base far to the north and west in Saudi Arabia near the town of Hafar-al-Batin. The five medics and I crammed into our little tent, which we also used as the new aid station. We dug in deeply because we were concerned about the Iraqis attacking before we moved against them. Our mission was to support one infantry brigade, and their mission was to stop a possible preemptive attack by an entire Iraqi division dug in just north of the border. Since we were only an infantry brigade and an attack helicopter battalion, saying we would stop the enemy seemed awfully optimistic. We might have delayed them, but as far as I could tell, if the Iraqis decided to attack, we were going to be just a speed bump on their march south.

The hardest part for me was trying to keep everybody else motivated and to convince them that our eighteen Apaches could handle an entire division of Iraqi tanks. For the first few days the weather was so bad that the helicopters were grounded and we were practically defenseless; we wouldn't have been able to fly either to fight or to escape. My medics all carried M-16 rifles, and I carried my 9mm pistol, and I suppose we could have stood in the bottom of the trench and tried to fight off an attack, but the odds would not have been very good.

I did occasionally imagine having to kill another human being, but my job was to save lives, not take them. As medical people, we were allowed to defend ourselves but we were not supposed to engage the enemy. The rules were a little hazy for people assigned to combat units like we were. If we had been assigned to a hospital, it would have been clear that we could not resist the enemy in force. We could have defended ourselves and our patients against terrorists, for example, but we would not have been allowed to man the barricades. In case of an enemy attack on a hospital, we would have been required to surrender. The policy made sense because if we tried to fight back with a hundred patients in the hospital, they might be killed in the crossfire. But when we were just one little tent of medics in the middle of a combat unit, the decision was more complicated. At one point we were asked if we could pull guard duty, but I drew the line there because that would have entailed defending a military position, not just defending ourselves and our patients.

The trouble with "rules of war" is that they only work if both sides abide by them. We wouldn't have attacked an Iraqi hospital, but I wasn't sure I could say the same for the Iraqis. I talked with the medics about these moral and policy dilemmas, and I told them to let common sense and their conscience be their guides.

One of my medics was assigned to the platoon that set up the forward area rearming points, which were at the front and were very likely to be attacked. One day I got a visit from Lt. Mike Pandol, the platoon leader. I've known Mike since 1988, and consider him not only a friend but perhaps the best leader in the battalion. He also brought out my wild side, and we had been kicked out of the officers' club at Fort Hood, and "asked" to leave the club at Fort Rucker on occasion. Pandol wanted every man in his unit, including my medic, to be trained for every job, including loading rockets and missiles onto the Apaches.

"No one ever knows every job," I said to Pandol. "I don't expect your guys to know about medical care. The regulation is clear. You can't make a medic load missiles. It would be an unlawful order to make him do anything offensive."

We both knew that the whole idea of "offensive" and "defensive" was becoming a more diffuse and ethereal concept. When did a weapon stop being defensive and become offensive? When was a medic serving in a medical position? The question of ordering a medic to fight had never come up in training, though, because there had always been enough people in the platoon to do the job. Now, with war so close, what was good enough for training was no longer good enough for us.

I sat down with the medic in the platoon, Sgt. John Middleton, and told him about my conversation with the lieutenant. "Do whatever you think is right," I told him.

He replied, "Well, that's what I'll do."

I don't know to this day what happened out there. I do know that I would trust Sergeant Middleton with my life. I knew he would do the right thing.

The ethical issue came up yet again when we were flying on a mission with Godfrey. We were flying across the desert, and he asked the medics and me, "Does everyone know how to operate the '60s?"

We looked at each other and shook our heads no. I had flown hundreds of times on the Black Hawk, but I had never fired the M-60 machine guns that were mounted in the side doors. That was the job of the crew chiefs, but they rarely needed the guns. The Black Hawk is a utility helicopter used for passengers, transport, and evacuating wounded. In no way is it an offensive weapon. In fact, we call the Apaches "guns" and the Black Hawks "slugs." None of us knew how to shoot the machine guns.

"Well, today's the day you are going to learn," Godfrey informed us.

We flew over the desert and Godfrey called out targets for us to shoot: a wrecked car, a fence post, a fifty-five-gallon metal barrel. He flew us back and forth over the sand, and we became reasonably good at putting bullets on the targets. I thought it was a good idea for us to learn to shoot, and I never thought about asking one of my superiors for permission; it was smarter to just do it. I firmly believe in the theory that it's better to ask forgiveness than to ask permission. Especially when we were about to invade Iraq.

3

The bouncing pickup truck finally stopped, and this time one of the guards lowered the tailgate so I could get out more easily. They led Dunlap and me about twenty-five yards across the sand toward the entrance to another bunker. I was having trouble seeing because it was dark, and my eye was pasted shut with dried blood and mud and hair. I couldn't control my arms at all, and although they didn't hurt too much if I was still, every time they did move it was as if I'd been stuck with a hot knife. One of the soldiers took what appeared to be a shoelace and tied my hands loosely in front of me again. Since I was clearly unable to use my arms, and obviously couldn't threaten him, perhaps he did it just so my arms wouldn't flop as I walked. We walked down into another bunker. The single room was about twelve feet long and six feet wide and had two feet of dirt overhead held up by timbers for protection from bombs. It smelled dank and musty. At the bottom of the steps there was a young officer, maybe thirty years old and probably a captain. When I entered this second bunker, the officer stood up from his wooden chair.

"Who are you?" he asked.

"Major Rhonda Cornum."

There were six Iraqis in the bunker with Dunlap and me, and we could stand easily. I was clearly the senior officer of the two Americans, even though I was a woman, and the Iraqis directed their questions to me. One of the Iraqis was taking notes on a clipboard. They wore uniforms with green sweaters and had their pants tucked into their boots. They were neat, well shaven, and well groomed.

"What is your unit?" the young officer asked.

I looked out at them, all a head taller than me. I knew I should tell them as little as possible, and I didn't want to give them the name of my unit. But I was wearing a green patch on my flight suit that had tiny black swords and little winged tigers (because of the "Flying Tigers" nickname). The patch read "2-229th Atk-Hel-Regt," which even the Iraqis could have figured out meant a battalion of the 229th Attack Helicopter Regiment.

"The 229th," I said.

"What are you?" the officer asked.

"I'm a doctor."

"A doctor in the army?"

"Yes," I said, figuring it was better to appear reasonable than to refuse to speak. I wasn't going to tell them anything important, but I didn't want them to beat me just to find out the obvious, like the name of my unit or my job.

"What are you doing here?"

"We were shot down on a search-and-rescue mission, sir."

"Who were you going to rescue?"

I looked him in the eye and told my first lie. "I don't know."

"What kind of airplane were you looking for?"

"I don't know that either, sir."

"What shot you down?"

"I have no idea."

I noticed again that my dog tags had spilled out of my flight suit and were lying across my chest. I could see my wedding ring. I looked back into the face of the Iraqi officer, but he had noticed the ring, too. He said something in Arabic to the soldiers and gestured at me. One of the soldiers took hold of my dog tags and tried to lift the chain up over my head. I leaned back so he wouldn't take it, but he yanked the chain off anyway. The officer didn't say anything, he just looked at my name and Social Security number on the tags. He held the ring, but made no comment.

While he was pondering what to do, his soldiers peeled off my name tag and the "Flying Tigers" patch, and cut off the XVIII Aviation Brigade patch, which was sewn onto the left shoulder of the flight suit. I don't know why they removed the markings from my uniform, except perhaps to strip me of my rank and drive home the fact that I was their prisoner. Maybe they wanted souvenirs.

Going through my pockets again, the soldiers found two little rocks. They handed them to the captain.

"What are these?" the officer wanted to know. "What are they for?" he asked, apparently expecting them to be some secret weapon.

"Well, as a matter of fact," I admitted, "they were going to be souvenirs of Iraq."

"What?"

"Never mind."

"You can leave now," the officer told me, and gave an order in Arabic to my guards.

"May I have my chain back? May I have my ring?" I asked.

He didn't respond, and the guards pushed me back up the stairs to the desert floor. They were less rough with me now; I think they realized that I was badly hurt. There was no advantage to yelling at me and kicking me, because I simply could not move any faster. I wasn't resisting; I was injured.

We walked over to the pickup, and luckily for me, they had left down the tailgate. I sat on it and swung my legs up onto the bed. Then I slid back along the gritty metal floor to the rear. Dunlap, whose hands were tied behind his back, climbed in after me and draped his legs across mine. We bounced down another track, a dirt road, but there was no way to know where we were going. It looked like a bulldozer had been through and carved roads out of the hard sand. Apparently, we had crashed in the middle of a Republican Guard bunker complex. I knew our AWACS radar plane had been in radio contact with us until the crash, so they must have known where we were captured. Outside the second bunker, I could hear what sounded like the crump of artillery in the background. They might have been bombs, but whatever they were, I figured they were ours. In a way it was comforting to know we were pounding the Iraqis, but at that point I was afraid we would be hit by one of our own munitions.

After about fifteen minutes, we arrived at the third bunker. This was turning out to be a *House and Gardens* tour of the desert bunker complex, but I don't think that was the Iraqis' intention. More likely they were trying to figure out what to do with us, and were sending us up the chain of command. Rather than make a decision about our fate, each officer we saw was passing us along to the next level of command. I understood that behavior very well.

The third bunker was a larger, two-room chamber that had walls lined with sand bags and was lit with a kerosene lantern. There was a burlap divider in the middle, with wooden supports holding it taut. My guess was that this bunker belonged to a battalion-level commander. It was obvious that someone lived there and also used it as an office. There was a Persian rug on the floor, books on the shelves, and a pallet made up as a cot on the ground.

A good-looking, neatly dressed officer, about thirty-five or forty years old, was waiting for us. Some of the Iraqi prisoners we had taken early in the war did not look very soldierly, but these men were all squared away and disciplined. One of the soldiers who had escorted me into the bunker led me to the pallet and tried to push me down to sit. I think he was trying to make me more comfortable, but I was rocked by a powerful wave of nausea. I was no longer as afraid as I had been in the first bunker, and I was trying to be very professional and polite, but now I thought I was going to be sick, from both pain and blood loss. I didn't want to vomit on my host's rug. I walked toward the entrance, expecting them to yell at me or push me down, but I was not going to stop. The Iraqis said nothing, and no one offered to help me.

The nausea came in waves, more like ripples, that pulsed through my entire body. I made it to the bottom of the stairs and leaned against the sandbag wall. Sweating and shivering, I tried to pull the cool air from outside down into my lungs. Slowly, the dizziness eased and I recovered. I realized that I must have lost a substantial amount of blood, but I still couldn't figure out where I was bleeding. I felt blood on my face, and I saw a little on my hand, but not enough to make me so weak.

When I could walk again, the guard pointed me back to the pallet to sit. I couldn't bend my leg, though, and wasn't sure how I could sit. Even worse, I was sure I wouldn't be able to get back up by myself, and I desperately wanted to avoid being raised by my arms again. The Iraqi guard thought I didn't understand what he was saying, so he pushed me harder. I fell with my back against the wall, trying to slide down as slowly as possible onto the pallet. This was the officer's bed, and it had a colorful quilt spread on top of the thin foam mattress. The officer stood in front of me and looked down into my face.

"What are you doing here?"

"A search-and-rescue mission, sir," I said coldly.

At that point, I didn't hate my captors or snarl at them, but I was not feeling very sociable. I was very mad at the one who had taken my wedding ring. I was obsessed with just how unfair it was, and I was afraid that Kory would be disappointed that I hadn't swallowed it. By that time in the war, we had taken hundreds of Iraqi prisoners in our unit, and we had not stolen anything from anyone. These guys stole my ring. There was no nice way to say it; they just flat stole it.

I didn't have a wallet with me, and I had purposely left my Geneva Conventions card and identification cards packed on our truck with the medics. I figured that if I was going on these kinds of missions, I had given up my protected status as a doctor. Technically, medical personnel are not supposed to be made prisoners of war. The Geneva Conventions state that doctors are to be returned to their side unless they are caring for soldiers from their units who also are prisoners. I didn't want to make a big deal of being a doctor, however, partly because I didn't want to be treated differently than other officers, but also because we all had heard the Iraqis didn't like doctors. The story was that Iraqi soldiers had been interrogated and tortured by doctors when captured during their bloody, eight-year war with Iran.

I couldn't lie about being a doctor, though, and like my name, it is printed on the badge I wear on my uniform. On the leather name tag, where a pilot has wings and a shield, I have wings and a caduceus. The insignia has the winged staff of Mercury, with two serpents coiled around it, and symbolizes the medical profession. The badge identifies me as a flight surgeon.

This officer appeared very professional to me, but he was tired, battle-weary. It seemed that they were still fighting, but he was not gloating at all about having two American prisoners. He gave the impression of being genuinely concerned about me, and if he resented Dunlap and me, it probably was only because we meant more paperwork for him. Most of the time during those first few hours in captivity was spent on logistical problems, trying to decide what to do with us and where to send us. No one seemed to care that I was a woman. The Iraqis apparently accepted the fact that there are women physicians, and that I was one of them.

They did not seem very interested in interrogating either of us. They asked Dunlap the same kind of questions: his name and what he was doing. That's all. I was relieved because I didn't want to tell them anything that could hurt the war effort or endanger people in my unit. Pilots in the air force, navy, and marines, as well as special operations, are given entire courses on what to do if they are shot down, what they can say and what they should not say. Kory had taken the course—known as Survival, Escape, Resistance and Evasion (SERE)—and told me about it, but to tell the truth, most of what I knew about being a prisoner of war came from old war movies: give only your name, rank, and serial number. No one ever asked me my serial number. I'm sure I had taken training on the military Code of Conduct at some point during my career, but I think it was thirteen years earlier at the Officer Basic Course, and all I could remember was that I shouldn't accept favors from the enemy and shouldn't do anything to hurt my fellow prisoners or the mission. I knew in my heart that I would refuse to make a video for Iraqi television denouncing the United States, but I also knew my captors could eventually make me do anything, just as they had the other prisoners of war.

I was thinking more clearly now. When the Iraqi patrol first pulled me out of the wreck, I was in a foggy daze and was easily led around by my captors. My focus was on survival. The longer I was conscious, the stronger I felt. They could have killed me at any time, but apparently they wanted me alive. What really sharpened my thinking was the theft of my wedding ring. It was the anger that finally snapped me out of my daze. Before then I had been responding, following their orders, but not really thinking for myself. Now my mind was working again.

The officer quickly tired of talking with me. I realize now that his world was collapsing around him, and the last thing he needed was two American prisoners. He said something to the guard, who reached down and pulled me up by the front of my uniform. Fortunately he didn't try to grab me by the arm. Another guard pushed Dunlap forward, and we went back up the stairs, outside and into the darkness.

They led us across the sand to a different truck. I think we were at an air field or some base not far from Basra, but there were no lights or markings to help me identify the location. The guards loaded us onto a pickup truck that had benches and rails on the sides. They put Dunlap on the bench across from me, and a guard sat alongside each of us. It was dark and cold—it must have been around 9 P.M.—and they put army blankets over us. I was wet, and I wondered if I had crashed in a puddle or a patch of mud. I shivered in the cold, even with the blanket over me. I sat leaning forward, hunched over, because if I leaned back against the side of the truck I felt a stinging pain in my right shoulder. In the cab of the truck, there were a driver and another soldier riding shotgun.

They drove out onto a paved road, and the cool air going by made me shake with cold. We passed thick sand berms and protected positions that formed a network of bunkers shaped like giant mole hills. We had to slow down to climb up and over some of these berms, and for the first time in months, I noticed bushes and trees growing in the sand. I thought we must be near the fertile Euphrates River valley. We had been doing missions there, but I didn't recognize anything.

The guard was sitting so close to me that our shoulders touched, and I tried to lean away from him. My arms hurt so much that I could not lean very far either way and, giving up, I tried to just stare ahead and ignore him. Dunlap, whose arms were tied behind his back, had one of his legs stretched across the bed of the truck, and I could feel his boot on the bench beside me. The guard next to me quietly reached under my blanket, and I could feel him untie my hands. What is this guy doing? I thought.

Suddenly he started pawing my head and face and trying to push the muddy, blood-caked strands of hair out of my face. He kissed me on the mouth and face. I could feel his clean-shaven face rubbing mine, and I could smell him against me. He actually smelled good. I thought, Why does he want to do this? I couldn't believe it. Normally I don't consider myself ugly, or even unattractive, but all I felt then was beat up and dirty. I certainly wasn't feeling amorous. I remember thinking, Hey, you could do better than this. I was not only repulsed by his advances, but amazed. But he wouldn't stop, and I moved my head around and shook it away from him. Then he tried kissing my neck and my ears. "No, no, no," I insisted. He pulled the blanket over our heads so we would not be seen and to muffle the sound. He reached in front of me, grabbed the zipper on my flight suit and clumsily pulled it down. I squirmed but there was no place to go. I had promised myself I wouldn't scream unless I was in life-threatening danger or something was so painful I couldn't stand it, but when he tried to yank the flight suit down over my shoulder, it was like a jolt of electricity had shocked me to the bone. My scream made him stop for a second, but then he started fondling my breasts and kissing me. When I leaned away again, he tried to push me off the seat and onto the bed of the truck, but the blast of pain made me scream again. He stopped. Every time I yelled, he stopped.

I realized then that he stopped not because of my pain, but because he was doing something he was not supposed to do, and he was afraid his comrades in the cab would hear me scream. Sergeant Dunlap could hear me and helplessly watched the battle under the blanket. It drove him wild with rage. My bigger fear was not so much being raped, but that Dunlap might try to do something stupid to defend me and get himself shot. I could feel Dunlap's boot against my side, and I reached down as best I could until I managed to lightly wrap my hand around his boot. I focused my energy into my hand and firmly squeezed the young sergeant's ankle. Even though the action sent bursts of pain through my arm, I desperately wanted Dunlap to know that I was conscious and that I appreciated him being there. "It's okay, sergeant," I tried to say with every painful squeeze of my hand, "I'll be okay."

We had heard the stories of what the Iraqi soldiers had done to women in Kuwait, so I had thought about the probability that I would be sexually abused if I were captured. I had never considered that I would be so badly injured, though. When I really was shot down, I was thinking of myself as a soldier, and a POW, and a very severely injured person. I was not thinking of myself as a woman. I was amazed that this Iraqi soldier could only see me as a woman.

My screams, and the fortunate impossibility of getting me out of my flight suit with two broken arms, kept the molester at bay until finally, after driving for what seemed like forever but in fact was probably only thirty minutes, we stopped in front of a squat, single-story building. In the darkness, it appeared to be a small prison. There were no lights on anywhere, but I'm not sure whether that was because the electrical grids had been destroyed by American and allied bombs or because the Iraqis practiced good light discipline, which means they switched off the lights to avoid attracting enemy bombs.

Someone from inside the darkened building came out to greet the soldiers driving the truck. They got out and pulled Dunlap and me down from the back. The molester said nothing, and he stayed with the truck while we were led through a door and down about seven steps. They marched us along a cinder-block hallway past two closed metal doors. At the third door, we stopped and they pushed Dunlap into a cell. I was led a few more steps on the damp, concrete floor. The thick, cool air made me think we were underground again. The guards opened a wide metal door and led me into my cell. It had a single, roughly eight-inch-square window above my head. There was a bar across the window, but even as small as I am, I could not have squeezed through the tiny hole. There was a small opening in the door covered with a curtain on the outside, so the guards could look in, but I couldn't see into the hallway. The metal door, as thick as the door on a bank vault, was secured outside with a deadbolt.

The entire room was about six feet by eight feet, and a wooden bench ran the length of one wall. The bench had been worn smooth and shiny by prisoners perched there. I managed to sit on the edge of the bench, but I couldn't lean back because my arms, left untied by the molester, would swing and I couldn't bear the pain. Also, there was something wrong with my back. I had a sharp, stinging pain, especially when I leaned against my right side. A faint light, probably from a lantern, came under the door from the hall. I could barely see, but when I looked carefully, I could make out the smeared remains of tiny bugs and mosquitoes that had been smashed on the walls by the previous occupants of the cell.

It was in that cell that I first realized I had not lost everything. For a few moments, I even found my sense of humor intact. That was when my concerns over the big issues of torture, captivity, the military Code of Conduct, and even death, evaporated in the face of a more immediate problem: I had to go to the bathroom.

I looked around the cell and didn't see a toilet, a bucket, or even a hole in the floor. I had last been to the bathroom about 1 P.M., and now it had to be about 10:30 that night. I couldn't be sure of the time, because the Iraqis had taken my watch, too. It was only an eighteen-dollar watch, but it had an alarm, and I remember hoping the alarm would go off and drive them crazy trying to stop it.

The guards had closed the door and left me alone. I sat on the bench for maybe fifteen minutes pondering what to do about my bladder, until I stiffly struggled to my feet and hobbled over to the door. I heard the guards talking in the hall, and I didn't want to interrupt. I'm naturally polite, really, and I was afraid of making them mad. When it finally was quiet, I called out for the guard. No answer. I yelled, "Guard!" and kicked the door, and the noise boomed down the hallway. A man wearing a white robe and leather sandals shuffled slowly to the door and pulled back the curtain on the outside to peer into the cell. He was forty-five or fifty years old and looked like he had been in bed when I called. I stepped away from the door, and he pushed it open.

"I need to go to the bathroom," I explained.

He looked at me quizzically.

"Bathroom. I need the bathroom."

"W.C.?"

"Yes, yes. W.C. Water closet. That's it. I need to go to the water closet."

He motioned for me to follow, but I said, "No. My flight suit."

He waved at me again and said to follow him to the water closet. I sighed in frustration. "I can't go to the water closet with my flight suit on." I couldn't move my arms, so there was no way I could get the suit off by myself. I couldn't even raise my hands to lower the zipper, and the pain had been unbearable when the soldier on the truck had tried to yank it down past my shoulders. I tried to point to the zipper with my chin, but I looked like a pigeon with my head bobbing up and down.

"Water closet," he insisted.

"Flight suit," I responded. I was afraid I would get to the bathroom, and he would leave without helping with the flight suit. I had to go so badly that I didn't think I could walk down the hall and then have a long discussion with him about how I was going to do it. I didn't want to talk with my captors at all, and I even considered going in my pants, but I didn't know how long this flight suit would be my only set of clothes. On the bright side, and this was the optimistic doctor in me, I thought that if I had to urinate so badly, it meant that my kidneys were still working. That meant I had not lost a truly dangerous amount of blood.

The gray-haired guard looked at me with a baffled expression on his acne-scarred face. Then he turned around, walked out the door, and closed it behind him.

He came back a few moments later with another guard, this one so skinny that his military uniform was hanging from his body. "Water closet," the first guard said.

"Take off my flight suit," I repeated, trying to point with my head to the suit. I had my fingers locked together in front of me to keep my arms from swinging, and I tried to knock my hands against the flight suit.

"Water closet," he repeated.

"You can say it as loudly and as slowly as you want to," I said, "but I can't do anything until you take off my clothes."

They spoke to each other in Arabic, walked out of the cell, and closed the door behind them. Two minutes later, I heard the dead bolt slide back and the door was pushed open. In walked the first guard in the robe, the second skinny guard, and now a third guard, also dressed in a military uniform but stout and strong. The new guard was carrying a dark blue robe with black stripes, the type of robe worn by the Arab men and made of a heavy wool. It had three buttons down the front and a little collar.

The third guard, apparently the brains of the operation, rolled up the blue robe the way a woman would roll up a stocking before stepping into it. He placed the rolled robe over my head and let it rest on my shoulders like a tire. The guards were very serious about this operation and were quiet except for a few traded words of instruction in Arabic. I stood quietly, hoping they knew what they were doing but mostly hoping they would hurry.

The front zipper on the flight suit was not damaged, and one of the guards pulled it all the way open. My arms were so sore and swollen, however, that the suit could not be pulled down over them. Every time my arms moved, the pain was excruciating. I gritted my teeth and vowed not to scream. I could feel the bones grinding together, and I had to force myself to relax the muscles to ease the bones back into place. The guards quickly understood the problem, and after more discussion in Arabic, the two uniformed guards reached into their pockets and pulled out folding knives.

I wasn't scared, even when I saw the knives. I could tell these men wanted to help me. They saw the situation as a problem to be solved, not an opportunity to be taken. Luckily, the molester was gone. The man in the white robe took hold of the blue robe resting on my shoulders, while each uniformed guard gently took one of my arms. They opened their knives and began to pick at the fabric of the sleeves, cutting slits up to the collar. I could not stand any movement of my arms, and each time they jerked, I felt a deep, sharp pain like being stabbed. Only the pain lasted longer than a stabbing. I made more noise than I wanted, and I felt bad, because they were trying to do the right thing.

The guards were careful with the knives, but I could feel the cold blades on my skin and little pricks when the sharpened points popped through the sturdy fabric. The men pinched the cloth between their fingers, pushed the knives through, and then pulled the blades back towards their chests, slicing open little gashes. I didn't know if they were cutting my skin along with the suit, but by then, with the goal in sight, I had to go to the bathroom so badly that I really didn't care.

When they reached the shoulders and started up the collar, the sleeves fell off. With that, the flight suit started to peel itself down my body like a banana. The robed man guided the blue robe over my shoulders, over the bra, and down my body. All three of them averted their eyes, or looked me straight in the eye, so I would know they weren't leering. The flight suit came down a bit, then down went the robe. A little flight suit, a little more robe, so I was covered every step of the way. These men were much more sensitive about my modesty than I expected them to be. In fact, they were more sensitive than some of my American colleagues, who had been known to catch a peek at the women soldiers going to the shower.

The guards were unable to maneuver my arms into the sleeves of the robe, so I kept my hands joined at the thumbs underneath the fabric. The robe itself fit me like a tent and touched the floor. Next they had me sit down, and one of them unlaced my combat boots. He pulled them both off, leaving me in my big green knee socks and finally able to step out of the rags of my flight suit. They pulled my boots back on, and the two soldiers walked out the door, triumphant.

I was left alone with the guard in the white robe. "Come with me," he ordered.

"No." I shook my head, smiling at him.

He looked at me with that quizzical face again and motioned toward the open door. "Water closet," he said hopefully, using his one expression in English.

"Not quite," I grimaced, flapping my arms underneath my robe, trying to gesture. But he couldn't see my hands. "Un-der-wear," I said. "I can't go with my underwear still on."

Finally, reluctantly, he got the message, and leaned over in front of me. He looked behind me at the wall, put both hands under the robe, hooked his fingers on either side of my orange bikinis, and pulled them down. Gentle is not the word I would use to describe the effort—I'm not sure if "gentle" was in his vocabulary—but he didn't try to knock me to the ground. He got the panties down, and I stepped out of them, one booted foot at a time. The guard tossed them on the bench and motioned to the door. This time I followed.

The wooden door was open to the small water closet and the guard pointed me inside. It smelled sharply of urine, excrement, and bad drainage, and I was glad they had put on my boots because the floor was wet and filthy. Apparently the aim of Iraqi soldiers in the bathroom is about as good as that of our own men. Instead of a toilet, there was an oblong hole in the floor with little foot pads on either side. The idea was to stand on the foot pads and squat over the hole. There was no toilet paper, but there was a black hose coming out of the wall at knee height. There was no way I would be able to clean myself anyway. Nor could I squat over the hole, because my knee wouldn't bend. I couldn't even lift up the robe because my arms didn't work at all. I had to keep from soiling the robe; it might be my only piece of clothing for some time. I looked down at the hole. After all those months in Saudi Arabia, I never had figured out which way to face when using those things.

I placed my feet on the foot pads with my back toward the closest wall. I stood straight, measured the distance, and started leaning backward, teetering actually, since my body was stiff. My head went back and clunked against the cement wall, and I was jammed there like a plank leaning against a barn. That position caused the robe to swing out away from me, clearing my trajectory to the target. My neck was stiff and my legs were trembling, but I managed to relieve myself without hitting the robe or my boots.

After congratulating myself on a mission accomplished, I realized I could not move. My head was mashed against the wall, and I was looking up at the ceiling, thinking I could not balance there much longer. My legs were tired and my arms hurt. One, two, three, I jerked forward and yelped from the pain in my leg. I thought my knee was going to collapse like a broken table leg as my body went forward. The pain shot up my right leg, and I shifted my weight to the left one. I caught my balance and stood there for a minute, breathing deeply so the pain would dissipate. My inability to perform that simple movement made the diagnosis of my knee for me: I had blown out at least the anterior cruciate ligament. Unfortunately, having the right diagnosis was of absolutely no value at that point.

Once I recovered and the pain had stopped surging through my leg, I pushed the door open with my shoulder. The step down was only about four inches, but I navigated it carefully because I was afraid of falling. I knew there were bone splinters or fragments in my arms, and

I was afraid of causing more damage. The white-robed guard was waiting for me and led me back to my cell. We walked inside and he picked up my orange underwear from the bench. He waved them at me and said something in Arabic that I didn't understand. I took his message to be that no green-eyed infidel woman in any of his cells was going to be naked under a blue wool robe.

"If you put them back on," I said, "you'll just have to take them off again when I need to go to the bathroom."

But he insisted, and one foot at a time, he slipped the panties up my legs and over my hips.

The guard closed and bolted the door on the way out, and I was alone. I sat perched on the smooth wood bench. I had only two available positions: standing, or sitting on the edge of the bench. It was too painful to lean back against the wall or lie down, which is what I really wanted to do. I hadn't slept much the night before our rescue mission, and this day had been fairly traumatic. At least I was not alone. Dunlap was in a nearby cell, although we couldn't communicate. I wondered if they would interrogate him separately. Would he be tortured? Too tired to think. My eyes burned and felt heavy; my brain was fuzzy. I was exhausted, frazzled. Sleep seemed like an escape. If I could just sleep until morning, life would have to get better.

Sleep was elusive, though, as the heavy door scraped open again in a few minutes. The skinny guard with a baggy uniform entered carrying a glass of water and a thick china plate holding a tomato and a fist-sized, brown roll. The guard set the glass and the plate on the bench beside me. This guard, maybe twenty-five years old, did not like me and was quick to make his feelings known. He never said anything, but I could feel the meanness in him. It was contempt, hate. He banged the plate next to me and waited for me to pick up the food and eat.

"I can't," I said. "Broken arms."

With a horrible, sour look on his face, he picked up the water glass and clinked it against my teeth. He resented me, probably as an American and as a woman. I imagine he didn't want to be there waiting on me, and I think by then the Iraqis knew how badly the war was going for them. I drank deeply. The cool water tasted so good and refreshing because I was dehydrated. He set the glass down and tore off pieces of the roll, dropping them into my mouth until the roll was gone. I watched his hands and noticed the dirt under his nails. Then he fed me the tomato the same way. I knew I should eat to keep up my strength, and the food actually tasted good. I had not eaten fresh, moist bread during those months living in Saudi Arabia, nor had we seen many fresh vegetables.

When I finished, the guard picked up the plate and glass and started out the door without a word.

"Thank you," I called after him, but he kept silent.

I appreciated what these men had done for me so far. They could have just left me alone in the cell, but they helped me. I didn't feel that way about all the Iraqis I had met up to that point. I did not appreciate the guy kissing me and touching me—I would've loved to let Kory spend a few minutes with him. And for the soldier who had taken my ring, I wished only the worst. I imagined our guys going in there and blowing up everything. I resented that they had taken my ring. I didn't have any problem with them capturing me; we would have done the same thing if we had shot down an Iraqi helicopter. Obviously, the military exists to break things and kill people, but stealing was not acceptable.

My blue robe was heavy wool, and I was grateful to have it, but I was shivering with cold. It was cold in the cell, probably just above freezing, and I had lost a lot of blood. I was happy to have my socks and boots. The skinny guard opened the door again and put a wool blanket on the bench next to me. I looked longingly at the brown blanket, but I couldn't grab it. The guard looked at me. He picked the blanket up, shook it out and draped it across my chest. A normal person would have put the blanket over my shoulders and across my back, but Mr. Helpful was not cooperating. I did not complain.

The guard left, and I sat as still as I could, perched on the edge of the bench and terrified the blanket would slide down onto the floor and leave me uncovered all night. I bent my head forward as slowly as possible and snatched the edge of the blanket in my teeth. I sat that way all night, half asleep and sucking on the edge of the blanket, fearing that if I drifted off too soundly, I would lose my toothy grip and die of exposure.

Perched in the darkness, the blanket in my teeth and my body shivering under the blue robe, I wondered if anyone else had survived the crash. There had been eight of us on board, and I had seen only one other survivor, Sergeant Dunlap. I didn't remember seeing any bodies in the wreckage. I felt lucky to be alive, and I didn't think anyone else could have survived the crash. The wreckage was in little pieces, thrown across the desert. Dunlap was in a cell two doors away, but I was afraid to call out to him.

I wondered if the two Apaches that were escorting us had made it back. My friend Lance was flying one of them, and I hoped he was safe. I knew he would be sick about what had happened to me. I knew he would feel responsible, especially after we had told Regan that Lance was going to watch out for me.

I met Lance in December, 1987, at Fort Rucker. At that time, and up until he volunteered to go with the 2-229th to Saudi Arabia, he was the standardization instructor pilot for D Company, which means he set the standard for the company that trains all the Apache pilots in the army. Lance was one of the first twenty people trained to fly the Apache when it was initially fielded, and he could make that helicopter do whatever he asked it to. When we had flown together, he told me, "You have to treat it gently, like a lover." Lance looks young for his age, 43, and in truth, he looks just like an Apache pilot—so much so that McDonnell Douglas, the company that makes the Apache, has a full-page picture of Lance in the company's book about the aircraft.

A twenty-two-year veteran, Lance had 283 confirmed kills in Vietnam. In the air force, when the pilots talk about "kills," they mean the airplanes they've shot down. We don't live under such illusions in the army, because in a helicopter you see the people fall when you shoot them. Early in the war with Iraq, Lance was the pilot who took the first group of prisoners. It was unheard of for an attack helicopter to take prisoners, and the capture had added to Lance's stature in the battalion. Lance told me he was glad the Iraqi soldiers had surrendered instead of trying to fight. He didn't want to kill them if it wasn't necessary.

In some ways, Lance is a typical attack-fighter pilot: desperately trying to grow up, but not quite there, seeking out every thrill from skydiving to scuba diving to hang gliding. In other ways he is very wise; he's seen a lot in a few years, and many of the younger pilots want to be just like him. Despite the constant, and sometimes serious, competition between the attack pilots like Lance and the utility pilots, Lance was well liked and respected by our Black Hawk crews. On an earlier mission, Garvey had commented that it was a good thing we had Lance. "At least," Garvey said, "there is one gun pilot with brains."

Sitting in the darkness, thinking about Lance and the fate of the other aircraft on our mission, I hadn't yet grasped the seriousness of my own situation. I was shivering with cold in a prison cell deep inside Iraq.

I was badly injured, perhaps permanently disabled. More interrogation, and maybe torture, lay ahead. I knew we were winning the war, but I didn't know how long it would last. I did know that long after the war in Vietnam had ended, Americans were still being held prisoner. In Lebanon, Western hostages had been held for years, chained to walls in dark cells, and used as bargaining chips. Still, I felt lucky to have survived the helicopter wreck. I felt lucky just to be alive, and I was confident I would get out of this mess.

Rhonda (left) with fellow members of the Presidio track team after winning a bronze medal for the one-mile relay, 1982. Rhonda's first assignment in the Army was in the Division of Experimental Surgery at San Francisco's Presidio.

Four generations: Rhonda with her father, her grandmother, and Regan in 1982.

The touchstone in Rhonda's life: daughter Regan was born during Rhonda's first year in graduate school; Regan was an independent fourteen-year-old when her mother left for the Persian Gulf. *Left:* Rhonda with four-day-old Regan in 1976. *Below:* Regan graduates from the sixth grade.

Rhonda and Kory Cornum met as medical students; they were married in the spring of 1983. The above photo was on their wedding invitation. *Below:* honeymooning in Jackson Hole, Wyoming.

Rhonda and Regan ride "Granny" and "Raisin," two of their thoroughbred race horses.

Steeplechasing is one of Rhonda's hobbies (she has a steeplechase jockey's license). Note Regan sitting under the brush jump.

An eighty-acre farm in northwestern Florida is home to the Cornums and their menagerie.

Rhonda and her thoroughbred mare, Granny, admire Granny's brand new foal.

Rhonda and the "wolf dog," Shemya.

Apache pilot Lance McElhiney (left) dropped in to the Cornum's Florida farm for a visit in spring 1990. Also visiting were Moshe Cohen (second from right) and Arnon Ronen (right), both Israeli pilots. Moshe is squadron commander of the only Israeli Apache unit.

The current Cornum project: a homebuilt experimental aircraft. Made of composite fiberglass, the aerobatic Glasair III will be capable of 300 knots.

Another hobby of the Cornum "adrenaline junkies"—skydiving. Rhonda waits for the jump, then is on her way.

Ready for her first F-16 flight with the Air National Guard in Montgomery, Alabama.

Rhonda has also flown in F-15s. This one is her husband's plane (note Kory's name on the side).

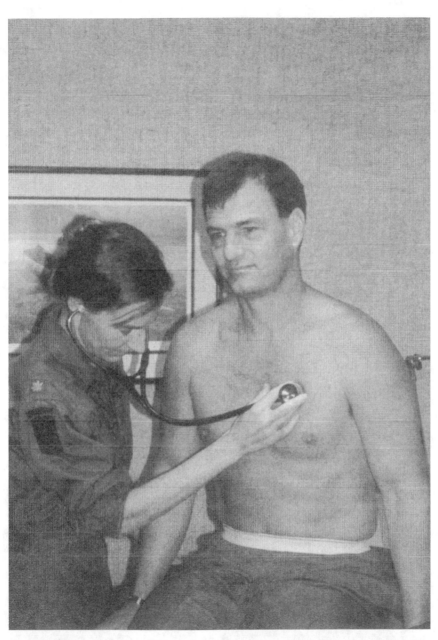

A flight surgeon's job is to keep the squadron's pilots healthy, flying, and able to operate effectively a myriad of sophisticated, sensitive instruments such as the night-vision device. Here Rhonda is performing a routine physical.

Lance, Rhonda, and Kory at King Fahd Airport before the war began. Kory, an Air Force flight surgeon, was stationed at Tabuk, and was able to visit Rhonda about once a month.

A Christmas photo for the folks at home: Rhonda and Kory strike a pose on an Eglin AFB F-15 at Tabuk, Saudi Arabia.

4

On the night the war finally began, after so many months of waiting, Lieutenant Colonel Bryan made us all stay up to watch the historic event. Helicopters from our battalion were not going to be involved that first night, but Bryan thought we should see the action. During the night of January 16 and into the dawn of the next day, we drank hot coffee to stay awake and hunkered down in our foxholes carved out of the sand, shivering in the 20-degree temperature. We scanned the dark northern sky above the desert and saw a few airplanes heading for Iraq, but it was very quiet. Helicopters from the 101st Airborne, the division we were attached to, had gone in ahead of the first wave of jets to knock out the Iraqis' early-warning radar and leave the enemy blinded. The fighters and bombers then roared in so suddenly, and in such strength, that the Iraqis were caught by surprise. The strike made all of us feel better, knowing that things had started and the uncertainty of the past months had ended. We knew what we had to do and were ready. Many of us realized that the only road home for the American soldiers was through Iraq.

After the first wave of the attack had ended, at about 3:30 A.M., I was freezing and decided to go back to bed. I figured that staying awake was not going to improve my ability to provide patient care the next day. Also, now that the war had begun, there was no way Saddam could launch a sneak attack and surprise us in the desert. Lieutenant Colonel Bryan did not exactly see it that way, and the next day he said something at the staff meeting about how some people "did not participate as fully as they might have." But no matter how much I concentrated on the first attack, or worried about the war starting, it was not going to affect the outcome. The first phase of the campaign belonged to the air force, and it didn't matter what I thought or did. I knew our chance would come very soon.

I had no doubt we were militarily ready to go to war. We had a well-armed force of five hundred thousand people in Saudi Arabia, and it was the right time of year for desert warfare. Even if we had to wear our chemical suits the entire time, we would not have suffered from the heat because the weather was cool and the skies were gray. The suits are as thick and bulky as snow suits, and they actually kept us warm. My only worry was that they would lose their effectiveness in a few weeks, especially in the rain. We had a solid logistical base and had stored enough Hellfire missiles to fight a long time with our Apaches.

In addition to my confidence that we were ready, I thought we *should* fight. I don't think taking over another country is right, and one country shouldn't be rewarded for taking over another. That, in fact, is another of my rules of life: do not reward bad behavior. It would have rewarded Iraq for taking Kuwait if we had looked the other way in the face of Saddam's absolute, naked aggression. That would have sent the wrong message to the Iraqi dictator: take Kuwait this week and go get another country next week.

Most of the aggression around the world lately has been internal, and I don't want us to involve ourselves in the civil wars or internal problems of every nation on earth. We certainly didn't think outsiders should have been involved in our Civil War. In the case of defending Kuwait, oil was part of the reason for fighting, but Saddam still would have been wrong if he had invaded a hundred years ago, before the oil was discovered. The fact is that Saddam invaded Kuwait because of the oil. He didn't need more rocks and sand; there's plenty of that in Iraq. We gave him every opportunity to withdraw peacefully, and the United Nations gave him until January 15, 1991, to leave Kuwait. I never thought he would withdraw without a fight, however, and he left no alternative but war. America can't go around fighting every battle in the world. There are only so many windmills we can tilt at, so it's better to tilt at the ones pumping oil.

Finally, I wanted to go to war to test myself. Almost all the soldiers, marines, sailors, and airmen wanted to test themselves. Out in the desert before the war, with the wind blowing stinging blasts of sand across the helicopters and our tents, I could not have articulated this desire to face the ultimate challenge. But now I know it's true. I never hoped for bad things to happen, and I certainly didn't want anyone to be hurt, but if there was going to be a war, I wanted to be there and do my part.

I tried to explain all those feelings to my family, in my usual glib way, in a letter I wrote on January 17 to my mother, father, brother, and sisters:

We are just in a defensive mode, waiting to move again when the rest of the division moves. . . . All I can say is—please don't believe everything you hear on the news. I can assure you it is probably not quite true, whatever it is.

Next, don't worry about the "anti-nerve-agent pills." Yes, we are taking them. Yes, the drug is FDA approved. No, not for this use, but then, nerve agent poisoning is not approved either! But most importantly, the stuff does protect you from the stuff. No, I am not really anticipating being gassed, but it is certainly a real threat and I'm very glad pyridostygmine bromide is available.

Also, if it gets press at home—don't worry about the anthrax threat. No, we did not get vaccinated, but it is a treatable disease (with plain old boring, high-dose penicillin) as long as someone recognizes that's what it is—and that "someone" in our battalion is me!

What else might anybody be worrying about? Well, I don't know, but stop, because #1) It won't help, #2) I want to be here, and #3) We are really kicking ass over here. That part of the news is true, anyway.

I love you,
Rhonda

A few days after I sent that letter, we moved much farther north and west to a camp near the Saudi town of Rafha. There we dug in and sat, waiting until February 24 when the ground war was to begin and we would move deep into Iraq. We lived in tents pitched on the sand, and now the parking garage seemed like luxury long in the past. Because our tent was a medical facility as well as our home, it had a plastic floor and double doors as barriers against the sand. But the blowing sand permeated everything and worked its way into the equipment, our sleeping bags, and even the food. We tried to keep the tent clean, but by the end of each day I could write my name with my finger in the dust.

To pass the time we played cards, and tried to get maps of the area and do some exploring. We visited all of the hospitals in the area and checked out their radio frequencies so we could communicate if we had to evacuate a patient. The OH-58 pilots looked for any excuse to fly, so they always were willing to take patients to the dentist, look for more supplies, or search for working X-ray facilities. A few times they asked me to "think up a mission" so we could stop for French fries in Rafha. One evening after Mike Pandol and I had been flying most of the day (and had stopped at the French field hospital for some really high-class rations) we went to the staff meeting. A notice had gone out that afternoon from the division commander, we were told, and he was not happy. Some soldiers in a small helicopter had not only passed him in his larger UH-1, but they were flying so low that truck drivers on the road could look into the cockpit. Mike and I glanced discreetly at each other. But for some reason, the entire staff looked over at us, and we all had to stifle a laugh.

Mostly we waited, and luckily I had become used to the hurry-up-and-wait element of military life. We had been waiting since August, but this time it was worse because we were so close. It reminded me of a horse that is calm before a race, until he gets to the course and sees all the other horses getting ready to go. He starts rearing and bucking, and it's hard to control him. That is how we felt. We were as finely tuned a fighting machine as we could be, and we wanted to get on with it. It caused much less anxiety to be doing something than to be waiting to do something. I knew we wouldn't be able to go home anytime soon, no matter how quickly we beat Iraq. I had been to the Reforger exercise in Germany, where we practiced sending reinforcements to Europe in case of a Soviet invasion, and it took us longer to clean up afterward than it did to run the actual exercise.

For the medical people, the most important piece of equipment that each of us had was an aid bag, which we packed and repacked obsessively. The night before we had a mission, we took everything out of the bags and repacked them. We always knew we had everything, but we wanted to see it one more time, just to be sure. It was a ritual we never failed to perform. My canvas aid bag was about as big as a bread box, army green, with a strap to carry it over the shoulder. The bag had a zipper on the outside and little pockets everywhere to hold bandages, casting material, IV packs, and autoinjectors of three types of nerve agent antidotes, which were shaped like felt-tipped pens. If a soldier felt queasy or nauseous and thought he had been exposed to nerve agents, he was to place an injector against the back of his thigh and push. The action would jab a needle full of antidote into his leg. The last injector was a heavy dose of Valium to prevent seizures in someone who had gotten his mask on too late and had received a full dose of nerve agent. As the weather grew colder during our movement north, I worried that infusing massive quantities of ice-cold IV fluid would kill a patient, so I stored the IV packs near the heater in the tent. When we went on a mission, I wrapped the IV packs in insulated socks before stuffing them in the aid bag.

Most days during the air war we had hot food, and the days and nights were so cold that everyone appreciated something warm to eat. We also had coffee twenty-four hours a day, and Kory was right: we drank a lot of it. Even on the days when we didn't have real food, just cold MREs, our cooks lovingly prepared their famous, world's best vegetable soup. I ate it from my canteen cup, and I always went back for three or four cupfuls. There was little to do, and we couldn't even run or exercise anymore because we always had to carry helmets, flak jackets, and gas masks. Whenever I boarded an aircraft, I also had to wear a survival vest. The vest was to be used in case we were shot down, and it is equipped with an emergency radio, knife, compass, and flashlight. Straps hanging from the vest secure the whole thing around the legs. If you are on the ground and need to be pulled out of a tight spot, a helicopter rescue crew can lower you a rope, which you hook on the vest to be jerked to safety.

The highlight of the air war for me was the first time I flew into Iraq—I came back with five Iraqi prisoners. It was February 17, and Lance and some of the other Apache pilots were flying armed reconnaissance inside Iraq. Two Black Hawks, one with radios to command and control the operation, and the other for search and rescue, hovered at the Saudi border to wait for the Apaches. The search-and-rescue aircraft, with me on board, was there in case one of the Apaches ran into trouble.

The constant bombing of Iraq had been going on for a month, and it had taken a heavy toll on the Iraqi troops, a mental as well as a physical one. When our Apaches flew over one Iraqi position, the soldiers fired a few wild shots in the air, but then stood up waving their arms, trying to surrender. The Apache pilots flew back and forth over the frightened Iraqis, not sure what to do. No one had ever heard of an Apache taking prisoners, and none of the pilots knew what to do with them. Lance landed close to the Iraqis and motioned for them to sit on the ground, which they did. The Apache only has room for the two pilots, so the commander called up our search-and-rescue Black Hawk to collect the prisoners.

We flew for fifteen minutes across the empty desert until we saw the Iraqis seated in front of Lance's helicopter. Several other helicopters were making low, slow circles to be sure it wasn't a trick and we weren't being attacked by anyone else. We touched down, and the Pathfinders jumped out to capture, search, and tie up the prisoners. The Iraqis seemed scared, but I think they were happy to get out of the way of the bombs. They were very docile as our soldiers put them on the ground to be searched. It was getting too dark to see, so the Pathfinders quickly emptied out their pockets and loaded the Iraqis onto the helicopter with me.

Five of the Iraqis were loaded on board, and I stepped to the ground, pulled out my 9mm, and chambered a round. I put one hand on the shoulder of one of the Iraqis to let him know I was watching him, and, with my finger on the trigger, I pointed the pistol at the head of another prisoner. I certainly was not going to kill him, but I didn't want him to move or do anything suicidal like throwing something into the rotor. The prisoners seemed more afraid than I was, and that gave me confidence.

The Pathfinders went back to tie up more prisoners, and one of the pilots suddenly asked in a panicky voice, "Hey, who's guarding the prisoners?"

The door gunner looked back, saw me with my pistol drawn, and casually answered, "The doc."

It was exciting flying back because this was the first group of prisoners anyone had captured. Later, when there were thousands of scared and hungry Iraqis giving up, it was not so thrilling. Once we were safely in the air, our intelligence expert went through the contents of the prisoners' pockets. He held up a piece of Iraqi currency, a dinar, with a picture of Saddam and showed it to one of the Iraqis. The prisoner spat at the picture. These men had not heard from their headquarters in weeks, and they felt they had been abandoned on the front lines. They looked like normal, very young soldiers in green uniforms, and I wondered how I would have managed on the receiving end of all those bombs. I didn't identify with them or feel any comradeship, but that was because they had not fought very aggressively, and it is easier to respect an enemy who fights well.

We were fired up, and it was almost a celebration when we got back to camp that night. This was our unit's first encounter with the enemy. We had flown several missions in Iraq, but we had never seen anybody. All the months of waiting and hours and hours of training had finally resulted in a successful mission. And we even had "home movies" to prove it. The Apaches are equipped with both regular video cameras and forward-looking infrared (FLIR) cameras, and we had filmed the whole episode. The tape was a big hit with the battalion and the whole brigade.

A few days later, we were called to pick up another Iraqi prisoner. He had gotten out of his jeep just before it was destroyed, and was more than happy to surrender. While we were there, a second Apache recon team asked us to come get their prisoners. We flew to the new site, where the Iraqis were still sitting in their bunkers.

This was not something we did every day, and we didn't even have any rope to tie their hands. The Pathfinders were so desperate that someone asked me if I had any surgical tubing to use for handcuffs, but I didn't. One of the crew chiefs had some plastic strapping material used to secure hoses on the engine or something, and that worked fine. By the time the Pathfinders had rounded up the prisoners and tied their hands with plastic strips, it was getting too dark to search them outside. They brought the Iraqis one by one to the helicopter, where I went through their pockets and searched them for hidden weapons before loading them onto our Black Hawk for the trip back to Saudi Arabia.

When we landed at the division military police station, which was protected by sand bags and razor wire, it was spilling over with dozens of prisoners who had been captured by other American units. I noticed that one of the Iraqis being loaded onto a bus for processing was limping badly, so I had two American soldiers help me carry him onto the bus. I gently unlaced his boot, which was squishy with blood, and found a piece of shrapnel dug into his foot. I didn't cut off the boot because he clearly had only one pair of boots. This soldier obviously had not surrendered without a fight, and the wound was still bleeding. I opened my aid bag and went to work. The other prisoners on the bus didn't talk much; they were scared. After I finished bandaging the wound, I looked down and noticed the sticky red blood on my hands. Iraqi blood. It was the first blood I had seen from an actual war injury, and it was the blood of an enemy soldier.

I had taken off my helmet to work on the Iraqi soldier. The prisoners on the bus must have noticed my long hair and realized that I was a woman. It probably came as a surprise to them because when I was in the field, I was so well covered in my helmet, flak jacket, and flight vest that only by looking closely could anyone tell if I was a man or a woman. Flying back to Saudi in the helicopter, with my pistol pointing at our prisoners, the Iraqis probably thought I was a scrawny, effeminate guy. None of the Iraqis on the bus said anything to me, though, and not one of our soldiers commented one way or another about me being a woman. That's how the army is: when we're busy doing our jobs, it doesn't matter to anyone if I'm a woman or a man. We're all soldiers; or as they say in the army, we're all green.

One occasion when my gender did become an issue was when I had presented the battalion medical plan a few weeks before. I had decided that during combat search-and-rescue missions, the medical officer (me) or the non-commissioned medical officer in charge would make the decisions about patient care. If we landed in enemy territory to care for a wounded soldier, it was the medical person who would decide whether to stay with the soldier. The pilot controlled the aircraft and would decide whether to wait on the ground or take the patient to a hospital. The plan also had a section on how we would care for our soldiers in the forward areas, and what to do if they were contaminated with chemical weapons. Army policy—and army politics—did not allow women in combat, even though the rules do specifically allow female medical personnel on combat aircraft. Whatever the policy, there was no way that I, as the flight surgeon, could avoid the combat zone if one of our Apaches was shot down.

When I presented the plan to Maj. Mike Rusho, the battalion's operations officer, he said, "Rhonda?"

"Yeah, Mike."

"Do you think Lieutenant Colonel Bryan knows you're a girl?"

"I think so," I chuckled. "I've been here six months, and if he doesn't know by now, why don't we not tell him 'til after the war?" Rusho agreed, and the issue did not come up again.

The weather was cold and the night was black a few hours before we launched the ground attack. We had packed and lined up all the trucks and decided who would go where and how to get there. I gathered my five medics in our dusty tent for one last meeting. I wanted to give them a pep talk, the one I always gave before a big mission. Everyone was excited, me included, and we were relieved to finally be doing something. We had worked so hard to get to this point, and now we were going in. The medics were talking fast and joking among themselves. They were young and they were primed, and really didn't need much encouragement from me.

"Listen up," I announced. "Everybody's going to look to you to save their lives, and that's a real important job," I told them. "I've watched you guys for six months, and I know you're the best medics in the division."

They shouted, "Huu-uh!" which I don't even know how to spell, but it was the young army way of saying, "Right on!" Some of my medics were very "huu-uh." Sgt. Eric Blaine and Sgt. Rodney Joyner had strapped on knives and wore bandanas around their necks in preparation for the invasion of Iraq. Their goal in life was not to work in a hospital somewhere; they wanted to be combat medics, and this was what we'd all been preparing for.

There was no question they were brave. One day on the flight line at King Fahd, a Hellfire missile accidentally flew off an Apache and landed in the ammunition dump, setting everything on fire. There was a truck parked near the ammunition, and no one knew if anyone was inside. The medics risked their lives to crawl over the berm to be sure the truck was empty, and it was. They might have been a little loud sometimes, and a little wild, but they were good. Sergeant Jackson was the only woman of the five. Sergeant Middleton was married with one child, and Sergeant Jodie Homan's wife had their second child while we were in the desert. Blaine and Joyner were single, very much so. In fact, I had told them early on that if they picked up some disease in Saudi Arabia, they were going to be in deep trouble. I didn't care about the details of their love lives, but I told them to please be careful. I wasn't going to have my medics needing shots of penicillin. If they did need shots, I promised them, it was going to be with the biggest needle in the whole division.

No matter how good the medics were, at first there were some missions I saved for myself because I was the only doctor. I figured that the mother of a wounded soldier would rather have a doctor who had actually done those things—tracheotomies and open cardiac massage—

working on her son or daughter. I was sure there would be plenty of business for us all, and they would be as experienced as I was by the end of the war. That night I felt very proud of them, and I had no doubt they would do well. None of them had ever been in combat before, and they felt the heavy weight of responsibility. It was one thing to pass out cold pills to our soldiers, our friends; it was another thing to hold one of them, crushed and bleeding, dying in our hands.

Standing before them in the tent, I looked out at their young faces, determined, anxious, and proud. "Our job is to bring everybody back," I said. "I know you guys can do it."

We began the air assault into Iraq at 6 A.M. on February 24, jumping off from our base camp near Rafha all the way to a place in Iraq we called Tactical Assembly Area Cobra. It took our trucks a whole day to catch up with us, even though it was mostly open desert and easy going. In the first hours of the ground attack, we met almost no resistance from the Iraqis. Now that we were inside Iraq, it looked a lot like Saudi Arabia: flat sand and gray skies. We were among the allied units farthest to the west of Kuwait. The heavy armored divisions were going up into Iraq to the east of us, and would turn right into Kuwait.

That night members of the battalion crammed into small tents, or slept inside the helicopters or on the ground. The Apaches had a few attack missions on the second and third days of the offensive, but we didn't have any patients except for a few soldiers with sore throats and coughs. No one was sleeping enough at that point, and the pace had shifted into real war. Everything was focused, all energy directed to a single goal. Our job was to get north as fast as we could to make sure the Republican Guard units did not sneak away toward Basra and up to Baghdad. Now that we had finally moved deep into Iraq and the resistance had been weak, I was confident the war would turn out better than we had expected. Going into the war, we had been prepared for large numbers of casualties, but now I began to think maybe we were not going to lose so many people. As it turned out, the only fatalities in our battalion were on my helicopter when we went on our final mission, on the fourth day of the one-hundred-hour ground war.

5

Morning finally found me perched on my wooden bench, the wool blanket still clenched in my chattering teeth. I hadn't really slept at all, afraid that I would drop the blanket. There was activity in the hallway outside my cell, the stirrings of a new day. The metal door squeaked open, and from the darkness of my cell, the daylight shone brightly behind the white-robed guard. He motioned for me to stand and come with him. We walked a few steps down the hall to Dunlap's cell. The guard opened the door and brought out Dunlap, whose hands were still tied behind his back. He was wearing his uniform with the patches removed by the Iraqis. Dunlap was thin and muscular, with a blond crew cut and a little scraggly mustache. For some reason, almost every American man sent to the Middle East, including my husband, tried to grow a mustache. The young sergeant and I traded smiles, but we were careful not to speak. It was Thursday, February 28, our second day in Iraqi hands.

We were led outside into the gray morning, and the guards directed us to climb into the back seat of a civilian, four-door sedan, which was not an easy maneuver for me because of my knee. I stood in front of the door, not sure how to get myself inside the car. Seeing my difficulty, one of the Iraqis grabbed a handful of my blue robe in the front and lowered me onto the back seat. When I was sitting, he helped push my legs inside and closed the door. I remember being surprised that I was not in very much pain, considering that I had two broken arms, both at odd angles; a smashed finger, which I hadn't paid much attention to; a blown-out knee; and various lacerations and bruises. I knew about the "gate" theory of pain, which means that a number of different factors control the entry of pain impulses to the brain, as if access were controlled by a gate. At that point, I figured my brain had closed the gate.

One Iraqi soldier got behind the wheel to drive, and the other sat next to him on the front seat, holding a stubby AK-47. As we prepared to drive away from the prison, the quiet, overcast morning sky suddenly erupted with red, green, and yellow tracers that streaked above us like fireworks or colorful shooting stars. The stillness was broken by the crack of automatic rifle fire and the deeper WHUMP of heavy explosions. Dunlap and I looked at each other in the back seat and shrugged our shoulders. The two Iraqis didn't react at all. I looked out the car window at the almost deserted streets, trying to figure out what was happening. There were no civilians to be seen, but a few soldiers standing along the road seemed to be blindly firing their AK-47s into the sky. I didn't know what they were shooting at. I would have assumed they were shooting at American planes, but we couldn't see or hear any jets overhead. There were explosions all around us, however, and Dunlap and I had the same fear: some of that Iraqi antiaircraft fire might rain down on us.

The two Iraqis guarding us, oblivious to the commotion in the street, drove us a few miles to a civilian-looking building that had a little fence around it and a front porch. They got out and carefully pulled me out of the back seat by my robe. Dunlap and I were led into the building through a screen door and down a hallway to the right. We turned into the first room on the right, which appeared to be an office, decorated with cheap wall-to-wall carpeting, a desk, and two couches. There was a bookshelf that held a few pieces of melted, twisted metal, and on the wall was a picture of Saddam Hussein. The two soldiers who had driven us installed Dunlap and me on a couch in the office and left the room.

A tall thin man with black curly hair swept into the room with an air of confidence and familiarity. He was thirty-five or so, wearing green wool pants and a green army sweater, but he had a distinctly civilian look about him. Soldiers of any country have a certain posture, a presence, and this man did not have it. He looked more like a college professor as he leaned back easily on the desk in front of us. In fact, he explained in very good English, he was a professional translator and had been mobilized in the army reserves. The whole building, which was a local office of the ruling Baath Party of Saddam, was filled with reservists, he said. There were teachers, merchants, and even some newspaper people who had been activated for duty. Some of the men were old enough to be grandfathers, and the youngest, a nervous teenager clutching an AK-47, guarded the door.

"Why are you here?" the translator asked, addressing the question to me but not waiting for an answer. "The Iraqi people don't hate the American people. Why do you come here to bomb us and to kill us?"

I felt my guard go up instantly. I sensed he would try to propagandize us, and the thought made me more tense than I had been dealing with soldiers. The soldiers didn't care what we thought politically, and with them I knew what the rules were. This man seemed different, and more dangerous. I sat stiffly on the couch, staring at the translator without speaking.

The Iraqi casually walked over to Dunlap and untied his hands. Dunlap rubbed his wrists and stretched his arms without speaking. The translator watched us both, but he seemed relaxed and did not seem concerned we would try anything.

"Do you need to use the water closet?" he asked me.

"Yes, sir," I replied.

"Do you need help?" he asked.

I nodded yes, deciding to speak as little as possible and only when spoken to.

He pointed at Dunlap and said, "You will help her use the bathroom."

Dunlap nodded and stood up off the couch. He walked in front of me, a serious expression on his face. He was not quite sure what to do with me, and looked a little uncomfortable. I leaned forward to stand up by myself, but my knee would not cooperate. I couldn't push off the seat with my arms, either, so I was stuck. Dunlap tried to help me, but he didn't know where to grab me or how to lift me without hurting me. I looked up at him and explained, "You have to grab the front of my robe and sort of pull me up." That's what the Iraqi guard had done to get me in and out of the car, and it seemed to work well enough.

"Yes, ma'am," he said. Those were the first words we had spoken.

At the time we were captured, I didn't even know the young soldier's first name. In the army, we tend to only use last names, except with good friends and people of the same rank. During the interrogations in the bunkers the night before, I had heard him tell the Iraqis his full name was Troy Dunlap. I didn't know much else about him. He took a handful of my robe and hoisted me off the couch. The translator pointed us to the bathroom, and we walked silently down the hall. Our mission was going to be rather embarrassing for both of us, but I needed to use the bathroom, and I preferred a little embarrassment to soiling my only piece of clothing.

The translator walked part of the way with us, but Dunlap and I entered the tiny bathroom alone. Again there was no Western-style toilet, just a hole in the soupy floor. I positioned myself above the hole and said, "What you sorta have to do is hike up the gown so I don't pee on it."

Dunlap was very matter-of-fact about the whole thing, but he was not used to taking care of broken people. He was uncomfortable touching me, and I didn't know if it was because I was older, or I was a girl or a major, or he simply did not want to hurt me. Probably it was a combination of all of those factors. After a couple of false starts, he took hold of the heavy fabric of the robe, and hesitantly pulled it up my legs. There wasn't much room in the bathroom, so Dunlap had to stand right next to me. Eventually he got the robe up high enough to clear the way.

Modesty was never something I worried about too much, and it had been forgotten completely during those months living in the desert. My modesty first began to slip away living in an open hangar at the Dhahran airport and then in the crowded parking garage at King Fahd. Not to say that I or anyone else flaunted nudity, but neither did we stay zipped up in our sleeping bags to change clothes. The little remaining modesty I had became an unaffordable luxury early in our final deployment to the desert. On one of those days, a rainy, miserable one, Lt. Mike Pandol and I took off in a giant truck used to move heavy equipment to see if we could find a spot where our convoy could ford a swollen river. We took turns, one of us walking ahead to test the depth of the water, and one of us driving. When we finally gave up, we were soaked and freezing. The convoy had to drive around the river, and I stayed behind to fly up later to the new site. By the time we had the evening staff meeting and had our tent set up, I was chilled to the bone and hypothermic. I couldn't bend my fingers and my words came thickly.

I walked into our tent for some protection from the environment, but the ground was covered with water, and there were puddles everywhere, turning the powdery sand into a runny chocolate milkshake. I climbed shivering up onto a stretcher, and balancing precariously, I peeled off my wet clothes until I was naked. I asked one of my medics to get a blanket, and another medic, Sergeant Joyner, gave me one of his uniforms to wear until I could unpack my things. All I wanted was to be warm and dry, and nothing else mattered right then. So while modesty is a player in my life when I'm living in civilization, it applies only after the life-threatening things are fixed.

Dunlap had my robe out of the way, but there was one more obstacle. "You need to take off my underwear," I told him, with a nervous grin.

He nodded at me, as if this were something he did all the time, and removed my underwear. We stood there together while I went to the bathroom, staring at the walls, at the ceiling, anywhere to avoid looking at each other.

"I feel pretty silly doing this," I muttered.

"It's okay. It's okay," he said, still looking away from me.

We were alone for the first time, and I whispered, "What did you say yesterday when we were captured?"

"Nothing, ma'am."

"That's good. Did you tell them there were other helicopters?"

"No."

"Are you okay?" I asked.

"Yeah." Dunlap shrugged. "But they had me tied up all night with my head tied to my ankles. They wrapped me in a blanket that was soaked with fuel. Every time these guys came in, they were smoking, and I thought for sure they were going to burn me up. I didn't tell them anything, though."

"Weren't you hurt in the wreck?" I pressed.

"I've just got this big bruise on my leg," he admitted. "Otherwise I'm okay."

"Good," I said. "I think we'll be okay if we just tell them the same thing."

Dunlap probably didn't know very much about the mission except that it was a search and rescue. He had been the last to get on the helicopter and had not heard any of the discussions about who we were going in to rescue or where he was located. That was better for Dunlap during the interrogation. There's no question that it's easier to say "I don't know," if it's true. All he knew when he got on board was that we were going on a real mission somewhere and it sounded neat. The problem was convincing the Iraqis that he really didn't know anything.

"Do you think anybody else is alive?" he asked.

"No. I think we're probably it."

Dunlap and I were both good about keeping our fears and emotions to ourselves. Part of the reason was that we wanted to support each other, and we were not going to do that by breaking down or being weak. A more sensitive person might accuse us of being a pair of emotionless fenceposts. We had no idea what was going to happen to us, but it seemed better to be strong, or at least act strong. Dunlap is a man of few words anyway, but no one ever accused me of being shy and retiring. For now, though, the fewer words the better.

When we finished in the bathroom and returned to the office, the translator was waiting for us. "Sit down, please," he invited.

"We are trying to get you a doctor," he explained to me, "but at this point, none is available."

"Thank you," I said, truly appreciative because no one had yet looked at my injuries.

"We would let you call home and tell your families that you are fine," the translator said, "except the American bombs have destroyed all of our telephones. We do not even have telephones in this country any more."

The translator mostly addressed me, so Dunlap sat quietly. I didn't argue about anything or challenge what he said, because I didn't want to make him angry. He looked at me, waiting for a response.

"I'm sorry to hear that," I said, my tone coldly polite.

He never raised his voice, but he was insistent.

"Why have you come here?"

"Sir, we are in the military and we were ordered to come. The same reason that Iraqi soldiers are fighting. It's because they have been ordered to fight."

"No, no," he said, waving a hand at us dismissively. "We are fighting for our homeland. We have been invaded by the Americans. That is very different."

"Well, that's above my level," I said. "We don't decide those kinds of things."

He walked to the bookshelf and picked up a piece of the twisted metal. "You see this?" he asked theatrically, shaking the burnt chunk at us. "This was part of a building. There were children in this building."

"I'm sorry that happened," I said sincerely. "Certainly there are innocent people killed in all wars."

"But why did you come? Why did you come?"

"Because we are soldiers, just like the Iraqis, and our countries are at war."

"But we are just reservists who have been called up to defend our country," he insisted.

"We have reservists in our country, too," I countered.

"But we just want to go back to our families and our villages."

"I understand that," I assured him. "I'm sure the war will be over soon."

"The Iraqi people don't hate the American people," he said smoothly.

"Well, I don't think the American people hate the Iraqis."

"Then why did you come?" he asked again.

"Sir, that is above my level. I don't make those kinds of policies, and I don't question them. I just go."

"Well, as I said, we do not have telephones in our country any more, but we will let you make video recordings to send to your families so they will know you are safe."

I knew about the infamous Iraqi videos of allied prisoners. The puffy, bruised faces of the pilots showed signs of torture, and the men seemed dazed or even drugged as they spoke broken English in monotone voices, obviously reading from prepared scripts. Saddam apparently thought he could upset the American people by putting our downed pilots on the air. He hoped people would protest the war, like during Vietnam, but the videos only stiffened American resolve to deal with Saddam once and for all.

"No, thank you," I said firmly. "We'll just wait until this sorts itself out, and hopefully we'll get to go home."

What I didn't know then, and what the translator apparently didn't know either, was that the war had ended a few hours earlier, at 8 A.M. that day, Thursday, February 28. President Bush had just announced that the ground war had ended victoriously for the allies, after one hundred short hours. I assumed the war was nearly over, but just that morning we had seen Iraqi soldiers filling the sky with tracers and antiaircraft fire. There must still be some resistance, I thought.

Sunlight streamed in through a big window that was covered with burglar bars. All day Iraqis walked by the window and looked in at us. There were old men, women, and children. Sometimes they yelled at us in Arabic, but mostly they just stared. Both Dunlap and I were worried that one of them might shoot at us through the glass. They were angry because of the bombings of their city and countryside. I could understand that. Besides, we were probably the only Americans who had been there since the war began, so the people were curious. For us in the room, it felt like being on the wrong side of the bars at the zoo. The translator also noticed the visitors at the window and pulled the heavy curtains closed.

The translator left the room, and Dunlap and I, weary because we had not slept the night before, dozed off on the couches. After a short time, a young man carrying a doctor's bag came into the room. He was wearing Western civilian clothes, but he looked like another reservist, and I took him for a medical student called up on active duty. He announced that he was going to examine my injuries. He stood me up in the middle of the room, and Dunlap looked the other way while the doctor helped me struggle out of my blue robe.

It was the first time since the crash I had seen my arms; they were swollen, but there were no open fractures. I was relieved to see the bones had not broken through the skin, but I still couldn't figure out how I had lost so much blood. I felt weak and slightly nauseous from the lack of blood. Perhaps there were internal injuries I didn't know about. The doctor did not have a clue what to do with me, but he did speak English, so I offered a few suggestions about my care. Normally I believe that doctors shouldn't try to treat themselves, but in this case, I thought I could be a consulting physician. He ignored me. His only contribution was to wrap a piece of gauze completely around my body so my arms were bound to my chest. That was much worse and more painful, and I tried to explain why, but he wouldn't listen. It was then that I became convinced he wasn't an orthopedics specialist. After a few more minutes, I wasn't at all sure he was even a doctor. I gave him the benefit of the doubt, though, and thought maybe he was a pathologist or worked in a lab, and I was the first living human patient he had ever seen. He did wrap a piece of gauze over the back of my neck and around my wrists to support my arms, which eased the pain a little.

The "doctor" gave us a pile of wool blankets and told us to sleep. It was the first time in days that we had been comfortable and warm. When the doctor left us alone, Dunlap stood in front of me, grabbed my robe in front and stretched me out on the couch with my head up at one end. He covered me with one of the blankets, and I finally escaped into sleep for a few hours.

The guards woke us for lunch, and we were served two rolls and a large plate of rice smothered with a lentil stew made with tomatoes and onions. I like to eat healthy food, and the dish looked very tasty and smelled delicious. Dunlap, on the other hand, is truly a member of the cheeseburger generation, and he turned up his nose. The translator and two other Iraqis were in the room and settled in to watch us eat, smiling and talking among themselves. Dunlap walked over to my couch and picked up the single plate. He sat next to me with the plate on his knees. He took one of the two metal spoons, scooped up the food, and gave me a bite. Then he daintily served up the tiniest bit of rice for himself and whispered to me, "I can't eat this."

"Sergeant Dunlap, you are going to eat every bite of this," I whispered an order in reply.

"Yes, ma'am," he grumbled.

The Iraqis watched the procedure closely, and they yelled at Dunlap each time he tried to use the same spoon for me and for himself. There were two spoons, and according to the Iraqis, one was for me and one was for Dunlap. We were eating off the same plate, so I didn't understand why it mattered if we used the same spoon, but it mattered terribly to the Iraqis. With me sitting there in a tent-sized robe and Dunlap feeding me, I felt like we were a comedy duo at a dinner theater. Dunlap loaded up a big spoonful of rice and lentils for me and pointed it toward my mouth.

"Wrong," I said.

He dropped his spoon and used the other spoon to prepare another bite for me. I opened wide and chewed gratefully, enjoying the warm rice and beans and knowing it was good for us. Dunlap put down my spoon and used the other spoon to feed himself a few grains of rice and one or two lentils. A few times he tried to be tricky and give me two or three bites in a row, so he wouldn't have to eat any. Each time I announced, "Wrong spoon." Then he would eat that bite, his face twisted in distaste.

"Sergeant Dunlap," I said very quietly, feeling six Iraqi eyes on us. "You are going to eat this. First of all, you don't want to offend these guys. Second of all, you don't know when you're gonna get anything else to eat. So eat everything."

"I can't eat this," he protested.

"Yes you can," I said firmly. I felt like his mother. It reminded me of telling my own daughter to eat her peas. When Dunlap and I finally finished, there was not a grain of rice left on the plate, and we both had eaten well.

I complimented one of the men, whom I took to be the cook, and he smiled and asked if I wanted a cup of tea.

"Oh yes," I said, with a big smile because a cup of hot tea sounded wonderful. He came back with two small glasses, not much bigger than shot glasses, filled with tea. It was sweet and hot and rich. I doubt that Dunlap had ever had a cup of tea in his life before, but he enjoyed his, too.

When we were alone again, I asked Dunlap to rearrange the way the medical student had bound my arms. Dunlap had seen me arguing with the doctor, and he understood what I wanted. He carefully unwrapped the gauze and firmly tied my elbows together in front. That way they couldn't swing behind me, which was the most painful position. My arms then felt more comfortable, although my back still bothered me on the right side near the shoulder. Whenever I leaned against it, there was a deep sting like from a giant bee.

With my elbows firmly tied, there was less pain, and the cup of hot tea had done a great deal to improve my mood. Things had been so rough since the crash that little details like a cup of tea and a strip of gauze made all the difference. We had been prisoners only twenty-four hours.

The translator returned in the middle of the afternoon and announced we were going to the hospital. I knew it was a good idea, because I had not yet seen a real doctor, but I would have been happy to sit on the couch all day, licking my wounds and regrouping. The guard tied Dunlap's hands behind his back, and they marched us out the door. We walked to a station wagon parked outside, and when we got close enough, I could see a stretcher in the back. There, with splints on his leg, was Sgt. Daniel Stamaris, a third member of our crew. So Dunlap and I were not alone after all. I knew Stamaris well, and he had been one of my patients. We had flown together on many missions in Saudi Arabia and into Iraq. He had been a crew chief on our final flight, and was pumping bullets at the Iraqi bunkers from the right door gun when we crashed. He was conscious, but the thirty-two-year-old chief, who normally has a healthy dark complexion, looked pale. I whispered, "Dan, are you okay?"

He didn't say anything, but he smiled weakly at me. Every time the car went over a bump, he was jostled and moaned in agony. I wanted to examine him, but I couldn't move, and I wasn't sure what our captors would say. Every time we talked, they would yell, "No talking! No talking!" I noticed that Stamaris had clean bandages and someone had done a good job splinting his leg. There was a pillow under him, but he was in a lot of pain. We drove for about twenty minutes before the driver stopped and announced that the road was closed. We turned around and returned to the Baath Party office, where Dunlap and I were taken back inside. The driver kept going with Stamaris, and we didn't see him again that day.

"I'm glad Stamaris made it," Dunlap said to me.

"Yeah, it was good to see him."

"Do you think there's anybody else that made it?" Dunlap asked.

"I don't think so, sergeant. To tell you the truth, I was surprised to see him."

That night the translator said the road to the hospital had opened, and we could try again. The night was very dark then, and my first thought was that driving along on an open road would make us a fat target for the Americans, maybe even for our own Apaches. I didn't want to survive the crash and capture, only to be killed by my own guys. I wanted the Apaches to come in and attack the people who were holding us, but not while we were still there. I also worried that in the darkness, the ride would be even bumpier than it had been that day. Every bump that made Stamaris moan, also was excruciating for me. If the car got stuck in the desert, it would be cold and I wouldn't be able to walk back. I had made it this far without much medical attention, except from the medical student. It appeared Stamaris had been seen by a competent person, so I thought we both could make it until the next day. At the same time, I didn't want to tip off the Iraqis that I suspected vehicles on the road would be a prime target that night.

"I can wait for the hospital," I told the translator. "It's too dark, and too bumpy, and if we get stuck we couldn't get back."

"Are you sure?" the translator asked.

"Yes, thank you."

"We can go tomorrow," he assured us.

I was glad that Stamaris had received some medical care. Dunlap and I figured he must have been the only other survivor from our crew of eight. I knew both of the pilots well, as patients and as friends. CW4 Phil Garvey was one of the senior Black Hawk pilots in the army. He had been one of the original pilots when the Black Hawk was first fielded, and he had flown Hueys in Vietnam. Before Desert Shield, he was not even a member of the 2-229th, but he volunteered for Saudi Arabia. "My kids are grown up," he said. "I'll go so someone else won't have to leave their family." His normal job in the Division of Evaluation Standards at Fort Rucker was to travel around the country making sure army pilots were training correctly. He was so good that he was called upon to test the instructor pilots.

There was a large group of senior pilots like Garvey, mostly instructors, who had volunteered for Saudi Arabia. They were great pilots, but at times there were too many chiefs and no Indians. Pilots are a special breed anyway, and Garvey had the delicate job of peacemaker among them. He was heavyset, fatherly looking, as nice as could be.

CW3 Robert Gary Godfrey was only 32, but he also was an instructor pilot. He was flying the left seat on our final mission. Godfrey was heavyset like Garvey, but that was where the similarities ended. While Garvey was calm and relaxed, Godfrey was pumped up and wild. I knew Garvey had seen a lot of combat in Vietnam, and that had left him seasoned and in control. Godfrey was too young to have gone to Vietnam, and his younger days must have been pretty crazy. We used to tease him about going bald, joking about how he had worn the hair off the top of his head. Godfrey had a good sense of humor, though, and he threw the barbs right back.

Sergeant Ortiz, the senior Pathfinder in our crew, was a stickler for detail. When we flew anywhere before the war started, even just to take showers at the nearby base called King Khalid Military City, Ortiz prepared checklists for us: the frequencies to call medevac in case of an emergency, the frequencies for the battalion, and the frequencies for the AWACS radar planes. Everywhere we went, Ortiz had a checklist. He constantly fretted about making everything perfect, and even out in the desert, his uniform was always crisply pressed. He must have shaved twice a day. He was a good-looking young man, only twenty-seven years old, but already he was worried about getting too old for flight school. When it was time to take the physical exam needed to get into the school, I told him to wait for me to smooth the way with the optometrist. But Ortiz was in a hurry and went by himself. The doctor got huffy and wouldn't see him without an appointment. Ortiz was so motivated, so eager to do things, that he could drive me crazy.

Billy Butts was the door gunner on the left side. I didn't know him very well, but we had been on a few missions before. He was not much taller than I am, but muscular. Sgt. Roger P. Brilinski was the other Pathfinder, and I had never met him. If people didn't get sick, I often didn't meet them, and these were healthy young men.

Dinner that night was more of Dunlap's favorite rice with stew, some brown rolls, and hot tea. The guards then led us to another room to sleep and gave us two piles of blankets. I thanked them, and the guards left us alone for the night. They let us stay together because I was helpless without Dunlap. Iraq was not as conservative as Saudi Arabia, where men and women were segregated in public. The Saudis never would have let Dunlap and me stay in the same room, no matter how badly I was injured.

Dunlap spread out a blanket on the floor and helped me lie down. He unlaced my boots, being careful with my right knee, and pulled them off. He took off his own boots, too, and used the four black boots to prop up my arms. I lay there for awhile, flat on my back, and tried to get comfortable. But just when I relaxed, my arms settled and the bones shifted, stabbing me with pain, or my knee ached or my back hurt. I groaned and shifted positions every thirty minutes, and Dunlap came running over from his place against the wall to adjust the blankets, or the boots, or my position. I don't think the poor kid slept all night. He was good at tending to me, and quickly learned which ways my arms would move and how to make me comfortable.

The Iraqis had placed Dunlap's blankets along one wall, and mine along another, but after a while Dunlap moved his blankets to be near me. We were so alone in that locked room behind enemy lines that neither of us wanted to be far apart. Once when he was adjusting my arms, he got behind me and I leaned against him. Finally I relaxed, my weight supported by Dunlap, and I wanted to stay there forever.

"This is the most comfortable I've been since we got to Iraq," I sighed. "Could we just sit like this for a minute?"

"Sure," he said, and I leaned against him, glad for the human contact, glad he was there with me.

I chuckled to myself about our relationship. I was the senior person, so I was expected to be responsible. But Dunlap had enough male ego that he was not going to appear weak in front of a woman or an officer. I certainly was not going to appear weak in front of a sergeant, so we reinforced each other's basic belief that we had to be brave. I was grateful to have Dunlap with me, and at the same time, my condition gave him something important to do and kept his mind off feeling sorry for himself. Dunlap knew that if I had not needed so much care, the Iraqis probably would have locked him in a closet with his head roped to his ankles.

People talk about male bonding in the military and how female soldiers supposedly will disrupt unit cohesion. Real bonding, however, goes far beyond whether the people involved are two men or two women or one of each. It's much deeper than that. Going to war with a unit, risking your life with them, builds an intimate and intense relationship. The soldiers don't all have to be men for that to happen.

The night was still, and we could hear only a few muffled voices speaking in Arabic outside the walls of our little room. We were quiet mostly, glad for each other's company but content to lie there without talking.

"Ma'am," Dunlap said quietly, "you're really tough."

"What'd you think, I'd cry or something?" I asked with a laugh.

"Yeah, I thought you would."

"That's okay, Troy," I said after a while. "I thought you'd cry, too."

That was the first time I called him by his first name. It seemed like the right thing at the time. Maybe I wanted him to know I knew his name. Maybe I thought it would feel like a friend was there.

During the middle of the night we heard scuffling in the hallway and raised voices. Dunlap grabbed his blankets and scurried back to the other wall. People were walking up and down the hallway. I waited for the door to burst open, but it stayed closed. The next day, the translator told us that some people from the town were angry about the American bombing and had come for us. It sounded like a lynch mob, but there was no way to know if it was true, or if the translator was just trying to scare us even more.

The translator was the only one of the reservists at the party office who spoke English well enough to speak to us, and he talked all the time. Once we got past the military questions, the translator asked the question that every Iraqi seemed to ask me.

"Are you married?"

"Yes," I said.

"Do you have children?"

"No," I lied. I had heard stories from the POWs in Vietnam who said that their captors had tried to collect personal information to use against them as an emotional weapon. I also worried that if there were a pro-Iraqi terrorist operation in the United States, and its members knew I had a daughter, Regan might be in danger.

"Why don't you have children?" the translator continued.

"I don't know," I improvised. "I guess we're too busy. Bad luck, maybe."

"What does your husband do?"

"He's in the air force."

"Is he a pilot?"

"No, he's a doctor."

I never denied being married because it seemed like everybody in the Middle East over the age of eighteen was married, and I didn't think my captors would believe I was single. Perhaps I also was trying to appear less desirable to them. I could imagine myself being recruited for some Iraqi's harem, and that did not seem like a good plan. Mostly I wanted to appear normal, not unusual. They seemed to understand that it was possible, however unfortunate, that I was married and did not have children. They probably thought the only reason a woman would be in the army was that she couldn't have children.

I was never sure whether the translator was trying to propagandize me, trying to get information to use against me, or was truly being friendly. I decided that I didn't care whether he was friendly or not; he was still the enemy, and he had the potential to hurt me. Maybe I had watched too many Gestapo movies, but I never trusted him. He seemed almost reptilian. I kept thinking he was the good cop, and the bad cop was waiting to appear.

"Saddam is really a great man," the translator gushed. "Why are you Americans doing this to us? Saddam has been the savior of our country. Before Saddam, our children had no shoes. We did not have education. But now we are strong."

I neither challenged nor agreed with what he said. Saddam's invasion of Kuwait never came up, and I certainly was not going to be the first to mention it. I was in no position to argue with this person, and all I wanted to do was get out with our lives. When we were alone, Troy and I talked about trying to escape, and we debated whether we could squeeze through the barred window. Even if we did get outside, though, where would we go? How far could a guy in an American uniform get with a brown-haired lady wearing a long blue robe? The Iraqi civilians we had seen so far did not look at all disposed to helping us. Lynching us, maybe, but not helping.

The morning of the third day, Friday, March 1, Troy folded the blankets and stacked them so we would appear to be neat, good soldiers. The translator announced that the road was open again, and we could try to make it to the hospital. The guards left Troy with the skittish teenager, who gripped an AK-47 in sweaty young hands. I nodded goodbye to Troy, and he smiled back at me. One of the guards wrapped a scarf around my eyes as a blindfold. If I tipped my head back, I could see my feet as the guards loaded me into another station wagon. Stamaris was there again, but he didn't look any better. I missed having Troy with me, and I hoped he would be all right alone.

We drove for about thirty minutes and pulled up to a small two-story clinic. Later, I learned that we were in downtown Basra in southern Iraq. I could see underneath the blindfold, and the guard took it off when we arrived at the clinic. I was surprised to see so many people in the waiting room, and there were entire families waiting with sick or injured loved ones. Some were bandaged and had limbs bound with splints. One man with a gauze patch over his eye sat with a woman in a black robe. The guards carried Stamaris on a stretcher and I walked through the waiting room with him. A young emergency room doctor used scissors to cut the sleeves off my blue robe. They made X-rays of my arms and my knee. The clinic's facilities were austere but seemed adequate.

Stamaris told the emergency room doctor that I was his doctor back home. The doctor spoke good English and invited me to look at the X-rays of Stamaris's leg, which looked terrible. There were so many fragments of bone it looked like dice spilled on a table. We were allowed to talk inside the clinic, and Stamaris told me that he had not had any contact with other prisoners and had been held alone since the crash. He said he was captured the night of the crash, but his captors thought he was going to die. They didn't want to be bothered with him, so they put him under a tarp and left him to die by the side of a road. Living in the deserts of Saudi Arabia and Iraq, we had always heard wild dogs howling at night, and Stamaris worried that he would be picked apart before dawn. He survived the night, however, and the next day another Iraqi patrol grabbed him. He was taken to an Iraqi field hospital before going to the Baath Party building where we found him.

The doctor wanted to re-splint Stamaris's leg, and he wanted me to convince Stamaris to consent. I explained the situation to Stamaris.

"Ma'am, what should I do?"

"If it were my leg, I'd let them do it, Daniel," I said truthfully. "They know what they are doing, and that's what I'd do if I were taking care of you."

There was no way I could do anything for Stamaris but give him advice. I did feel good about the doctors at this clinic: they were intelligent and articulate. Stamaris consented and they took him to a treatment room.

The doctor also showed me my own X-rays. The left arm was a classic displaced spiral fracture between the shoulder and the elbow. "Yep, that's why it hurts," I said.

As he was looking at the X-ray of the other arm, he asked me, "Major? Did you always have a piece of metal in your shoulder?"

"No," I said. "Not before the other day."

He showed me the film. He had to hold it to the light for me because I couldn't move my arms. There it was: a bullet lodged in my shoulder. There was no way to tell what kind of weapon it had come from, maybe an AK-47. I also saw small pieces of shrapnel surrounding the bullet under the skin. The bullet must have passed through the fuselage of the helicopter before hitting me. That slowed the velocity and probably saved my right arm, which also had a displaced, fractured humerus, the bone between the elbow and the shoulder. The bullet wound solved the mystery of how I had lost so much blood. I had lacerations on my knee, face, and hand, but none of the cuts looked bad enough to account for the fact that I was so weak. The bullet would have caused massive blood loss, and it also explained why I felt like I had a giant bee sting in my back.

The Iraqi doctor and I determined the extent of the damage: besides the two broken arms and the bullet wound, I had a crush injury of my right pinkie, with a piece of bone missing. The ligaments were torn in my right knee and there was a deep laceration. The cut on my hand was so deep that I could see the tendons. My face felt tender, and the doctor said I had facial lacerations and multiple bruises. I was sure I had black eyes, but I had not seen myself in a mirror since the crash. By then my arms were swollen and colored black, blue, and yellow. As long as I didn't move my arms, they didn't hurt badly. I still had pulses to both hands and I could feel my fingers, which meant the nerves were not badly damaged.

The doctor removed the bullet and put plaster splints on my upper arms and cradled them in slings. He didn't set the arms in the correct orientation, but at least they moved much less in the splints and there was less pain. I sat quietly, because the doctor seemed competent. Doctors usually are bad patients, but this one knew at least as much about orthopedics as I did. I don't even like orthopedics, so I let him do his job. The doctor already had cut off the sleeves of my blue robe, and the nurses helped me out of what remained. They found an old Iraqi military uniform, cut the sleeves off the shirt so my arms would fit, and dressed me. When they had finished, the orderlies wheeled Stamaris out on a stretcher and we left the clinic.

"How am I gonna do?" Stamaris asked me as I walked alongside his stretcher.

"I think you're gonna do fine," I told him. Stamaris had terrible X-rays, but there was no point discussing the medical aspects of his condition right then. The foot at the end of that badly broken leg still had pulses, and he could move his toes. Like my arms, I thought, his leg will heal, if he gets surgery in time.

Back in the car, they covered my eyes again, and we drove back to the Baath Party office. As soon as I walked into our room, I could tell by the tense expression on his face that Troy had endured a bad couple of hours. He had been left alone with the teenage guard, who was even younger than Troy. The young guard took our presence personally, and his attitude seemed to be, "You have invaded my country, and I would love to do something about it." When I sat down on the couch next to Troy, he whispered, "This guy's gonna kill me." I just laughed, but I confess Troy didn't think it was very funny. We both relaxed when the young guard took his post outside the room.

Troy asked about Stamaris, and I said I thought he would be fine. I told him about the clinic, and how everyone had stared at us. Walking in with Stamaris, I had tried to smile at the Iraqi patients and hospital staff. I had concentrated on looking straight ahead, never at the ground, as I walked through the waiting room to have my X-rays taken. I'd wanted to be strong for Stamaris, because he needed a lift. He had been alone with the Iraqis the whole time, and that would have been tough for anyone, even someone who hadn't been badly injured. I also wanted the Iraqis to know that we were proud and had not been broken. They'd looked back at me. Maybe I imagined it, but they seemed to understand.

Now I was back with Troy, and I felt safe. I had been fed a decent meal and had sipped a cup of hot tea. I was alive and my captors had given me medical care. I was a prisoner of war in Iraq, and I had no idea how long I would be there, but all things considered, life was not bad.

6

life has always been good to me. Even deploying to the Middle East, I had a great experience—until the final week. While I never expected my life would lead me to an Iraqi prison cell in the middle of a war, there is little I can complain about during my thirty-six years. I can't find a clear thread to explain the path my life has taken, no indication in my childhood that I would become a doctor or a soldier. The only constant in my life has been a burning desire to do the best, to seek new challenges and conquer them.

I was born in Dayton, Ohio, when my parents were still in their early twenties. My father was an electrical engineer who always seemed young and energetic enough to play with my friends and me, to help us build a tree house or to care for a baby bird that we had found. While he worked in his shop in the basement, I sat on the workbench separating the screws and nuts and bolts and putting them in the right little jars. We had fun together, and I think my father considered me his first-born son.

Many of my favorite memories from early childhood include my father's parents, who lived on a farm in Ohio. We had left Ohio for New York when I was little, but I returned to visit my grandparents as often as my parents would let me. My grandparents were restoring a dilapidated old farm house, and I helped paint the barn and repair the roof with my grandfather. He was an electrician, and in the evenings when he came home from work, we would sit at the kitchen table and talk. He was an emotional man who read books, cried over poetry, and knew history. He showed me how to shoot a gun and taught me that an unloaded gun was the most dangerous thing a person could have. A gun was not a toy but a weapon to kill. Carrying an unloaded gun was dangerous, he said, because someone was likely to shoot at you first thinking it was loaded.

My grandfather was from Kentucky, where the Hatfield and McCoy feud was not just something in books. He knew first hand about tradition and loyalty to family, feelings that were cemented during four years in the Marine Corps and at Iwo Jima and Guadalcanal. He never talked to me about the horrible things he must have seen during the war, but he did talk about integrity, friendship, and honor. He told me about virtue and how a person's word meant everything. There were many things worse than dying, my grandfather said, and one of them was living with dishonor.

Like my father, my grandfather didn't consider me a girl, at least in the traditional sense. My grandfather grew up during a time when women were protected and sheltered, but he didn't expect his own women to be weak. My grandmother came from a line of strong women. She had worked every day of her life but never used that as an excuse for not being a good mother or not having fun; she thought a woman could work hard and raise children. Her mother (my great-grandmother) had been a pilot in the 1930s, had married multitudinous times, and knew Amelia Earhart. Women in our family did not burn their bras, they just went out and did what they wanted to do.

Growing up, I was what most people would call a tomboy. I built dams in the creek and floated on rafts and collected frogs, toads, and snakes. When I was thirteen, my parents bought me a dog, and she became my constant companion. I had read *Big Red* and *Irish Red* and all the Irish setter books, but I didn't want to be just like them, so I chose a Gordon setter. She was my birthday present and Christmas present combined that year, and I named her Reba. I had a few friends as a girl, but I wasn't a member of any of the cliques in our town, East Aurora, located about twenty miles from Buffalo. Our community was a stable, white, Anglo-Saxon Protestant enclave where everyone, us included, went to church on Sundays.

My first sister came along when I was six, followed by another sister when I was eleven and a brother when I was already fifteen. So for a long time, I was the only child. I use the word *child* loosely, because my parents always acted like I was a small adult. Treating me like an adult—my mother says I was an "old lady" when I was a little girl— was to become the biggest cause of friction in our house. When I became a rebellious teenager and thought I could make my own decisions—just like my parents had taught me to do—they tried to clamp down on me.

The big fights I had with my mother were over my image. I probably was not as restrained and conservative as my mother would have liked. My mother is slim and attractive and dresses well. We didn't always value the same things, however, and she worried about my reputation and my choice of friends. I didn't care how I appeared to other people, and if they didn't like me the way I was, they could find someone else to like. That was the opposite of what my mother believed, and we clashed. Even when I was mad, I never cried, screamed, or threw a tantrum. Control was always one of the greatest virtues in our family. The women, as well as the men, were to be strong and in control. Fortunately, my mother and I have mellowed. Now I have a teenage daughter of my own, and I understand what my mother was trying to teach me about image. At the same time, my mother cares less what other people think about us.

I entered my teens in the 1960s, when people my age said we should not take society and school seriously. I felt conflicting pressures to conform to my own generation—the dropout generation—to my parents' expectations, and mostly to my own overwhelming need to excel. I didn't want to drop out of society as some of my friends urged; I wanted to do everything and said I didn't care what anyone thought. Like every young girl, inside I really did care what other people thought about me, and I wanted to be liked and respected. I resolved the conflict by being friends with a group of people who were not very academically oriented, but who didn't say anything if I did my homework and earned good grades. Older people mistakenly thought I was a troublemaker and a rebel because of my friends, but the teachers were always satisfied with my school work. That was the only way to please everyone, including myself.

By the end of high school, I was no longer embarrassed about being smart. I read all the time, mostly novels and historical fiction, plus *Agamemnon* and all the works of Shakespeare. When we were about fourteen, my friend Kathy Koningisor and I practiced *Romeo and Juliet* until we could recite all the lines, and she later became a professional actress. I always assumed that I would go to college, and I thought maybe I would study to become a veterinarian. I loved dogs and rode horses, I was good at science, and I loved to learn new things. Maybe

I could become a scientist, I thought. I didn't know any real scientists, but it sounded neat to have a job that would pay me to learn.

I graduated from high school after my junior year in 1971 and was accepted at Wilmington College in Ohio with a full tuition scholarship for academics. I wasn't eligible for financial aid because of need, but I wanted to pay my own way through college and held out for a scholarship. I had decided to become a scientist. My chemistry teacher in high school was the best teacher I had had, so chemistry and organic chemistry were interesting to me. I also liked chemistry because it was difficult. I wrote well and got A's in all my English courses, but I considered them too easy. My friends said I should be an English major, but it wasn't a challenge, and that was when I realized one of the things that still guides me: just because I'm good at something doesn't mean I'm obligated to do it. Another reason for going into science was practical. I didn't go to college for the social life; I went to get an education, so I could get a job. I didn't know what kind of job I could get as an English major.

After two years, I had taken all the courses I was interested in that were offered at Wilmington, and had legally established financial independence from my parents. That meant I was eligible for state education loans when I transferred to Cornell University. I had wanted to go to Cornell from the beginning, but I couldn't afford the tuition. There I finished my bachelor of science degree in microbiology and genetics at age 20, and had already started my graduate research. Research was the perfect and passionate focus for my energies in those days. I could define any problem and solve it, and there was no limit to the problems I could find. I thought scientific research was what I wanted to do forever.

At the time, I was in love with a future botanist. I met Marvin at Wilmington and he followed me to Cornell, where he studied botany and earned a living installing car stereos. We were young and we were poor, and we married as seniors in college. Our daughter, Regan, was born at the end of my first year of graduate school. Life was pretty rugged in our little log cabin in Freeville, in the middle of a state forest in upstate New York. We cut eighteen cords of wood for the winter, because that was our only source of heat. We grew our own vegetables, canned our own tomato sauce and green beans, and even put up venison. We raised chickens, and Regan was weaned on milk from our goats. We were "back to the land" types, and some of the lessons I learned—

"you can do anything and everything if you try hard enough," and "you won't die without indoor plumbing"—have been invaluable.

I am the first to admit, the U.S. Army was the farthest thing from my mind in those days. My first exposure to the army came during my second year of graduate school, when I was invited to present an abstract about amino acid metabolism at a conference in Atlantic City. It was the first conference I had ever attended, and before going I had to shop for a new outfit because the only clothes I owned were blue jeans. After my talk, a man in a green uniform introduced himself as a lieutenant colonel in the army. He said he worked at the Letterman Army Institute of Research at the Presidio of San Francisco.

"How long are you going to be at Cornell?" he inquired.

"About a year or two more," I told him.

"Have you ever thought about being in the army? We're looking for someone to do amino acid metabolic research."

I was surprised and flattered. I'd never been to a conference before, and for all I knew, job offers always flew around the corridors. But the army? I had never considered the army as a place for me. Two of my uncles had been to Vietnam and had come home safely, but that war had been fought and finished without really affecting me directly. At the time of the conference, my attention was focused on research, horses, Gordon setters (by then we had several), and my baby. I ignored the rest of the world. Even during the height of Vietnam, I didn't follow the news about the war, and I never thought about the military at all. It wasn't that I was antimilitary like some of my college friends; I just didn't think about it, and I certainly never imagined I would join.

"Would you at least consider it?" asked the man in uniform.

"Sure," I grinned. "I've got to find a job doing something."

A few weeks later I received a letter inviting me to San Francisco to learn a scientific technique related to work I was doing at Cornell. I suggested to my professor that I learn the technique and bring it back for the university's research program. He agreed, and I flew to the West Coast.

Letterman was a wonderful place with a great lab and equipment. It didn't seem at all like I had imagined the army: the scientists wore civilian clothes and the atmosphere was just like at any lab. None of my colleagues at Cornell knew anything about the army, and I certainly didn't, but I was impressed with what I saw, and it seemed like a good place to work. In April 1978 I signed the papers, raised my right hand, and swore to defend the country as an officer in the U.S. Army. The way I saw things, I was swearing to do research, not fight. I would have had the same reaction if I had signed up to be a staff scientist at the University of Wisconsin.

I had a Ph.D. in nutrition and biochemistry from Cornell under my belt, but my army education began soon after I was sworn in, when I flew to San Antonio for the Medical Service Corps Officer Basic Course. The army gave me time toward promotion for the years I'd spent in graduate school, so technically I was a first lieutenant (with only two months to go to make captain), but I truly was a neophyte army officer. Almost everyone else at the school had just received their bachelor degrees and were new second lieutenants, fresh out of their college Reserve Officers Training Corps (ROTC). They had studied military science and attended military camps to learn soldier skills, drilling, and leadership. I didn't know anything about the military.

I was so green that I had never even put on a uniform and had to buy my first pair of fatigues. In those days, the women's fatigues had buttons up the side instead of zippers in the front. I was slender, so the roomy trousers came up easily and fit fine. We lined up for our first formation under the hot sun at Fort Sam Houston. I imitated the others standing at attention and stared straight ahead, until I noticed my colleagues giggling and pointing at me. One of them informed me that I had my pants on backwards.

The army also introduced me to organized exercise, what they called physical training or "PT." I had never run anywhere in my life, but I was strong from riding and baling hay, and I liked to exercise. "PT" was just one of the new expressions I picked up; there was a whole new language to learn. I've always liked to learn new things, and I studied hard, but this new world was so alien to me. One day during class when an instructor called on me, I was stumped for the answer. I turned desperately to the student next to me for help, and he whispered, "S.O.L." I turned back to the instructor and proudly answered, "S.O.L., sir." The room erupted in laughter, and even the stone-faced instructor smiled. I didn't know at the time that "S.O.L." was an old army expression that stands for "Shit Out of Luck."

The first time I took all this soldiering to heart was on a week-long field problem, which is what the army calls playing war games in the woods. I had been dirty and miserable plenty of times before, but this was the first time I went camping in a squad and was forced to de-

pend on another person for survival. Camping had always been a chance
to be alone, to get away from other people, but in the army we were
forced to work together, to grow closer. For example, in order to navigate,
I had to take a compass reading and send another soldier out to mark
the spot. Then he would take a reading, and I would leapfrog past him,
on and on until we reached our destination. We built tents together
and learned to carry litters with wounded soldiers. It took teamwork
to load the wounded onto the helicopters. On the fifth day, I was riding
in the back of a 2½-ton truck, which by then I had learned to call a
"deuce-and-a-half," and I was hot and dirty and surrounded by my new
buddies. It felt great. I had never been a member of a club or a group
in school, and I'd never had much school spirit, but all of a sudden
in the army, I found that spirit and I loved it.

The other thing I learned being on my own for basic training at Fort
Sam Houston was that I didn't want to be married anymore. Not that
it was a mistake to have been married; it was just that a chapter of
my life had ended. The hardest part of basic training was being away
from Regan. I knew that moping around missing her was not at all useful,
however, and I became efficient at putting those feelings into a drawer
and closing it until I could see her again. That's an emotional survival
skill that would serve me well later in life. Although we went as a family
to San Francisco for my first army job, it soon became clear our marriage
would not work out, and Marvin and I split up soon after. Regan stayed
with me.

Working at the lab in California, I quickly realized I was one of
the few people who were gung-ho about the military. Many of the others
were civilians or people who, like me, had joined the army to be scientists, not soldiers. The medical department as a whole (at least in
San Francisco) seemed much less "militaristic" than other branches
of the army, such as the infantry. To remind myself that I really was
in the army, I went with a gung-ho friend to take the course and exam
for the Expert Field Medical Badge, which signifies that the wearer
can actually perform the skills needed for operational field medicine.
The badge is the expert infantry badge of the medical department, and
of all the schools I have been to in the military, this was by far the
most difficult. Very few people who try for the badge ever earn it.

We had a week of classroom instruction and then a week of field
testing in first aid, preventive medicine, evacuations, and other tech-
niques we would need on the battlefield. We not only studied the medical

skills, we had to be able to perform them under rough conditions. The course culminated in a twelve-mile forced march, which we had to complete in less than three hours while carrying heavy packs. Our class had sixty people when the course began, but only eight graduated. I was the only woman who finished. There were women who washed out, but most of the men also failed. Earning that badge made me feel good about the army, and about myself.

Another thing I was proud of was being selected by the army as an astronaut candidate. I've always loved the idea of "Star Trek" and going where no one had gone before, so space travel was my idea of real fun. My goal was to some day reach the space station, if I lived long enough and we flew fast enough. I went for a week of interviews at NASA in Houston. There were medical tests and a full day of psychological screening. I was not chosen, but I considered it an honor to be one of the few people who made it to the interview. I was picked for a second interview in 1987, but again I wasn't chosen to be an astronaut. I was disappointed, but I guess it was better to find out I wasn't what they wanted before I moved the whole family to Houston.

Life in California was pleasant. I rode my two horses and showed five dogs all over the state. I joined the women's basketball team at the Presidio, even though I'd never played before. We travelled to other bases, and while we weren't the best team to ever suit up for a game, we did have a lot of fun. I was the only officer on the team, and I didn't understand why. Maybe the others were too busy to have fun. I also joined the post track team and ran the quarter mile. All these activities were new for me, and I did them because of a new sense of belonging I felt in the army. I had never felt such a sense of ownership in an organization in school or anywhere. I liked the camaraderie, being part of the team. My father thought I was an idiot because I could make more money outside the army. I told him that making money was no more important to me in the army than it had been in graduate school. Anyway, even with the modest pay in the army, I was earning ten times what I made during graduate school.

I worked in the lab's division of experimental surgery, and the other scientists were physicians. I noticed they made more money than I did and had higher rank, even though all of them did not necessarily do very good research. I reached an impasse when I wanted to do research on humans: the army wouldn't let me unless I worked with a physician. I decided I could work with rats and chickens the rest of my life, or I could go to medical school and become a physician myself. I studied hard and took the entrance exam for medical school. I was accepted at several schools, but I already had decided I liked the army after four years, so I enrolled in the military's Uniformed Services University in Bethesda, Maryland, near Washington, D.C., for the fall of 1982.

Before going to medical school, it was time once again to remind myself that I was still in the army, so I signed up for the Airborne School at Fort Benning, Georgia. The course was physically demanding—by then I was in very good shape and could do pushups all day—and it also was militarily demanding. Airborne School was supposed to teach us how to jump out of an airplane, but that was not the most important skill I learned. In fact, jumping out of an airplane was easy: they pushed us out the door. Jumping was scary the first time, but none of us was going to refuse because we would have been embarrassed. What I really learned at Airborne School was pride and leadership. When addressed, we no longer answered, "Yes, sir," but "Airborne, sir!" When something was going well or was fun or satisfying it was simply "Airborne!" If we passed the difficult three-week course, we would be distinguished from the rest of the soldiers in the army by the wings on our uniforms.

As the third most senior captain in my Airborne class, I was given a platoon of about two hundred people to lead. On the first day I looked out across this ocean of people and had no idea what to do with them. At the lab, I had a little group of technicians under me, but I didn't have to lead them, and I certainly didn't make them march in formation. This was the real army, though, and I was out of my league. I had a relatively high rank compared with my classmates, but I knew far less than they did about military skills. I was unusually quiet and tried to listen to what the other leaders did, but I didn't have a clue.

That night the class leader, another medical service corps captain, but one who had been an enlisted marine in Vietnam, came to my room. "I watched you today and I tried to decide what to do," he confessed. "I could either try to humiliate you and get you to quit. Or I could try to help you. I've decided to try to help you."

"Thank you," I said, and we went to the parking lot and practiced drill and ceremony commands all night. There was no way to memorize so much so quickly, but I learned the secret was to find a noncommissioned officer who knew all this stuff and make him the platoon sergeant. We never did become the most "strack"—or squared away—platoon in the army, but we got through the course. On one maneuver we didn't do so well, and I rightly got the blame. As punishment, one of the instructors yelled at me to hit the ground and start doing push-ups. When I got down on my hands and started the first push-up, I saw the whole platoon get down and follow me. They could have just watched me do my push-ups alone, but they chose to follow me, and it was a wonderful feeling.

During the early part of the course, the "black hats," as the instructors were known, were very tough on me. When they saw I didn't know how to make formations, they were visibly aghast. I felt they were trying to harass me into quitting or at least breaking down into tears. I didn't know if they didn't like women or they didn't like me or they thought I was a wimp. I wasn't going to give them the satisfaction of making me cry, but the constant pressure was getting me down, and during one of the daily six-mile runs, I decided I was ready to quit. As my feet pounded the hard, endless road, I had a cramp in my side, my lungs burned, and all I could think about was dropping out and going home. It would have been so easy. It wasn't unusual to drop out of Airborne School, and no one at the lab would have thought less of me. They thought I was crazy to go in the first place.

"I'm gonna quit," I told the sergeant running alongside me.

We were running hard, but he caught his breath and asked, "What would all these troops think if you dropped out?"

That got to me. I wanted to be a leader, and being a leader meant setting an example. I couldn't quit now. I smiled at the sergeant, and kept running. I earned an "Airborne" badge to wear on my chest.

I started medical school that September with great expectation, but I soon found myself depressed and lonely. Biochemistry and other subjects were easy for me because of my science background, but some courses, particularly anatomy, were very tough. I had been out of school for a long time and resented being made to remember things for which I could see no value. I missed research and simply didn't enjoy being lectured to and tested on my ability to memorize the excruciating minutiae of all the parts of the human body.

During the first few weeks at school, I made two good friends, both of them air force students. Peter Demitry and Kory Cornum had been friends since their days together at the Air Force Academy. Peter learned soon after we met that I had a Ph.D. in biochemistry, and he immediately suggested that we form a study group. He invited Kory, who like Peter could barely spell *biochemistry,* and they came to my house every Sunday afternoon for some "E.I."—an academy expression for extra instruction.

Peter and I actually studied, while the ever-confident Kory generally snoozed on the couch. I ended up helping Peter get an "A" in biochemistry, but falling madly in love with Kory. So much so that we were engaged by November.

I was single again when I met Kory, but thought I had no time or inclination for romance. He first won the heart of six-year-old Regan, which was probably a good strategy. It all began because Kory was doing better than I was in our anatomy class, and he volunteered to watch Regan one night while I went to study. I came home at about 12:30 A.M. to find this enormous rugby player asleep on my couch. I wasn't sure what to do with him, but he woke up and drove himself home. The next morning all I heard from Regan was what a wonderful guy this Kory was. The two of them had stayed up after doing her homework and built houses from our old packing boxes in the basement. "Mother, he has a Corvette," Regan announced, as if that should have been enough to convince me.

Very soon after, I invited Kory to a dinner of chicken Marsala at the house and took him to a movie, *Chariots of Fire.* He normally preferred comedies, but I thought he needed a little drama in his life, and this was a good movie for two people who liked to run. Before the show started, we sat in his car and talked, passing a cold bottle of champagne between us. One thing I liked about him right away was his self-confidence. This was a man who was not going to be bowled over by me. We returned to my house after the movie to talk a little longer, and at a reasonable hour, I walked him to the door.

"I'd kiss you good night if I was nine inches taller," I told him, looking up at the huge man in the open doorway.

With that he stepped off the stoop to look me in the eye and said, "Now I'm nine inches shorter." I gave him a little peck on the lips.

We started jogging together and Kory came to dinner more often, so often that I let him buy groceries because he ate more in one meal than Regan and I ate in a week. Regan and I had little money left over every month after we paid the rent on our house and her tuition at a private school. The move to Washington and the temporary demotion to second lieutenant, which was required by the medical school, both had taken a toll on our finances.

I first began to suspect things were getting serious with Kory when, out of the blue, my lab partner commented, "You know, Kory really likes you."

I looked at the woman and said, "Really?"

"Yeah," she continued. "He went out with me for two years, and he never went running with me."

Our relationship had gone from just friends to good friends to very serious in only one month. I worried we were going too fast, but Kory said, "When it's right, it's right. If it is, we might as well do it. If it's not, we could wait forever, and it still won't be right." We were married on March 29, 1983, at the Air Force Academy chapel in Colorado Springs.

There was one part of medical school that made me very nervous, and that was giving my first physical exam. As students, we got to practice on real patients, people who volunteered to help us learn and were probably bored being in the hospital. I was anxious the entire day trying to imagine myself walking in on a patient, someone I didn't even know, and asking questions that would make me look like an idiot. Normally I like new experiences, but I like doing them well. For example, I practiced for months before my first dog show, and when we got to the show, we won. But the only way to practice for a physical was to actually perform one. My first patient was understanding, though, and he made it easy. The more patients I saw, the more I came to like dealing with people instead of mice.

When I finally made it to the third year and was doing real medical things such as surgery and internal medicine, I began to enjoy my classes more. My grades got progressively better, and I went from the bottom third of my class during the first year to graduate in the top third. I've always had a practical view of grades, and my grade point average for all my academic life—through high school, college, graduate school, and medical school—has been virtually the same: B+. I figure there is a certain amount that I need to know. After that point, the amount of work required to score better will not result in learning much more, or make me better at doing something, and therefore is not worth the effort.

During our fourth year, Kory convinced me to join him for the army's Aviation Medicine Basic Course to learn to be flight surgeons. He went

on and on about how it would be fun and exciting to be a flight surgeon—basically a general practitioner who cares for pilots at home
and in the field. Flight surgeons are medical doctors who have extra
training and experience in aviation, altitude physiology, field sanita-
tion, and combat medicine. Kory was more excited than I was, because
the army school at that time taught the flight surgeon students to fly
helicopters. He loved flying and had wanted to fly jets since he was
at the Academy. I still thought I wanted to return to academic research,
but I agreed to give it a try.

When time came for flight training, I was nervous because I had
never flown anything, while many of the other students, including Kory,
already knew how to fly at least a fixed-wing airplane. I was insecure
at first, but I had a terrific instructor pilot. He was a smoker, but army
regulations prohibited smoking in the aircraft. We made a deal that I
wouldn't tell on him for smoking in the cockpit if he didn't yell at
me while I was learning to fly. I have never liked being yelled at, and
have long thought it is not a very effective way to teach anything. I
always want to do the right thing; I just need to learn how.

When I climbed into the cockpit for the first time, it felt strangely
familiar. I realized it was just like being on horseback, something I'd
been doing for 25 years. Only instead of two reins and stirrups, there
were pedals and controls called a cyclic and a collective. I treated the
helicopter just like a horse, making small corrections before it got out
of control, using my weight and arms and legs to direct it. Just like
riding a horse, I learned to look straight ahead instead of at my hands.
Looking forward between a horse's ears felt just like looking out the
windshield of the helicopter. I loved flying from that first day, and I
graduated first in my flight surgeon class.

Flying a helicopter felt different than flying a plane, partly because
we always flew with the doors off, but also because a helicopter doesn't
so much glide through the air as beat it into submission. My interest
in flying grew quickly. I love the fact that no matter how much I practice,
there's still room to improve. Besides that, I love to go fast. I learned
to solo in a small Cessna 150, and since then I've flown F-15 fighters with Kory's squadron and an F-16 with the Alabama National Guard.
They wouldn't let me land or take off, but I got to fly upside down
and roll both high-performance aircraft. Going air-to-air and practicing dogfights with air force pilots made me appreciate just how good
they are. Flying aircraft seemed to lead naturally to jumping out of

them. I had learned to parachute in Airborne school, and Kory and I took up skydiving as a hobby.

After graduation from medical school on May 17, 1986, I spent a year as an intern in general surgery at Walter Reed Army Medical Center in Washington, D.C. I tried pediatric surgery, orthopedics, neurosurgery, and urology. I had begun to consider myself a physician during the third year of medical school, and I truly enjoyed being an intern and actually practicing medicine. I didn't miss being a student at all. I liked being responsible again, both for myself and for other people. I like to feel that what I am doing matters in some way, and to me, being a doctor matters very much.

When the internship was completed, Kory, Regan, and I moved to Florida. Even though Kory was in the air force and I was in the army, it was not hard to find assignments that would allow us to live together. The trick was to convince the personnel people in the army and the air force that we were essential to military medical care, and to ask for places that were not unreasonable. Our first choices were in North Carolina: the army's Fort Bragg for me and Seymour Johnson Air Force Base for Kory.

That was the first time I had a problem in the army because I am a woman. Fort Bragg is the home of the 82d Airborne Division, one of America's first-to-fight units. The 82d is a high-speed unit, and I thought that if I was going to be a flight surgeon, I wanted to be with a good, busy unit. The only positions open were battalion surgeon positions in the aviation brigade or Special Forces. Army policy excludes women from all those jobs, however, because they are considered combat slots. I was told to look elsewhere.

One of the few other times I had faced discrimination in the army was several years earlier at Letterman. I was receiving my regular officer evaluation report, and the colonel who did the rating said, "You know, Rhonda, if you were a man, you could be a general."

"Thank you very much, sir," I said, wondering how to react. "Some of us will just have to live with these physical handicaps."

I was upset about being denied the 82d Airborne, and instead of Fort Bragg, I went to Fort Rucker in Alabama in July of 1987. Kory became a flight surgeon at Eglin Air Force Base in the Florida panhandle, and we bought our farm in DeFuniak Springs, Florida, which is about halfway between the two bases. Fort Rucker is the home of army aviation, and I expected to be assigned to the research lab or the aviation medical clinic. Instead, I was named chief of Primary Care and Community Medicine at Lyster Army Community Hospital. Rather than caring for pilots, my job was to care for their families, even though I had done only a month of family practice in medical school and never liked it.

The job turned out far better than I had imagined because my boss gave me the freedom to run the department. I decided how to staff the emergency room and clinic, who took time off, and how we would handle sick call. I had observed other doctors run clinics, but now I was the one in charge of a physician's assistant, three military doctors, and several civilian doctors who helped in the emergency room. I was a captain by then and jumped to major that year.

In October, only three months after arriving at Fort Rucker, I volunteered for my first big field exercise: Reforger in Germany. Reforger stands for Return of Forces to Germany and was a massive deployment from the United States into Germany to defend against a simulated attack from the Soviet Union. I was given the choice of working in a comfortable hospital or in a battalion aid station in the field. Being with the troops sounded like more fun, and it was. We saw many injuries at the aid station, often because there were fights every night in the German beer tents, or drunken soldiers had rolled off the top bunks onto their heads.

One night the MPs brought us two soldiers who were very drunk and abusive. They were kicking and screaming and calling me every name in the book, but they were so drunk they didn't even know where they were. They should have been locked up in the stockade, but I was afraid they would hurt themselves or someone else. I couldn't sedate them, because they already had severely altered mental states. We sandwiched the two sotted soldiers between pairs of litters, and zipped them inside big furry body bags we used for transporting people in the cold weather. We put them in a tent with a medic who happened to speak Russian, and he spoke to them only in Russian all night. We all played along so they thought they had wandered across the border into East Germany and been captured. By the next morning, they were scared to death and very sober.

When I returned to Fort Rucker, I became chief of the Physical Exam Section at Lyster Hospital. At the clinic, we gave the pilots the physical exams needed to be allowed to fly. My greatest innovation was a simple one: I made everyone on the staff smile. The clinic had been receiving more complaints from patients than any other in the hospital, but after a few months of my "smile policy," we went six months without a complaint. We didn't perform more physicals, and we didn't spend more money; we just changed the attitude.

I finally was part of aviation medicine, and Kory was right: being a flight surgeon was the best job in the world. Pilots, particularly fighter pilots and attack pilots, are different from other patients and even from other military people. They tend to be very outgoing and active, not introspective, lots of fun and a little arrogant. In many ways, attack pilots are not unlike surgeons, who are the attack pilots of medicine. I'd always liked the surgeons, and I took to the pilots from the start. One of the beauties of pilots as patients is that they are very motivated to be healthy. When they seek medical care, they really do have a problem, and they want it fixed. Frequently, they show up later rather than earlier because they are afraid of being grounded, or taken off flying status. This generally threatens not just their careers but their whole self-image. It's like a doctor being told he can never practice medicine again. Because I keep that thought in mind, I built a great deal of trust among the aviators I cared for, and I was honored to be named Fort Rucker's Flight Surgeon of the Year in 1988 and Flight Surgeon of the Year for the entire army in 1990.

When I went to Fort Rucker, the hottest piece of aviation equipment in any army in the world was the Apache attack helicopter. The first day I met an Apache pilot was August 21, 1987, the day we had a terrible wreck on the range. We worked for an hour trying to resuscitate one of the pilots and only gave up after the X-rays showed his injuries were incompatible with life. I didn't know much about the Apache, except that it was very expensive and had new technology. Only a few battalions of Apaches had been fielded, and it cost something like three thousand dollars an hour to fly them, compared with only a few hundred dollars an hour to fly the older aircraft.

Everyone admitted it took extra time and resources to take care of the helicopters themselves, but as far as I could see, we virtually ignored the most important components: the pilots who flew them. Since the capabilities of the aircraft, and the optical system used to employ it, were vastly different from other aircraft, it seemed like a good idea to invest some extra time and energy on the pilots. Morally it might have been right to treat all the pilots the same, but practically it didn't make sense. The Apache was the most expensive and most difficult helicopter to employ, and like all new aircraft, it had a high rate of accidents at first. It seemed to me that the pilots might need special care.

I started a campaign to change the relationship between the flight surgeon (me) and the Apache pilots. Eventually I planned to add the pilots of the other attack and scout helicopters. First, I went out of my way to meet the pilots outside of the clinic, in circumstances where they were more comfortable. If one of them needed stitches removed or something minor, I went to the flight line for the treatment so the pilot wouldn't miss a day of flying. Eventually I "adopted" the entire 1/14 Aviation Training Battalion, one company of which trained all the soldiers who came to Fort Rucker to learn to fly Apaches.

I hadn't lost my interest in scientific research, and I saw research potential in this group of trainee pilots. The Apache had systems that had never been studied. How were the pilots adjusting to the Apache optical systems? What problems did they experience? What could be done to improve their performance? To find out the answers, I had to convince the trainees to let me study them. One of the instructors, Lance McElhiney, had some outstanding advice for me: If I wanted to win over the trainees, I should first try to win over the instructors. If the teachers went along with my plan, Lance said, the students would follow.

I started holding sick call at 6 A.M. every day at the airfield. If the pilots had to wait until the clinic opened at 7:30 A.M., they could miss the entire morning of flying. Say a pilot was playing basketball in the evening, twisted his ankle, and went to the emergency room. To be able to fly the next morning, he needed a note from a flight surgeon. Instead of making them go to the clinic, I went to them. Soon I was invited to brief each new class of Apache pilots on what health problems they might expect from flying the aircraft. The briefing always included my home phone number, which I encouraged the pilots to use if they had a question about anything. If they were willing to pay for a long distance call to DeFuniak Springs, I was surely willing to talk.

As it turned out, I benefited more than they did: the pilots became my friends, they took me flying, and I got a terrific, if informal, education about army aviation. Because a large number of the most senior instructor pilots in the army were at Fort Rucker, I met a large group of men (only men could fly the Apache) who had flown all different types of aircraft, with every conceivable unit and mission in Southeast Asia. I learned to fly many kinds of aircraft with night vision goggles that turn the darkest night into a cool green. I learned to use the "heads-up displays"—where the instruments are shown on an eye-level screen instead of on gauges on the dashboard—and the forward-looking infrared (FLIR) system, which is a camera mounted outside the Apache that sees the slightest amount of heat, such as from a tank engine.

I was promoted in 1989 and became the chief of aviation medicine at the medical center. I enjoyed the administrative duties, but to keep my medical skills sharp, I also performed all the vasectomies at Fort Rucker—about a hundred operations in all. I did the little procedure well, and my patients appreciated it.

In July of 1989 I went back to the U.S. Army Aeromedical Research Laboratory and became chief of the Crew Life Support Branch in the Biomedical Applications Research Division. That is a long-winded title for a terrific assignment. I could still do all the clinical medicine I could make time for, but I also was involved with standardizing aircraft equipment among the services and some of our allies, evaluating how the pilots worked with existing technologies, and evaluating some of the experimental helmets and visual displays for the LHX helicopter, which was the scout/attack aircraft then being developed by the army to follow the Apache.

That was the job I had enjoyed for one year, when Lt. Col. Bill Bryan—whom I had met at one of my briefings for Apache trainees—asked me to trade my lab coat for a flak jacket and deploy to Saudi Arabia in August, 1990.

7

After I returned to the Baath Party office from the Basra clinic that third afternoon, the translator came in for his regular attempt at convincing me of the error of my ways and converting me to his side.

"Why are you here?" he asked again. Again, I told him I was a doctor in the army and I had just followed orders.

"How can we make the Americans stop the bombing?" he asked, pleading for an explanation or a way out of this war. There was no way for me to know if he was sincere or if this was yet another propaganda effort.

"I don't know," I said. "I don't make those kinds of decisions."

I didn't think it was my place to suggest that all the Iraqis had to do was leave Kuwait if they wanted the bombing to stop. Later, I learned that by then they already had been driven out of Kuwait, but listening to the translator, I assumed the war was still being fought.

"We are going to take you to another place," the translator announced. "Somewhere more safe than here."

"You could just take us back to where the helicopter was shot down," I suggested, trying to sound innocent. "You could just leave us there. I know we would be safe, and I'm sure someone would find us." I knew that we had been shot down near U.S. lines, and would be found by friendly forces if we could just get back to the crash site.

"No, no. We cannot do that. Soon you will go to another place."

Troy and I were blindfolded and led outside into another gray afternoon. Troy's hands were tied behind him and my arms were wrapped in splints and bandages from the hospital. I was wearing the Iraqi army uniform, sans sleeves, that they gave me at the clinic. The blindfold was loose, and I could see a small school bus waiting.

At that point, I had no idea how long we were going to be held. So far our captivity had lasted only three days, but it felt like much longer. I had forced myself to accept the fact that it could be weeks or months before we were freed. I refused to consider the possibility that it might actually be years. I felt very confident we would be released reasonably quickly, barring unforeseen difficulties like being bombed by allied planes or kidnapped by terrorists. As I had written in my poem: "All we ask is your promise, we'll be allowed to win this time." In my mind, and for our leadership, winning this war meant getting all of our POWs back safely.

When the battalion first went to Saudi Arabia, other people thought we would be there for only three months. When three months came and went, they set their sights on six months, and then a year. At each stage they were disappointed and depressed that we were staying longer than they had expected. I went to Saudi expecting to stay one year, and made myself believe that anything less would be going home early. So now I imagined being held prisoner for weeks or months, secretly hoping that I would be released earlier. I tried not to think about home, where spring would soon be showing in the pastures; or Kory or Regan, and how worried they must be. Keep them in the family drawer. Keep them safely out of mind. Be thankful you are still alive to hope, I told myself, and focus on staying alive.

I tipped my head back so I could see under the blindfold as we walked toward the bus. The advantage of a large nose was that it pushed the blindfold off my eyes and allowed me to peek at the ground. The guards pushed Troy on the bus first and I followed silently. With broken arms and a smashed knee, I needed all my concentration to navigate the stairs and aisle. Hobbling down the narrow aisle, I tipped my head back and saw a large leg set in a splint and wrapped with bandages. The leg was connected to a big man, almost as big as Kory, who measures six feet five inches and weighs more than two hundred pounds. The man had a bushy mustache under his blindfold and was wearing an American flight suit. He was sitting with his back to the window, and his bad leg was stretched out on the seat into the aisle. I walked slowly and managed to read his name tag: "Capt. Bill Andrews."

"Hey, Troy," I whispered. "That's the guy we came to get."

"No talking! No talking," one of the guards interrupted.

It was a relief and a pleasure to see Andrews. We had not rescued him, but he was still alive. Now I thought we had at least accomplished half of our rescue mission: now we had our pilot. Admittedly we were a few days late, and I was not exactly in control of the situation, but at least the doctor was with the pilot. The doctor had two broken arms and would not have been very useful in surgery, but I felt great. I couldn't help smiling at Andrews although he was blindfolded, too, and couldn't see me. In the rear of the bus, Stamaris was on a stretcher, and Troy was tucked into another seat.

The wind blew through the open windows of the bus when the driver pulled onto the road, and I heard Andrews say loudly, "It's cold. Could someone close the window, please?"

Underneath my blindfold, I saw one of the guards stand up and shut the windows. Andrews said, "Captain Bill Andrews thanks you, and the United States Air Force thanks you."

"No talking!" the guard said.

Andrews must have known there were other allied prisoners with him on the bus, and he gave us some remarkable news.

"The war is over," he announced. "Everybody needs to know the war is over."

"No talking!" the guard screamed at Andrews.

How could Andrews know the war had ended? He had been shot down a few hours before we were, and the war was not over then. He seemed pretty sure, though, and I wanted to believe it. Maybe he was trying to boost our spirits. Maybe he was told before his last mission that the war was close to ending. Or he wanted to demoralize the guards. Troy and I hadn't seen him before, and it was possible he had been held somewhere where he had access to the news. Maybe, just maybe, the war really had ended.

Pretending to sleep with my head tipped back on the seat rest, I could see under the blindfold and out the window as we drove through Iraq. Darkness was falling at the end of another long day. No one had told me where we were going, but the road signs, written in English and Arabic, were clear: we were headed to Baghdad. I thought about what Andrews had said. If the war really was over, we would be going home soon. But the war had been fought mostly in Kuwait, not Iraq. Now we were heading deeper into Iraq, and maybe it didn't matter if the war was over in Kuwait. The fighting might have ended, but the war was not over for us. In his maneuverings to outwit the allies before the war, Saddam had used foreign hostages as "human shields." He was not above trying to use prisoners of war to pressure the allies for concessions. Saddam had studied the American war in Vietnam, so he knew that American POWs could be useful as leverage in peace talks. Nearly twenty years after the Vietnam War ended, more than two thousand Americans were still unaccounted for in Southeast Asia. Wars end, and then there are negotiations and peace talks. The missing and the dead from both sides must be identified and exchanged. The process could take months. Or years.

Suddenly there were two dark brown eyes looking into mine. I jumped back from the face of the Iraqi guard, and he roughly pulled the blindfold further down my face over my eyes and tied it tighter in the back. I couldn't see anything for much of the rest of the journey and concentrated on keeping my arms still as the bus jostled. Another distraction was the growing pressure on my bladder.

"Water closet," I said, hoping the guard would understand.

"Be quiet. No water closet," he replied, ending the discussion.

The guards allowed Andrews and Stamaris, neither of whom could walk, to urinate in a water bottle, and they let Troy get off the bus to use the bathroom. I was told to wait.

The bus rumbled and bumped down the nearly empty road, and every movement hurt my arms. I tried to sit as still as possible. I was afraid to peek out from underneath the blindfold again, so I stared straight ahead with my eyes closed under the tight cloth. Seeing Andrews was a boost for my spirits, just like when I discovered Troy and Stamaris. I felt bad because of the loss of our crew and the fact that three of us were prisoners, but it was a great consolation to know that Andrews— the person we had tried to rescue—was safe. We had failed in our mission to rescue him, but we had tried, and we had done everything we could have done. I never thought we had wasted the lives of our crew members trying to rescue him. Every one of us would go again if we had the chance.

On the other hand, I never liked failing, and I never liked feeling guilty. At least I didn't have to feel guilty that Andrews died of his injuries because I didn't get there in time, or that he was killed on the ground by the Iraqis. I didn't feel guilty about being captured myself, because there was nothing I could have done to prevent it. I was just baggage on that helicopter. Our pilots and crew were the best in the army, and they had done everything right. Once we crashed, I had not been inept and lit a fire in the desert or failed to cover my tracks in the sand or any other dumb thing. Maybe Andrews felt bad about being shot down. Fighter pilots frequently feel bad when they have to eject, and often they blame themselves for being shot down. Usually there is nothing they could have done differently, but that rarely makes the guilt disappear. I knew that some POWs from Vietnam and other wars, especially pilots, suffered from survivor's guilt because they had lived and their crews had died. Or they felt they were failures because they had been captured. I knew from experience with wrecks at Fort Rucker that even in peacetime pilots feel bad if they survive a crash and someone on board doesn't.

I was fortunate to have had other experiences that prepared me to live with that kind of failure. A new doctor learns fast that if a patient has a disease and doesn't do well, it isn't the doctor's fault. If the doctor does everything he can, and the patient still does badly, the doctor can't take that home and feel guilty. Now, if something happens because the doctor doesn't do everything he can, or he does something stupid, or doesn't pay attention or is in a hurry, and something bad happens, *then* he should feel guilty. I considered Andrews my patient from the second we got the order to get him. I had done everything I could for him, which wasn't much, but I had tried. If I felt guilty every time one of my patients did badly, I couldn't be a doctor. Most doctors have that attitude, and it gave me an advantage as a POW.

Darkness fell completely—there were no lights inside the bus or on the road—and we rode in silence. I tried to sleep, but my mind was racing and the pain in my arms was like a constant stabbing that kept me awake. I felt like I was sitting next to an obnoxious passenger who kept punching me in the arm and filling my ear with bad conversation. During the long night I began to shake with hot and cold flashes and I knew I had a fever. I diagnosed that I was septic, or infected, and tried to do a self-examination, even though I couldn't see and could barely move my hands. Obviously there was some infected wound that wasn't draining, and I was suffering from what we commonly call blood poisoning. If I didn't do something about it, the infection could kill me. Now that would have upset me: to survive the crash and a bullet wound, then die from an infection. Something had poisoned my blood, and I had to find the source.

My right hand and little finger hurt and felt swollen. I slowly looked down under the blindfold, hoping no one would notice, and saw my smashed finger was bloated. The Iraqi doctors had done nothing for the finger or the gash across the top of my hand, concentrating instead on the broken bones in my arms. I inched my hands together on my lap and used my good left hand to bend the joint of my little finger. When I did, creamy pus drained from the finger onto my leg. So that's where the infection started, I thought. The finger hurt when I bent it, but I knew it was good to drain the pus. I also worked my hand, and more pus spilled from the crusted-over gash. I flexed the finger and my hand as long as I could stand the pain. Then I would rest and start over a few minutes later. The bus was dark, and no one seemed to notice my discreet efforts at self-treatment.

The bus seemed to stop once an hour during the trip, which I figured lasted about fifteen hours. It was afternoon when we boarded, and the sun had risen on a new day by the time we arrived at our destination. During the frequent stops I could hear voices, and guards stepping off the bus to talk with people on the road. I didn't know if they were changing guards or checking paperwork, or if our guards were just showing off their prisoners. At one point, we slowed to navigate deep water that had flooded the road. Under my blindfold, I saw the water climbing the stairs of the bus as we pushed through, and I wondered if we would be swept away. The main focus of my attention for the final hours was my bladder, which had swollen into a giant ache. The Iraqis ignored my pleas to step off the bus to relieve myself.

It was morning when we arrived in Baghdad, on our fourth day as prisoners. The blindfold had loosened again by that time, and I could see we had driven into a military-type complex. There were heavy gates in front and neatly trimmed grass between the buildings. The buildings appeared to have survived the bombing without a scratch. The guards led us off the bus and into a clinic or a small hospital. They put each of us—Troy, Andrews, Stamaris, and me—onto a separate gurney and ordered us not to move. The guards removed our blindfolds, and I noticed the waiting room had wooden floors and windows without bars. Finally they let me use the bathroom. I was sorry I wasn't wearing the long blue robe instead of the Iraqi uniform. My arms were supported by the slings, and I managed to inch my fingers down to unfasten the pants. By pushing gently with my fingers and rubbing my hips against the wall, I scraped the pants down to my knees. I felt like a moth trying to escape from her cocoon. Getting back into the pants was even more difficult. Imagine the same moth trying to return to her cocoon.

When I returned from the bathroom, my mood had improved. But only for a moment. Then the guards came for Troy and marched him into another room down the hall. After a few moments, I heard Iraqi voices yelling in English from the room, shouting questions about what we were doing in Iraq. I imagined Troy in the room surrounded by Iraqi soldiers, but he said nothing. Then came the sound of a loud slap as someone hit him across the face. They asked another question, and when Troy didn't answer, they slapped him hard. Again and again, shouted questions; silence as Troy refused to speak; and loud, stinging slaps. Shouting. Silence. Whap, the sound of a hand across Troy's face. I felt terrible, helpless. I remembered being molested on the truck, and how Troy had felt so frustrated because he couldn't protect me. Now I was the one who was unable to protect him. I had been helpless from the moment we were captured because of my injuries, but it was far worse to feel helpless for someone else, for someone I cared about. This was the man who had done everything for me: feed me, cover me from the cold, even help me use the bathroom. I couldn't do anything for him. The slaps came more frequently, then suddenly stopped.

My turn was next. A guard came for me and helped me off the gurney. He led me into the interrogation room. I saw Troy sitting on a stiff wooden chair. There was a rope around his neck, and his head was pulled down between his legs and tied to his boots. The Iraqi officer in charge, about thirty-five or forty years old, ordered a guard to remove Troy. The guard bent to untie him and pulled him from the room. I tried to catch Troy's eye but he was led outside quickly. He seemed dazed but not badly injured.

When I was alone, the officer ordered me to sit on another wooden chair in the center of the room. I walked slowly, stiff after the long bus ride and unsure of my knee. I eased myself onto the chair, realizing again how bruised and battered I was. There was rope on the other chair, but no one moved to tie me. I concentrated on sitting up straight and watched the officer. He held his hands behind his back, his face stern, as he paced silently back and forth between me and his desk, which stood in front of a picture of Saddam. His uniform was neat and he had a professional bearing. I didn't know what he was going to ask, or what I was going to say. My stomach tightened in the silence between us. This man was nothing like the translator, who had tried to ingratiate himself to us and win us over to his point of view. The translator was slimy, but I wasn't afraid of him. This man was deadly serious, and I knew he could hurt me. During the past few days, I had almost grown accustomed to being a prisoner. It was inconvenient, painful at times, but I knew I would survive. The sight of this man was like a slap in the face, a wake-up call. I was still a long way from home, and people like him were going to decide if I ever made it.

"What is your name?" he snapped.

"Major Rhonda Cornum, sir."

"What is your unit?"

"The 2-229th Attack Helicopter Battalion," I said.

Even though I was no longer wearing my uniform with the unit patches, everyone before him had known the name of our unit, so I figured he must already know. I sensed that he was feeling me out, trying to see if I was going to cooperate or play hard ball.

"Where are they?"

"I don't know, sir," I said, honestly.

"Where are they in relation to where you were captured?"

"Sir, I don't know where I got captured, so I don't know."

"What direction were you going when you were captured?"

That's when I started to lie. I didn't think it through; it just came out of my mouth. "Straight north," I said.

We actually had been going almost due east from Iraq toward Kuwait, but I thought I could get away with lying. He wouldn't have known what direction we had been flying, and it seemed like a good POW should give the enemy misinformation. What I couldn't understand was, why was he asking such basic questions? If, like Andrews had announced on the bus, the war really was over, why was this Iraqi questioning us so harshly? Why did he care about the direction we were traveling? Why did it matter where our units were located?

There must still be fighting, I thought, and I can't tell him anything. Information is power. It's the only thing I have, the only thing still in my control. What is in my mind is the only thing that is truly mine. They can take my wedding ring, my uniform, and my freedom, and control when I eat, sleep, and go to the bathroom. They can't take my mind. But I knew they would try, and I didn't want them to beat me.

My bones were broken and I was covered with bruises. If this man beats me, I thought, he could disable me permanently. I knew this officer was the one who had been hitting Troy, and I sensed he wouldn't hesitate to do the same to me. If he did hit me, I was afraid I would break down under the pain and talk. I had to make him think I was cooperating, make him think he was winning. I had to keep him talking, keep him at ease. Make him think I was just a doctor who knew nothing.

"How old are you?"

"Thirty-six."

"Are you married?" he asked.

"Yes," I said.

"Do you have children?"

"No," I lied again.

"So where was your unit going?"

"I don't know."

"Where were they when you left them?"

"In Saudi Arabia," I said. That, too, was a lie, because we had been in Iraq for days before going on the rescue mission.

"What were you doing?"

"We were on a search-and-rescue mission, sir."

"Who were you trying to rescue?"

"I don't know."

"What kind of aircraft were you looking for?"

"Sir, I don't know."

The officer walked to the door and opened it. He motioned for me to leave. I creaked to my feet and walked stiffly out the door. Was that it? Was it over? The officer said nothing. His face was a mask and he ignored me, apparently already thinking about his next prisoner.

The guard led me back to the gurney, and I sat down, my heart pumping fast. I smiled weakly at Troy. The guard chose Andrews next, and wheeled him into the interrogation room. The door closed behind him, but I could hear clearly through the thin walls.

"Who are you?" the Iraqi interrogator yelled.

"Captain Bill Andrews of the United States Air Force," Andrews said, in a voice as strong and clear as if he were sitting right next to me.

"What kind of airplane were you flying?"

"The Geneva Conventions say I am only required to give you my name, rank, and serial number."

"Answer the question! What was your mission?"

"The Geneva Conventions say I am only required to give you my name, rank, and serial number," Andrews repeated in a flat monotone. I sat in the lobby, staring straight ahead, listening to the interrogation and feeling both horrified and fascinated. Troy was with me, but we didn't want to risk talking.

Question after shouted question, Andrews answered the Iraqi with that phrase: "The Geneva Conventions say . . ." I suddenly felt guilty that I had not done the same thing. The walls were so thin that Andrews and Troy must have heard everything I had told the Iraqi officer. I hadn't given him any useful information, but the way Andrews handled himself seemed more professional. I had thought I could reason with my captors, try to beat them psychologically. If I just appeared reasonable, they would let me survive. Andrews handled it better.

A guard came for me and motioned for me to stand. "We are leaving," he said.

"Sergeant Dunlap needs to come, too," I suggested.

"No."

"Yes," I argued. "He needs to take care of me."

"No."

I looked at Troy and shrugged my shoulders. Stamaris stayed behind with Troy. The guard loosely blindfolded me again and led me outside. He loaded me into the back seat of a civilian car. I was tired of traveling, tired of moving from place to place and being asked the same questions again and again. By now the fever and chills were intermittent, but I was exhausted. I worried about what would happen to Troy and the others. If Troy wasn't taking care of me, the Iraqis might decide he was no longer useful. They might beat him again. I went along silently; there was nothing else to do.

I sat quietly in the car. The engine wasn't running, and it appeared we weren't going anywhere for awhile. I knew there was a driver in the car because I could hear him fidgeting at the wheel. With the blindfold on, I felt my other senses, especially my hearing, get sharper. The driver must have been waiting for orders. We sat there for a few minutes before he spoke up: "So what do you think of Iraq?"

"I haven't seen very much of it," I said, referring to the blindfold that covered my eyes but trying not to sound too sarcastic.

"You know, we do not hate the Americans," he said.

"I don't think the Americans hate the Iraqis, either," I replied.

"We know the reason this war has happened," he continued. "It is because of the Zionists."

I sat back and kept my mouth shut. This was clearly not the time for a conversation like this, and I was glad I wasn't carrying any letters from my Israeli friend. The driver's reality was so different from mine that there was little common ground for conversation. We had been sitting in the parking lot for about twenty minutes when someone approached the car. He said something in Arabic to the driver, who started the engine and pulled onto the road.

"Would you like to see my country?" the driver asked, as if we were out for a Sunday drive.

"Yes, I would," I nodded.

He stopped alongside the road, leaned back across the seat and gently pulled the blindfold off my eyes so it hung down around my neck. The two of us were alone in the car.

"I will have to replace it before we arrive," he said, sounding apologetic.

"I understand," I assured him.

The driver appeared to be in his late twenties, clearly a civilian and very handsome. He spoke good English, and he seemed glad for the chance to show someone from America another side of Iraq. He knew I could not have a very favorable opinion of his country, but he was proud of Iraq, and he wanted me to see it in a different light.

"This is Baghdad," he said, smiling and looking up at me in the rear-view mirror.

The city was not flat like the Saudi cities I had visited. There were dips in the streets, and most of the low spots were filled with water. It seemed older than the Saudi cities, most of which appeared to have been built of concrete and glass the night before. Old men walked along the side of the road, and the women wore black robes but did not have their faces covered. I noticed the street signs and stoplights were not working, so there must not have been electricity. Most of the buildings were undamaged, but occasionally we passed one that had been bombed. Driving past a block of buildings, all of a sudden one would be missing—only girders and the shell of the structure left on the lot. I was impressed with the accuracy of the allied bombers. They obviously didn't hit individual buildings by chance, and they had taken great care to minimize civilian casualties.

The driver pulled to the side of the road. He leaned back and replaced my blindfold. "We are almost there," he informed me. "I have to cover your eyes."

"That's okay," I said. "Thank you for the tour."

By now it was late afternoon, and I had not eaten or had anything to drink since the evening before. I was hungry, dehydrated, tired, spent. We drove into another complex of buildings and stopped in front of a door. I said goodbye to the driver, and a guard led me inside, still blindfolded. We walked down a hallway and turned into a room that smelled of disinfectant and medicine. The guard removed my blindfold and left me alone, closing the solid metal door as he left the room.

This cell was much larger than my quarters in Basra. The floor was cement, and the cinder-block walls had at one time been plastered and painted. The ceiling was high, maybe ten or twelve feet, and there was a small fan built into the wall far above my head. There was no window. The room held three metal hospital beds, only one of which had blankets, and a small nightstand. I was apparently in the prison ward of a hospital, or the infirmary of a prison. I couldn't tell which. Once again, I found myself in a strange place, trying to establish my location by piecing together the few clues at hand.

I walked to the side of the high bed and leaned back against it. Slowly I managed to wiggle back until I was sitting on the edge of the bed, my feet dangling above the floor. I was truly weary. I didn't want to go anywhere else; I didn't want to get into another car or bus and go to another place to be asked the same questions. Who am I? What was I doing? Was I married? The same questions, over and over, and my same answers, some true and some lies.

The room was cleaner and better equipped than any I had been in so far, but it also was the farthest away from the friendly forces. The conditions had been austere back in the desert bunkers, but we were only thirty minutes from the most forward American troops. Now I was in Baghdad, and I knew the good guys would never make it here. What I knew of the war plan did not include an invasion of the Iraqi capital. I still wasn't sure what was happening in the war. I had not heard a single bomb up close since being captured, so I was confused. Had the war ended? I knew we had been bombing Iraq for six weeks, and this building did not seem damaged, so apparently it had not been a target. Even if the fighting continued, this place, whatever it was, probably was safe from American attack. Still, after four days in Iraqi hands, no one had told me what was going to happen to me. The only question I had was, When am I going home?

I heard the deadbolt slide open on the heavy metal door, and an older man wearing a clean white robe walked in slowly, carrying a glass of water and a cracked white plate piled with bread and sweet, sticky dates.

I was still perched on the edge of the bed with my feet dangling just above the floor. The man stood in front of me and tried to explain in a few words of broken English that he had my dinner. He smiled and held out a date, which I took in my mouth.

"Is good?" he asked.

"Yes, very good. Thank you very much."

I was starved, and had to concentrate on chewing the date slowly instead of wolfing it down. I knew I had to eat. I needed food to keep up my strength. I needed to heal. The guard took the pit from my mouth when I had finished. He held the glass of water to my dry lips and I drank gratefully.

"Doctor coming," he said.

"Okay. Thank you."

I asked to use the bathroom, and the old man led me down the hall. I could walk if I went straight and slow, but I was afraid my knee would come unhinged. My greatest fear was falling, which might do more damage to my arms. The man who fed me stood in the hall while I walked into the bathroom, which, like the other Iraqi bathrooms, had a single hole in the floor below a single dim light bulb hanging from the ceiling. This bathroom was not as dirty as the others, but still it looked more like it belonged in a gas station than in a hospital. The first thing I noticed that was different about this bathroom was a metal-rimmed mirror over the sink.

"Oh my God," I gasped, staring into the mirror. The light was dim, but I could see my face: I looked like a raccoon with two black eyes. My hair was matted with blood and mud, and a pirate's patch of hair was plastered across my left eye. Above the eye was a laceration that was starting to heal. My hair looked like an abandoned bird's nest, and my first thought was that I'd never get a comb through it and I'd probably have to chop it off. My teeth were all in place, but they were scummy after four days without brushing. I was still dressed in the Iraqi uniform with the sleeves cut off. I hadn't seen myself since the crash four days ago, but I remembered asking Troy how I looked when we were being held together in the office. He claimed I looked great, although he did laugh when he said it. Now I understood.

In Saudi Arabia before the war, there had been days in the field when I got pretty dirty. I would look at myself in the side mirror of a truck and joke that it didn't matter how bad I looked, as long as I could recognize myself. Well, I was still recognizable, but I wasn't going to win any beauty contests. On the positive side, my nose wasn't broken. In the past, my nose seemed to attract attention during accidents, and I had broken it at least twice. The last time, I had fallen off a horse during a race, and my helmet tipped forward, pushing down my goggles and crushing my nose. This time it had survived in one piece.

Staring at myself in the mirror, I was dying to wash up, or at least splash a little cool water on my face and rinse out my mouth. But I couldn't move my arms enough to turn on the water. I walked out of the bathroom, and the man in the white robe was waiting to lead me back toward my room.

We walked by the open door of the room next to mine, and I glanced in and saw Stamaris being loaded into a bed. "Hey, Dan," I said as we walked passed. Stamaris didn't say anything; I'm not sure if he heard me. I didn't see Troy anywhere, but I was not surprised because this was some kind of medical facility, and Troy had not been badly injured. I didn't know when I'd see him again, if ever.

The attendant helped me back to my perch on the hospital bed. "Doctor coming," he said again, and closed the door behind him. In the next room, I could hear people—they sounded like doctors—talking with Stamaris. I couldn't quite make out the words. Then my door opened and three men entered. The leader of the group, a husky man in a white lab coat, was very authoritative and clearly in command.

"How do you do, Major Cornum?" he inquired.

"I'm fine," I said, being polite rather than honest.

He introduced himself as the chief of orthopedics at the hospital, the Rashid Medical Center. One of the other men was a resident or a physician in specialty training, and the third looked like a medical student or an intern receiving on-the-job training. He reminded me of being an intern at Walter Reed when we trooped around after the residents and staff doctors on their rounds.

"Doctor Cornum, please tell us what happened to you," the chief of orthopedics said.

"Well, sir, I was in a helicopter crash four days ago."

"We are going to take X-rays and see how bad your injuries are," he said. "Tell us please what you know about your injuries."

"I have two broken arms; a bullet wound in my right shoulder; a broken, infected finger; and I have at least an ACL tear," which is a tear of the anterior cruciate ligament in my knee. "I also have an MCL," which is a tear in the other knee ligament, the medial collateral. "I don't know very much orthopedics," I said, "but that's how it feels."

"Anything else?"

"My eyes hurt. I think there is just stuff in them, hairs maybe, that I can't get out, but they sting."

"What is the most serious problem you have?"

"I think the worst thing about me is that last night I was septic, fever and chills and all that, and I'm pretty sure the site is my right hand."

"Oh yes, antibiotics," the chief said. "We will get them for you. We will look at everything. We are going to take care of you, Doctor."

"Thank you very much."

The chief did not smile much, but he was kindly. There was no ethical problem for him in treating me, even though technically I was an enemy of his country. We had taken care of many Iraqi wounded, and I myself had bandaged the foot of one Iraqi soldier. A wounded person is a wounded person. Once they are wounded, they cease to be combatants and are no longer considered the enemy.

"Are you married, Doctor Cornum?" the chief asked.

"Yes," I told him, wondering why this was so important to them.

"Do you have any children?"

"No," I lied. I felt bad lying to this man, though, because he seemed to be straight with me and truly concerned about my care. Still, it was too late to change my story. I was not out of danger yet, and I wanted my story to be consistent. Anyway, it probably didn't matter to him if I had children or not.

"We will return after your X-rays when we have your films," he promised, and they continued on their rounds.

In the next room I heard a machine go "whir, clunk, clunk." Then I heard Stamaris moan in pain. I heard voices speaking Arabic, and each time the machine sounded, Stamaris groaned. I was pretty sure the machine was not an Iraqi torture device, however, because I recognized the sound: it was a portable X-ray machine. The technicians must have been taking a lot of film and moving Stamaris often, because he groaned loudly. Poor Dan, I thought. I hope they have pain killers for him.

I heard the squeak of the wheels as they rolled the machine down the hall to my room, but the camera was too wide to pass through the door. The technician pulled the machine up to the doorway and ordered me off the bed and into the hall. He was not very gentle when he made me lean over and shoved my head under the mechanical arm that took the pictures. I didn't think I had a skull fracture, but he insisted on taking X-rays of my head. Always the doctor, I had asked the guards in Basra to bring the X-rays taken at the clinic there. They had tucked the film under the blankets on Stamaris's cot, but somewhere along the journey, the film had been lost. I had to laugh about that because the same thing always happened when we evacuated someone: the films seemed to fall into a black hole. When the X-ray technician finished, he closed the door and left me alone.

I managed to get completely onto the bed by sitting on the edge, putting my good left leg under the bad right one and hoisting them both up and over the side. The head of the mattress was inclined forward, and I leaned back against the white pillows with my legs stretched in front of me. My heavy, splinted arms rested on my chest and stomach. This was the first time I had been alone and able to think since the crash. That first night I had been in shock. The second night, Troy and I had talked and slept fitfully. The third night we spent on the bus traveling from Basra to this hospital in Baghdad.

I stared at the blank walls in the large empty room. The acoustics ought to be pretty good in here, I thought. I sang a few words and it sounded nice. It reminded me of singing in the shower. Boy, would a hot tub be nice! My singing grew louder, and louder, until it was bouncing off the gray walls. I sang the rock songs I liked from high school— Simon and Garfunkel, Gordon Lightfoot, and Cat Stevens. I sang the scores of *Evita* and *Jesus Christ Superstar*, and "Summertime" from *Porgy and Bess*. I've always liked to sing when I'm alone. Unfortunately, my life back home didn't allow me much time by myself. The only time I sang was on the long car rides between our farm and work at Fort Rucker. Sometimes flying on a helicopter, I turned off my radio mike and sang, my voice drowned out by the thumping noise of the rotors.

From my bed I could hear people talking in the hallway and noises coming from the other rooms. I knew the Iraqis could hear me singing. It seemed like a positive thing to do, and I was feeling positive. I felt I was going to get out of Iraq someday and go home. I had no clue when that would be, but I guessed a few months. I knew being a prisoner would be hard, but it was better than being dead. When we were at the Baath Party office in Basra, I thought we would be held only a few weeks. Now I resigned myself to months.

Since I was badly injured, I figured a hospital was a good place to recover. I was not in much pain unless I moved, so I sat as still as possible. Sometimes when I dropped off to sleep, I shifted my weight without realizing it, and pain shot up my arms. I couldn't move them except by very slowly walking my fingers across my chest. I tried to hook the fingers of both hands together so my arms wouldn't fall to the side. I couldn't do anything for myself, and I wouldn't be able to for some time. I had never been so helpless in my life. I was helpless both because I was a prisoner and because I was injured. The combination was almost unbearable. Think positive. Don't let it get you down. Stay strong.

At every place we had been held so far, the Iraqis had asked for my name and my unit, so I assumed that I had been reported as a prisoner to the Americans. The battalion must know that I was safe, and Kory, too. That was a relief. But I couldn't think about home now. Instead, I consciously tried to remember everything that had happened to me since the crash, down to the last detail, so I wouldn't lose track of time. It seemed important to stay oriented to time. There was no natural light in the room, and I didn't have a clock. I didn't think the Iraqis were trying to throw off my biological clock by playing with the time, but I couldn't be sure.

I sang some more and prayed. I didn't ask God to do anything else for me; He'd done His part. Over and over I repeated, "Thank you, Lord. Thank you, Lord, for getting me here."

When I sang my favorite song, "The Wind beneath My Wings," I couldn't help but think of Kory, and the memories came sharp and clear. I liked that song so much the first time I heard it that I wrote down the lyrics and sang them until I knew the song by heart.

That's how I felt about Kory: he was my hero, the wind beneath my wings. He made so much possible for me. Finally I let my mind drift back home, back to my husband and Regan. They would be worried, but at least they would know by now that I was alive. The word must have gone up and down the chain of command, and Kory would have been notified. I wondered how the other people in my unit had fared, not just on the aircraft flying on our mission, but also in the two other attack companies that were on a different mission when I left.

I wondered if they were still fighting, and if any of them had been killed. I was sure my medics had done well, and I looked forward to drinking a beer with them and hearing about their adventures. I thought about Lance, who had been our escort when we were shot down, and I hoped he had made it back safely. I felt sure that he had, but occasionally I would contemplate the worst, that maybe he'd been shot down and had died in a crash. I knew that if he did get back, he would be suffering horribly, thinking he had let me down, and that he had let down Regan as well.

I felt saddest for Regan, fourteen years old and her mother a prisoner of war in Iraq. She was a strong girl, but I didn't know how she would react. How long could she stay strong? These kinds of things were always harder on the people at home, especially the children. What if I were here for months? Her teenage years were supposed to be fun and free of worry. How could she live her life normally, worried about me in Iraq? I had to get word to her, let her know I was okay. I wouldn't be coming home for awhile, but I was with her in my thoughts. I didn't want her to be sad. I saw her pretty face so clearly in my mind. I focused my energy and tried to turn myself into a human radio antenna. I will radiate and project good, positive thoughts. I tried to imagine which way to focus, trying to direct the beam at my unit and my family. I hoped Kory and Lance would be sitting quietly somewhere, still enough to pick up the signal. I didn't imagine the signal would make it all the way across the ocean to Regan, but I knew that if somehow I made Kory believe I was safe, he could relay the message to Regan. Think hard, project energy. I'm fine. I love you.

In the months prior to the war, the UH-60 aircrews regularly practiced combat search-and-rescue and evacuation of casualties. *Left to right*: Sgt. Roger Brilinski, Sgt. Patbouvier Ortiz, Maj. Rhonda Cornum, and the "patient," Pvt. German Batista.

New Year's Eve in Saudi Arabia—a good way to release tension while waiting for the war to begin. Rhonda celebrates with Eric Pacheco (noisemakers in ears) and Mike Pandol.

CW3 Gary Godfrey (*above*) in the pilot's seat of a UH-60; *below*: CW4 Phil Garvey in the pilot-in-command position. Both men wear night-vision goggles and standard flight gear. Godfrey and Garvey, both instructor pilots at Fort Rucker, were killed when Black Hawk 214 was shot down.

Lance straps into an Apache attack helicopter. The air war had just begun.

The five Pathfinders attached to the 2-29th Attack Helicopter Battalion from C Company, 509th Infantry (Airborne). *Left to right*: Sgt. Patbouvier Ortiz, Sgt. Roger Paul Brilinski, S.Sgt. Dennis Smith, S.Sgt. Larry Richardson, and Sgt. Troy Dunlap. The antiaircraft gun was captured on February 16 when the battalion participated in the first armed reconnaissance missions.

Troy Dunlap and Billy Butts retrieve hand-held grenade launchers and other spoils of war left on the desert by captured Iraqis, February 18, 1991.

Last photograph taken of Black Hawk 214 before it was shot down in the desert.

The aircrew of Black Hawk 214: *Left to Right*: Gary Godfrey, Phil Garvey, Dan Stamaris, and Bill Butts. The mission crew on February 27 also included Rhonda Cornum, Patbouvier Ortiz, Paul Brilinski, and Troy Dunlap.

Tail boom of the crashed Black Hawk.

Crash site: debris was scattered over a wide swath of desert. Personnel from the 101st who combed the wreckage thought no one could have survived the impact.

March 6, 1991: Finally released after eight days as a POW, Rhonda is safely aboard a Red Cross flight from Baghdad to Riyadh, being pampered by crew member Lorenz Probst. While in captivity, her broken arms had been set.

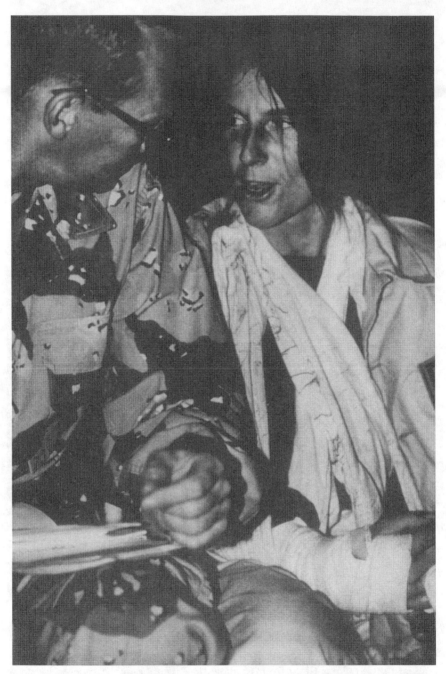

In Riyadh, after a welcome home from General Schwartzkopf, the POWs boarded a C-141 transport for the flight to Bahrain and the U.S. Navy hospital ship *Mercy*.

Rhonda and Kory on the USNS *Mercy*, reunited after much red tape and many psychiatric interviews.

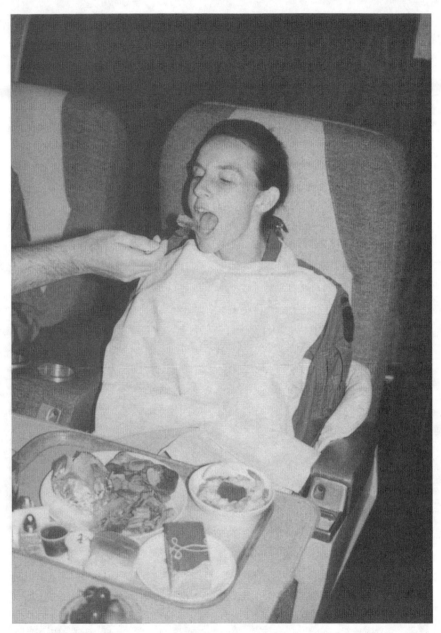

Kory feeds the "baby bird" a steak dinner on Air Force One, winging back to the U.S. Unable to use her arms, Rhonda submitted with difficulty to the indignity of being fed and cared for.

The "Welcome Home" overwhelmed Rhonda and her family—an outpouring of love and pride from all over the country.

Reunited at last: Regan carefully hugs her injured mother at Walter Reed Army Medical Center.

The Fort Rucker "Welcome Home Parade." The crowd cheers as Rhonda and Kory go by perched on a convertible.

Troy Dunlap, Rhonda, and Kory at the reception at Fort Rucker on March 14, 1991, to honor the returning POWs.

Lance gives Rhonda a bear hug at the welcome home ceremony for their unit at Fort Rucker.

The Army-Navy Game, 1991. Rhonda was honored to be the featured speaker at halftime ceremonies. *Photo courtesy Don Schwartz, Lancer Photos.*

The Cornum family poses in a captured Iraqi tank in Kuwait, December 1991.
They had been invited by the Ministry of Defense to visit Kuwait.

8

The love that Kory and I have for each other is strong and true, but during the long months deployed in Saudi Arabia we were not ones to dwell on sentiment or indulge in frequent expressions of emotion. We were not always like that, and during medical school our friends used to tease us about being mushy and romantic. But life in Saudi Arabia was hard enough without the constant heartache of long-distance love. I tried to keep Kory tucked away in a corner of my heart, always with me, but not too close to the surface. I didn't worry about him being injured, because he wasn't flying combat missions and his base at Tabuk was out of range of Saddam's missiles.

At least we were in the same country. The separation was harder for our friends who had spouses back in the United States, which seemed so very, very far away. The lives of family back home proceeded normally, apart from the worry, while our lives were so different from what we had ever experienced. Those of us who were deployed were busy and challenged, which made the separation easier for us. Even though Kory and I were apart, I knew he was doing what he loved, and he knew I was just where I wanted to be. Some of our friends had civilian wives who never understood why we actually wanted to be in Saudi Arabia. Other friends tried to manage their houses long distance, and they went crazy. Our house was on autopilot, and our relationship was fine.

Despite my best efforts to keep Kory in the "family drawer," he sometimes escaped without warning and jumped right in front of me. One of those times was November 4, and I wrote him this letter from my dusty parking stall in the King Fahd garage:

Dear Hubby:

I know you don't like gooey, emotional letters (or tears on phone calls, etc.), but sometimes my loving-ness gets too big and I have to tell you. I've been humming "The Wind beneath My Wings" for the past two days, and it sort of applies to us, except you are very well known and well respected in your own right. But in my little army world it sort of does apply. And I know it's true— I would never have been able to have the potential to be as great a success at anything if it wasn't for you. That is being a mother, daughter, a doc, a wife, an officer, a neighbor; all things that you have shown me (by example & word) how to do better. I can never say Thank You enough for that. And on top of all that, you love me. Other people say things like, "I don't care what you do for a living, etc. I just love you," but I can't see how people separate what you do from what you are. And you seem to love the whole package—and I appreciate that.

Why did I start thinking about all this? I don't know. Perhaps it was due to one of our captain's comments after you left. He said, "Ma'am, I only met your husband for a little while, but he is just an amazingly nice guy." And I thought, Yes, I've known that for over eight years. But it's like saying goodbye at a funeral—it is too late. So I don't want it to ever be too late for me to say how much I love, admire, respect, like, and cherish you.

Bye for now,

Wifelet

At Tabuk, a squeaky clean and modern Saudi base built on the sand near the border with Jordan, Kory was the flight surgeon for the 58th Tactical Fighter Squadron, which belonged to the 33rd Tactical Fighter Wing. There were thirty-five pilots in the wing, and for the first two months in Saudi Arabia, Kory was the only doctor for nearly seven hundred people. That was good for him because he was so busy he had no time to be lonely or worry about me. I was able to get away first and visited him during the last weekend in September, which was nice because later I could imagine where he worked, where he slept, and what he did in his daily routine. I had fun enlightening Kory and his air force friends about what it was like for us army types living in the real desert instead of at an air-conditioned base. For about one week after my visit, he told me later, they stopped complaining about their pool, the gym, and eating real cooked food.

Kory also had more access to telephones than I did, and he was able to talk regularly with Regan, who was living with her father in North Dakota. She followed our progress on television, and Kory gave her regular updates on what was really happening. During one call in February, she said she was impressed that Kory's pilots had so many kills against the Iraqi air force, but she was feeling left out of all the excitement.

"It's just not fair," she whined.

"What do you mean?" Kory asked.

"You and Mother are over there having fun and getting to play war, and I'm up here."

Kory and I talked as often as we could, but there were long periods when my battalion deployed far into the desert, which left us out of contact. One of those times, during the height of the air war, Kory decided he wanted to visit me, but he wasn't sure exactly where we were living. All he could determine was that we were seventy-five kilometers southwest of Tapline Road near the Saudi town of Rafha. Kory already had flown on a British C-130 to Dhahran to try and fly with the F-15s from Langley Air Force Base. He desperately wanted to see and understand what the war was really like. Then he had taken a USAF C-130 to Rafha. Only someone as sure of himself as Kory would set out hitchhiking across the empty desert during the middle of a war, and only Kory would have never once doubted that he would find me. The roads were filled with military vehicles during the final positioning for the ground campaign, and hitchhiking was easy. He got a lift part of the way from a young army captain. The captain soon became nervous about transporting an unauthorized air force doctor, however, and wanted to unload his passenger. When they saw some helicopters off in the distance, the relieved captain dropped Kory in the desert. But the helicopters belonged to another unit; they weren't ours. A second army officer said "No problem," and offered to take Kory to the door of my tent. This guy delivered Kory to the wrong division: the 24th Infantry Division (Mechanized), instead of the 101st where I was living. The whole experience further eroded Kory's already minimal confidence in army officers.

Luckily, Kory found a flight surgeon he knew with the 24th Mech—

they had played rugby together in medical school—and the fellow doctor gave Kory a cot for the night. Camped out in the middle of the empty desert in the heart of an army division, Kory, like an animal drawn inexplicably to its own species, managed to find the only other air force guy within miles. He was a sergeant with a vehicle, and he offered to give Kory a ride to my unit, if they could find it.

They drove for hours across the open desert, down unmarked roads, and between armed camps. When they finally found our battalion, Kory had a good laugh over our defenses: we only carried enough barbed wire to go around part of the camp, so much of the rest was wide open. Kory and his air force sergeant drove in without being challenged until they spotted a soldier lying in a lawn chair. It was Lance, who was pleasantly surprised to see Kory at our little outpost. I had gone on a mission that day, but Lance found Kory something to eat and a lawn chair so he could work on his tan. I came back and found him late that afternoon, and we spent the night joyously in my tent.

Kory told me about the sixteen air-to-air kills made by the pilots in his squadron, more than any other unit in the war, and he was proud of them. They had been so successful that allied planes now controlled the skies over Iraq, and Kory was able to leave the base for a few days. Things were too quiet for Kory, though, and he was afraid the war was slipping by without him doing anything exciting. So far, his life had been almost unchanged by the war. None of his pilots had been wounded, thank goodness, and their medical needs were minimal. He treated people for aches and pains and colds, but that was not how he had imagined going to war. Visiting me was Kory's one chance to be on the front lines, and the next day we made a fairly unusual request of Lieutenant Colonel Bryan: could my husband fly on a mission? Bryan agreed, and that was how Kory came to climb on a Black Hawk helicopter and fly into Iraq.

The battalion was doing armed reconnaissance before the ground war, but the soldiers had more fun searching the desert for souvenirs that the Iraqi soldiers had left behind. When Kory's helicopter landed in Iraq, the soldiers with him hit the ground running and quickly scrounged 9mm pistols, bullets, grenades, and even a rocket launcher from abandoned Iraqi positions. They loaded everything on board and were ready to head back before Kory found anything. He was crushed; the mission was going to be over without anything to show for it. Sitting in the helicopter flying back to our base camp, Kory noticed a cloth tag printed in Russian on a grenade launcher. That would make a good wallet-sized souvenir, he thought. He took out his knife and started to saw off the little tag. One of the young sergeants on board nervously eyed this crazy air force doctor playing with a loaded RPG. The crazy doctor also was a captain, however, so the sergeant kept quiet. But he never took his eyes off that grenade launcher. At the time, Kory had no idea how grateful he would be one day to that young sergeant: Troy Dunlap.

Kory left the next day on a French airplane, but not before he saw the battle plan and learned that our mission in the ground war would take us deep into Iraq. He might have been a little nervous for me, but mostly he was envious. Kory's only regret was that he couldn't do more to help the war effort. He had done his job by keeping his pilots healthy and flying, but it didn't seem like enough. Out here in the desert was where the action was, and he would have loved to stay with us. He had to get back to work, though, and we hugged goodbye one last time. He's so big that I only come up to his chest, and he had to bend over to hug me properly. He kissed my face again and I smiled up at him. We knew the war would be over soon, and in a short while we would be together again. In fact, we thought that pretty soon everyone would be packing up to go home.

When the long-awaited ground campaign finally began on February 24, Kory watched the war on television back at Tabuk and attended the intelligence briefings to follow the action. Looking at the maps, he could see that our battalion and the entire 101st Division were moving fast and taking no casualties. His first hint that something had gone wrong came on February 27, the last full day of the ground campaign. Kory watched General Schwarzkopf on television giving a live briefing from Riyadh about the results of the war. After his summary of the lightning advance of the coalition forces and their relatively easy victory, Schwarzkopf said:

> I would remind you that the war is continuing to go on. Even as we speak right now there are incredible acts of bravery going on. This afternoon we had an F-16 pilot shot down. We had contact with him; he had a broken leg on the ground. Two helicopters from the 101st—they didn't have to do it—but they went in to try and pull that pilot out. One of them was shot down, and we're still in the process of working through that. But that's the kind of thing that's going on out on that battlefield right now. It is

not a Nintendo game—it is a tough battlefield where people are risking their lives at all times. There are great heroes out there, and we ought to be very, very proud of them.

Kory told me later that when Schwarzkopf mentioned the helicopter, his first thought was: I'll bet Rhonda's on it. He figured I might have known the F-16 pilot who had been shot down and volunteered to rescue him. On the other hand, he rationalized, there were lots of helicopters in the 101st, and I was probably not involved. A pessimistic person would have gone berserk right then, convinced that I was dead, but Kory is a true optimist. There was no way he could call the battalion out in the desert to be sure; he didn't even know where we were anymore. All he could do was wait for news. There were some anxious moments when his mind wandered and he thought of me, but the night passed and no one appeared to inform him that I had been shot down. The next day came and went without any bad news, and Kory put his worries behind him. He assumed I was celebrating with the battalion out in the desert, miles from a telephone, and that we would get together in a week or so.

With the war over and America victorious, Kory's squadron was told they would be going home in about twenty days. They threw a party to celebrate in Kory's room that Saturday night, March 2. That was the night I was alone in my room in the Baghdad hospital, singing "The Wind beneath My Wings" and trying to turn myself into a human radio antenna. My message apparently got through to Kory, sort of. He said he woke up early the morning after the party because he thought he should call Regan. He wanted to tell her that we were fine and would be coming home soon. It was already dark in North Dakota when he got through, and Regan came to the phone.

"The war's over and everything is fine," Kory assured her. "I saw Mother a couple of weeks ago and she was fine."

"When are you coming home?" Regan asked.

"I don't know," he said. "It won't be too long, but I'll let you know."

Kory said goodbye to Regan and let her go back to sleep. He returned to his cluttered room, which smelled of stale drinks. His roommate, Sly, was asleep in the top bunk. Kory stepped into a hot shower, still trying to recover from the party the night before. Feeling a little better when he finished, he walked out of the steamy bathroom into his room and found the wing commander and the squadron commander, both wearing serious expressions on their faces. Oh no, Kory thought, we're in trouble for having a party. Then Kory noticed the chaplain was with them. And an unexpected visit from the chaplain usually meant something was very wrong.

"We have some bad news," the wing commander said. He read from a computer printout that said Maj. Rhonda Cornum had been shot down while on a rescue mission for a downed F-16 pilot west of Kuwait. Her status was missing in action. "That's all we know," Col. Rick Parsons said.

Kory stood there looking at the slip of paper.

"What are you going to do?" Parsons asked.

"I'm going to get dressed and see if I can get through on the phone to her battalion commander to see if he knows what's going on," Kory said.

"That sounds like a good plan," the commander agreed. "Let me know if you need anything or want to use my phone."

The senior officers left the room. Kory looked over at his roommate, who was awake now, the color of green grass after the party, and lying in the top bunk. "I'm sorry they found the room like this," Kory apologized.

"Don't worry about that now," replied Chuck "Sly" McGill, a Marine exchange pilot flying F-15s with the air force. The roommates had become good friends. They had grown matching mustaches and were quite proud of them.

Kory had been strong and brave when his commanding officers were in the room, and the news had come as such a shock that there had been no time to react. Kory usually sees the bright side of things, but everyone in the military knows that "missing in action" is usually a euphemism: it means the person is dead but the body has not yet been found. How could Rhonda be dead? he thought. It's not possible. She's indestructible. Alone with his roommate, Kory leaned up against the bunk bed and rested his big arms on Sly's legs. He put his head down and cried.

Sly forced himself out of bed and volunteered to spend the day with Kory. The two of them hurriedly dressed and went to work the phones, trying to determine just what had happened. They soon learned that my helicopter had indeed been shot down. The crash was very bad, but my body had not been found. Just as Kory had suspected: killed in action, body not recovered. Kory knew he would have to tell Regan and my parents, but first he wanted to be sure of what had happened. He would wait a day or so until things were clarified. But when he called the Military Personnel Command, he was told that an officer already had been dispatched to inform my parents. Kory couldn't stop the notification, but he could head off my parents before they called Regan. He thought he should be the one to tell her. Kory dialed North Dakota and braced himself for the hardest telephone call of his life. It was very early Sunday morning there, and Kory knew Regan would still be asleep. Regan's father answered the phone.

"Marvin?"

"Hi Kory, what's up?"

"I've got some kinda bad news, not absolutely terrible news, so don't say anything to Regan," Kory said. "Would you go get her up, put her on your lap, and put the phone to her ear."

After a few moments, Regan came to the phone.

"Howya doing?" Kory asked her.

"I'm asleep."

"Well, I have some bad news."

"What?"

"I just got notified that Mother is missing."

Regan began to cry and couldn't stop. "Is she alright? What happened? What happened?"

"Regan, all I know is that she's missing. I don't know any more than that," Kory explained. "But remember, Lance was there with her, and I'm sure he's doing everything he can to find her."

"But will she be okay?" Regan pleaded, choking on her tears.

"You know she always had her gun with her," Kory said. "So if she's out there in the desert, and they're trying to sneak back, she'll do alright. Mother's tough."

"When will we know where she is?" Regan asked.

"I don't know," Kory said, tears in his eyes, but trying to be strong. "I'll be calling you back once or twice a day until I hear something. As soon as I hear anything, I'll call you first. Don't worry."

Kory wanted to keep up Regan's hopes, but he didn't know what to believe. He tried to keep busy and ran twice a day, but it was agony to wait for news and not be able to do anything. Everyone at the base knew what had happened, and his friends offered whatever help they could, but there was nothing anyone could do. Kory's friends said I was too tough to be dead, and he wanted to believe them. From his

phone calls to my battalion, Kory began to piece together more details about what had happened. He learned that five bodies had been
found with the wreckage. The crash was really bad, so bad that it didn't
look like anyone could have survived. Three people—me, Dunlap, and
Stamaris—were missing. That was strange. Why would the Iraqis leave
five bodies and take three others? The worst thing would be if the Iraqis
had buried the three bodies out in the desert. Would they ever be found?
Would anyone ever know what had happened? But maybe they were
alive, Kory thought. Maybe there was hope. He got a boost of encouragement from a televised briefing given by Gen. Colin Powell. The
chairman of the Joint Chiefs of Staff, asked about the missing and the
POWs, declared that the war was not over until every single person
was accounted for or safely back home.

Back in Buffalo, New York, my mother learned the news the hard
way: with a knock on the door from a man in a uniform. This is the
wartime nightmare of every mother and father, wife, husband, and child.
I had tried to prepare my family in case something happened to me,
but there really was no way to prepare them. I knew they worried about
me, often needlessly, and I tried to calm their fears in my letters. On
February 22, I had written to my mother:

Dear Mother:

I have gotten several letters from you lately (Thank you, by
the way!), and I have been debating about what to write. I could
lie, and say I am safe in a nice quiet medical job somewhere, but
A) I don't lie, and haven't for twenty years; and B) I'd rather
you know what I'm really thinking and feeling about being here.

Five days ago I was (I think) the first American female service member to fly into Iraq, get out of my aircraft, be a part of
taking the first prisoners of war that the 101st took, and fly back
out with these guys in my helicopter. No, I wasn't scared. It was
in fact the most exciting thing since sex I've done. No, this is
not a particularly romantic war, but going into combat is the real
reason people stay in the army. It isn't the money because I could
not possibly make as little as I do if I was a civilian. It isn't the
lifestyle, because I haven't lived like this since Freeville, New
York. But it is in some ways—it is a personal test to see if you
have the "right stuff." And let's admit it—that's me. I seem to

gravitate to doing things that are difficult just because I crave challenge. And the army likes me for it! And I like, no, I love what I do. It was like being a surgery intern at Walter Reed. That is the most difficult internship offered by the army—and I liked it!

I feel what I'm doing here is important, and I am very proud to be doing it. My family (husband and daughter) are happy with me. . . . So go to the library or something—but it doesn't help me focus on what I need to do here to worry about you worrying about me!

I love you; I'm glad you are doing well. Please, just laugh at some of my stories, be proud of me doing my patriotic thing, fly your flag. Sure, we've got body bags—I'm even considering using one as an outside liner for my sleeping bag, warm and dry!

Love always,

Rambo Rhonda (it's a joke)

Even my strictest admonitions were not enough, however, to prepare my mother for that morning, March 3. She told me later that she was still in her robe and had the Sunday paper spread across the floor of her home. She has lived alone since she and my father separated, and she enjoys those quiet mornings by herself. There was an unexpected knock at the door. Maybe it's the paper boy, she thought. She tightened her robe and straightened her hair. When she opened the door, she saw a man in uniform and froze.

"Are you Mrs. Scott?"

"Yes," she said, coolly inviting him in. Tensing, she already knew what his message would be.

The officer, an army major, stood at attention and formally read from a piece of paper: "I regret to inform you that your daughter, Major Rhonda L. Cornum, is missing in action." He explained that my helicopter had been shot down in Iraq, and I was missing with two other soldiers. The officer was straight and correct, which was lucky for him, because otherwise my mother would have broken down completely, or possibly attacked him. Instead, she stood there stunned, her face blank.

My mother asked the major to go with her to tell my father, who lives a few miles away. They drove to my father's house, and my mother stood by crying while the major repeated his brief message. My father did not cry. He pressed the major for details about what had happened. Where exactly had they crashed? What were they doing? He took notes on a piece of paper. The way my parents dealt with the news says a lot about their different personalities: my mother wanted to cry and feel bad; my father wanted to feel like he was doing something positive to solve this problem. Together they called my youngest sister, Eden, and she came to the house with my brother Paul. When my mother called my sister Loren in New Jersey, she never doubted I was alive, and her reaction was, "Darn, now I'll have to write her a letter."

My father did not break down until later. He was telling my mother that he was worried about one of his missing cats, named Hork, and he had designed all kinds of crazy traps and trip wires to catch him. He had planned to write a story about the adventures of Hork and send it to me out in the desert. His voice broke and he began to sob, saying that he never got around to writing the story and now it was too late. He quickly recovered, though, wiped the tears off his face, and got down to business. He started by firing off letters and telegrams to every important person he could think of, including President Bush, General Schwarzkopf, and General Powell, demanding that they find his daughter. Right now. If my mother was going to scream and cry, he was going to pack his bags, get on the next plane to Iraq, and personally lead the rescue mission. That is exactly the kind of thing I had feared he would do, exactly what I had warned my sister against. I had worried that he would embarrass me, and he was about to. I guess I never really thought my sister, a mere mortal, could stop our parents from doing what they thought was best, especially when it involved one of their children.

Until that time, my mother had regarded my job in the army as just that: a job. I was a scientist who worked in a lab that happened to be run by the army, and it was not particularly dangerous work. The army was not the life she would have chosen for me, but she had accepted it and was glad that I was happy. Now, she drove alone in her car and screamed, screamed at God and declared to Him that she refused to outlive her children. She suddenly was furious with the people who protested the war and called it a war for oil. The small protests had not affected her before, but now that I was missing, protesting was no longer allowed. This was a good cause, a just war. This war must have a purpose for my mother, otherwise my death would be meaningless. All she could do was scream.

Kory waited until he was sure my parents had been notified before he called them. He dialed and dialed, but the number at my father's house was always busy. When he finally got through, Kory tried to calm them down and explained there was nothing anyone could do except wait for news. My father, however, wanted to know about flights to Saudi Arabia. In a voice that was increasingly firm, Kory told him to stay put and also to stay off the phone. Kory said that if he did get news, he would call, but he wouldn't be able to get through if the phone was busy all the time. They talked about Regan and decided she should stay with her father in North Dakota. Kory was the calm one in the family, as I knew he would be, and he tried to be an anchor for the others. He suffered, but quietly, forcing himself to wait for news and allowing only the slightest hope that I was still alive.

By then I had been a prisoner for four days, and I was alone in my locked room in the Baghdad hospital. I had sung until I was hoarse, I had thanked God for being alive, and I was wondering how long I would be held against my will. I was injured, and I was a prisoner of war deep in the enemy's capital city, but I was very much alive and had every intention of getting back to my husband, my daughter, and the rest of my family.

2

The morning of the fifth day, my friendly hospital attendant in the white robe entered the room with a plate of pita bread, jelly, and a hard-boiled egg. There was the usual small glass of hot, sweet tea, which never failed to improve my outlook. I knew I should eat, and the man patiently fed me, tearing the bread into bite-sized pieces and waiting for me to swallow. After breakfast two pretty young army nurses, wearing green uniforms and patent-leather high heels, arrived with instructions to bathe me. They were the first women I had seen in the Iraqi military. I was glad for the chance to clean up and get out of the Iraqi army uniform I had been wearing since the clinic in Basra.

The nurses, wearing makeup and with their dark brown hair tied neatly in back, led me down the hall to the bathroom. They did not speak a single word of English, but we understood each other well enough. After the three of us squeezed inside the cramped bathroom, they gently and competently helped me out of my Iraqi uniform. I looked down and noticed my white bra was stiff with blood. Rather than try to pull the crusty bra over my arms, one of the nurses cut it off with a pair of scissors and threw it in the trash. When I saw the scissors, I thought about asking them to cut off my matted hair, but Kory likes it long, so I decided to let them try to wash out the dried blood and dirt. That was an indication of how confident I was that I would be going home soon: I didn't think I would be in Iraq long enough for my hair to grow back. Or maybe I just didn't want to be a bald POW. The nurses stood me on a pair of sandals on the damp floor, as helpless as a small child, while they dipped rags in cold water and began to scrub at the dirt and blood that was caked on my body. The water was icy, but it felt good to be cleaner, and the nurses clearly were experienced in caring for the wounded.

"Thank you. Thank you," I told them. They smiled and nodded back at me. Conversation was limited by our lack of a shared language, and even sign language was difficult because I couldn't move my arms, but I was learning to be fairly expressive with a few gestures and a smile.

My arms were still in splints. The nurses held them away from my body while they cleaned everything else. I closed my eyes, and they scrubbed my face and neck. When I saw how dirty the rag became, I realized how much dirt I had picked up in just a few days. I looked into the faces of these women while they worked and thought how pretty they were. During all those months in Saudi Arabia, I had never seen more than the dark eyes of an Arab woman because the Saudi women always were veiled in public. When they had cleaned my face and body, the nurses sat me in a chair, tipped my head back into the sink, and washed my hair. Even when my hair was relatively clean, they still couldn't pull a comb through it and just shook their heads at me apologetically. I gestured back that they shouldn't worry. One of the most wonderful things they did for me was to brush my teeth, which had not been cleaned in five days. After they finished, and I had gratefully rinsed my mouth in the sink, the nurses presented me with the brush and a tube of toothpaste as a gift. Be very careful with them, they made me understand in whispered Arabic, because toiletries are scarce since the war.

I was clean and back in bed, dressed in a fresh hospital gown, when the chief of orthopedics and the resident I had seen the day before came back for a visit.

"Doctor Cornum, we are going to operate on your arms later today," the chief announced.

"Well," I said, "let's think about that for a minute, Doctor."

"You need to have it done," he insisted. "But I think if we just align them, set them, and cast them, you will be home in time to have the definitive surgery done in one of your own hospitals. If you want to wait, that would be fine. If you want me to do the surgery, I will do it."

I thought about what he had said and realized this was great news. Here was a man with enough authority to know what was in store for me, and he thought I would be going home soon.

"I think I'll wait for the definitive surgery," I said, glad that he had given me a way out without hurting his feelings. "I would appreciate it if you would align them and put them in casts."

"That's fine," he said. "We'll do it later when we have power."

I was not sure I wanted any complex procedure done in a hospital that did not even have electricity twenty-four hours a day. The doctors told me that they only did surgery at certain hours because that was when the generators produced enough power. I also knew they didn't have intravenous antibiotics, and their choice of screws and rods for my arms was extremely limited. The chief wanted to plate my arm, which probably was a reasonable thing to do, but since he said it was safe to wait, and that I would not have any neurological or structural deficits, then I was willing to wait. I doubted he had enough surgical supplies anyway, and he probably would have preferred not to use them on an American if his own people were waiting for care. I could not leave my arms the way they were, however, because they were at odd angles and unstable. If anyone was going to set them, I was glad it was this man because he seemed quite capable.

"What about Sergeant Stamaris?" I asked.

"We must operate on him because he is in bad shape. We also are giving him blood," the chief said.

We talked for a while, doctor to doctor. He mentioned he had presented some of his work, the results of orthopedic research, at the Mayo Clinic in Minnesota, and he clearly was treating me with professional courtesy. For a moment, I felt like a normal patient talking to her doctor. After a few minutes the chief excused himself to continue on his rounds, and I thanked him again.

The resident returned alone to my room. He was a little chubby, with curly black hair. Like any good resident, he started to do a routine history on me, and a physical. He asked the right questions and methodically checked my reflexes and pulses. He and all the doctors appeared worn and resigned. I imagined they had been busy during the past six weeks. They had not been able to check my blood pressure because my arms were splinted, but I told him I didn't think I had a problem. The resident wanted to draw a little blood, and he searched my bound arms for a place to insert the needle.

"Try my left ankle," I said, knowing I had a good vein there. In fact, when I was teaching medics and other people in the battalion how to insert an IV, I used to let them practice on me. I knew where to find all my good veins.

The resident drew a little blood from my ankle and left, only to return a few hours later saying he needed more blood.

"Why do you want more blood?" I asked.

"We typed and crossed you with the sample I took, but we want your hematocrit," which is a measure of how much blood a person has.

"Don't bother," I said. "I don't want a transfusion anyway." I was still weak, but not so weak that I wanted to risk tapping into the Iraqi blood supply. I was not afraid it had been stored improperly, but hepatitis and the AIDS virus would have worried me anywhere. I figured that if I had needed blood after the wreck, I already would have died. I knew I was no longer bleeding, so I didn't want any blood.

"But Doctor Cornum, I was supposed to prepare you for a transfusion."

"That's okay, really," I insisted. "I don't want a transfusion."

He paused and asked hesitantly, "Will you promise to say that you did not want me to do it?"

I smiled because I knew the problem. The chief had ordered the resident to take my blood, and he was afraid of being reprimanded. "Don't worry," I assured him. "I'll say I wouldn't let you give me a transfusion."

"Thank you, Doctor Cornum," he said gratefully. He said goodbye and left the room.

Later an ophthalmologist came to see me. I had complained to the chief that the vision in my left eye was blurred, and both eyes were stinging. After an examination, I was relieved to hear that my eyes were fine, and that none of the lacerations around the eye had cut the muscles required for opening or closing the lid. My vision would soon return to normal, the eye doctor said.

A pair of orderlies appeared later that day with a wheelchair, and I gathered they were taking me to the operating room for my arms to be set. The resident walked in with them. "I'm sorry, Doctor Cornum, but we will have to blindfold you."

"That's okay," I assured him. "I've been blindfolded everywhere else."

The resident helped seat me in the wheelchair with a blanket over my legs. Then he placed a surgical mask over my eyes so I couldn't see. I felt the orderlies wheel me out the door and down a hallway. We passed through another door and we were outside. I felt a sidewalk underneath the wheels and heard birds chirping along the way. By peeking out from under the mask, I could see grass and trees on either side of the path. There were thick bushes and honeysuckle. It felt wonderful to be outside again. This was the first clear day that I could remember, and the sunshine felt warm and healthy on my pale skin. I heard people talking as we wheeled by, perhaps other patients enjoying the day. After about two glorious blocks outside, we turned inside again. They removed my blindfold and helped me onto a stretcher. Lying there, I stared up at the dripping pipes hanging along the water-stained ceiling. We must have been in the basement of the hospital. Doctors and nurses, scrubbed for surgery, bustled through the swinging doors that opened onto operating rooms. This was a solid old hospital, and I felt oddly at home. My mind filled with memories of another solid old hospital, Brooke Army Medical Center in San Antonio, where I had done general surgery as a medical student.

Someone rolled me into the operating room, and the nurses removed my gown and covered me with a sheet. I looked up at the doctors and nurses in their blue scrubs and caps. It was a familiar scene, except that I was on the wrong end of the procedure. The first problem they had was finding a place for the IV. They normally would have put it in my arm, but both arms were splinted and were going to be fixed.

"You can use my jugular," I suggested. I turned my head to the side, and one of them inserted the needle.

The anesthesiologist politely introduced himself, and I thanked him.

"I'm sorry that the nurses we sent for you did not speak English," the chief of orthopedics said, making small talk before going to work.

"Sir, that's okay. I don't speak Arabic," I said. "Before I come back to Iraq, I'm going to learn, though."

Everybody froze. The scrub technician, the nurses, the chief of orthopedics—everybody stopped and stared at me. Finally the chief said, "Doctor Cornum. Please. Please don't ever come back to Iraq."

"Well, how about if I come back as a tourist?"

They laughed and said I would be welcome. The anesthesiologist was getting ready to put me under. I'm sure he had given me an injection of something already. I said to the chief, "Sir, I lied to you yesterday."

"Yes?" he said, looking at me.

"I told you I didn't have any kids. I have a daughter."

I saw him smile before the plastic mask went over my face and I fell into a deep, drugged sleep.

When I woke I was back in my room. I didn't have a clock, but the room was dark, and I felt like it was very late. My mouth was dry and cottony, but my throat wasn't sore, so I knew they had not put a tube down my throat during surgery. Instead, they had used the mask and "bagged me," which meant the anesthesiologist had kept the mask on and used a squeezable bag for every breath. I noticed I had new casts on my arms, which rested on my chest. When I moved my head to the side, I was startled to find the IV catheter still in place in my neck. That made me a little nervous; I never would have left a capped IV in a patient's jugular vein. I didn't want the needle to spill blood, so I kept my head very still and tried to ignore it. The rest of the hospital was quiet until I heard the doctors returning Stamaris to his room. Dan must have had surgery tonight, too, I thought. A while later Stamaris began to moan in pain; soft, muffled sounds that gradually grew louder and more anguished. I figured that his drugs were wearing off after surgery. I heard someone go in his room, and soon he grew quiet again. Morphine, I thought. After a time, I too drifted off to sleep.

The morning of the sixth day, two very young women in crisp white uniforms whisked brightly into the room. The older one, still only in her early twenties, spoke a little English and was excited to have a captive audience on whom to practice.

"What are you?" she asked me.

"I'm a doctor in the army."

"Bombs? Drop bombs?" She made arm motions to show an airplane flying overhead.

"Oh no," I said. "Doctor."

She nodded that she understood.

"How old are you?" I asked.

She scrunched up her face quizzically.

"How many years?"

She counted in Arabic on her hands and then tried to translate the number into English. I think she was saying twenty-four.

"You?"

"I am thirty-six," I said.

"Are you married?"

"Yes," I said. "What about you?"

"No, I am a student."

"What is he?" she asked.

"My husband?" She nodded. "He's in the air force."

"Pilot? Drop bombs?"

"No, he's a doctor, too."

"Do you have children?"

"No," I said.

The younger girl did not speak any English and whispered questions to the older girl to be translated.

"Saddam is good. Very good," the older girl said. "He takes care of our country." She spoke of him in reverent tones. "The bombing is very frightening."

I didn't say anything, but I thought sadly that this girl had been thoroughly brainwashed by her government.

The girls led me down the hall to the bathroom to wash me and brush my teeth. My knee still bothered me, but I felt stronger. I smiled at the girls, and they giggled and chattered away while they washed me, careful not to splash water on the new plaster casts. They noticed my matted hair, and I just shrugged. They were young but competent, and I assumed they were nursing students.

We returned to the room, and they fed me breakfast of an orange, a roll, and a glass of milk. The milk was very hard to get, the older girl said, and people outside the hospital didn't have any at all. They peeled the orange and fed me the fat, juicy sections. The girls cleaned up the breakfast dishes, sat on the bed next to mine, and settled in for a good visit. They laughed and smiled at me the entire time, and they seemed to be enjoying themselves. They were supposed to be taking care of me, but I felt more like their mother.

A thunderous explosion rocked the building. The girls shrieked and jumped to their feet, landing on my bed and huddling next to me for protection. I laughed and told them, "Don't worry, they're not going to bomb this building." They calmed down after a few minutes, but clearly they were shaken. I wasn't sure what had caused the explosion. I didn't think coalition pilots would be bombing a hospital, but I had no idea what was happening outside the walls of my room.

The girls left me alone for a time, but they returned later in the day with a brush to work through the knots in my tangled hair. While one brushed, tugging hard at the rope-like bunches, the other held up oranges and other objects from the room so I could pronounce the names in English. The girls then repeated the word in English and pronounced it slowly for me in Arabic. I repeated the word in Arabic, and they giggled. The language seemed to have a lot of raspy sounds that came from the back of the throat, but I liked the way it sounded. I figured that if I was going to be in Iraq for the near future, it would be helpful to learn Arabic. There was no reason my captivity had to be entirely negative, and maybe I could squeeze out some benefits. Imagine how great it would be to go home speaking Arabic.

"Chai," I said for my favorite tea. "Bai chai," I said, meaning "more tea." The girls giggled with pleasure.

The chief of orthopedics came in the room to brief me about my surgery. He said it had gone well, and he had realigned my arms. Because the bones were broken, the muscles had started to contract, and that had made the bones start to overlap painfully. He had successfully pulled the bones back into place, he said proudly, obviously pleased with the results.

"Thank you," I said.

"We sewed the lacerations on your hand and knee, but it is not a very plastic job," he apologized, meaning the stitches were not like a plastic surgeon would have left them.

"That's okay," I reassured him. "I'm not a very plastic person."

I had noticed that the chief had sewn me up with thick needles and silk sutures, which normally would not have been used on skin. Apparently silk sutures were all that remained after the economic sanctions and shortages caused by the war. We chatted for a few minutes, and he mentioned that he had a brother, also a physician, living in the United States. I remembered hearing someone bring Stamaris back to his room the night before, and I was curious about his surgery.

"How is Sergeant Stamaris?"

"He was badly injured, but I think he will do well," the chief said, very business-like.

After the doctor left on his rounds, and the young nurses had gone, boredom settled on my gray room. The day had been busy and full of visitors, but now I had time to reflect by myself. I didn't feel like singing. There was nothing to read. I had read stories about POWs, and I knew I should develop a physical training program to keep in good condition. There wasn't much possibility of exercise in my room, but I thought I should at least walk a little, which I could do now without my arms hurting so badly. Getting off the bed took some effort, but I used my good leg to lower the bad leg onto the floor. I rocked myself up to a standing position and hobbled across the room. I counted nine steps to the wall. Then I walked back. Then forward. That got boring pretty quickly, so I tried walking in little triangles.

On one of the turns, I noticed marks on the wall next to the door. I bent to look closer and saw tiny hash marks in groups of four with a diagonal line through each block. Each of the blocks represented five— I guessed five days—and there were six blocks across and six down.

That seemed like a lot of days to be in this room. I had been a prisoner long enough for only one block of five plus one day. I debated keeping my own calendar, but even if I had a pencil, or a nail to scratch the wall, I still couldn't use my hands to write.

I was sobered to think someone had been a prisoner here before me, and had been held so long. I wasn't sure exactly what this facility contained. I assumed it was a military medical center, but I didn't know if my wing was a military complex with a hospital or a hospital with a prison ward. Nearly everyone I had seen so far was military, but they were medical people, not soldiers. The explosion, too, was a mystery. As I told the girls, I didn't think the Americans were bombing the building. If our war planners had wanted to destroy this complex, it would have been done long before now. Besides, we were not in the business of bombing hospitals. But I did worry there was something important near the hospital that had become a target. Maybe the war had started again, or maybe it had never ended. Maybe it wasn't even an allied bomb.

The explosion was less frightening than the hash marks scratched onto the wall. Now I began to think about spending years in Iraq, not just weeks or months. So far I had been concentrating on getting well, and that had taken most of my energy. What would I do with myself when my health was restored, and I still couldn't leave this place? I'm the kind of person who is moving constantly, always doing something. I thought it entirely possible that I would die of boredom. I could study Arabic, that would keep me occupied mentally. Maybe I could get some books. The chief of orthopedics ought to have some books in English, even if they were medical texts. I would have to develop an exercise program. Pacing was not very exciting, but it was better than nothing. The chief had said I would be going home soon, but maybe he was just trying to keep up my spirits. I myself had been known to give my patients only the good news at first, particularly if they were injured and I was evacuating them somewhere.

Another fierce explosion shook the building that day. What are they up to? Seeing how the first explosion had scared the girls made me wonder what it must have been like for them during the war. They had been under constant bombardment since January 17. I felt bad for the girls and their families, but I never thought we had done the wrong thing. We did not bomb Baghdad because we were bored or had nothing else to do that day; there were solid, key military targets here. The only way Saddam was going to leave Kuwait was if he could no longer support his army in the field. That meant going to the source, not just bombing the troops in Kuwait.

I rarely got philosophical in my musings, but when I did, I never thought this war was immoral or wrong, even if I did feel sorry for some of the individual Iraqis I had met. In fact, I thought the war was a good idea. I don't have time for people who say there should be no war. In an ideal world, that would be wonderful, but one side can't simply say, "No more war." That would leave control of the world to the people who like war, and there are plenty of them. It seems so self-evident to me that I can never understand people who want America to disarm unilaterally. What would happen then? They never seem to think that far ahead. The people who feel that way don't have a logical sequence to their thinking, and I have a hard time dealing with illogical people.

Eventually the girls returned, and I was happy to see them, glad to stop my mind from wandering. They carried a women's magazine in Arabic, and were excited to show it to me. They got comfortable alongside me on the bed. Arabic reads from right to left, so they flipped through the magazine "backwards" to show me the pictures. I couldn't understand the writing, but I did recognize a lot of the people. There was Jackie Onassis. There was a story about the movie *Total Recall.*

"That's a good movie," I told the girls, pointing my face at the picture. They looked at me, blankly, apparently confused about the word "movie." They turned the page.

When we finished the magazine, which didn't take long, they brushed my hair again and neatly arranged it in a clip. Gradually they were straightening all the knots, and I was glad I wouldn't have to cut it. The girls apparently didn't have enough work to do, so we practiced Arabic. Then they fed me lunch of an orange, a roll, and a glass of milk. The meal was the same as breakfast, but the food tasted good and I knew it was healthy. Eventually the girls said goodbye, promising to return later.

Alone in my room again, I stared up at the ceiling, sang a little, and let my thoughts carry me beyond the four walls. I tried to practice the Arabic I had learned so far, but I couldn't remember anything. "Chai" was tea. That I could remember, but nothing else. My brain did not seem to be working well. I was still weak from losing so much blood and from surgery the night before. I was pretty confident I'd recover eventually, but I was impatient. I was ready to be better. Now. A radio blared in the hallway, but my Arabic was months away from being able to understand the lyrics, and the music was an annoying twang. The room. The walls. The ceiling.

Mosquitoes buzzed around me like tiny vultures or miniature attack jets, pleased to have such a helpless target. I watched them calmly fly humming orbits above my body, searching for choice morsels of exposed flesh. They would spot a likely place and circle closely before landing. Slowly, carefully, they touched down and moved their little feet into position. Then they stuck me and drank deeply of my blood. They grew fatter before my eyes as they gorged themselves, and I imagined them bursting from their gluttony. There was not a darn thing I could do about it. I bounced on the bed and shook my head like a horse, but it did not dissuade them. I hated those mosquitoes.

This was it. This was life as a POW. This was my life for the near future. This room, those walls, that ceiling. My reality. At least I was not in pain. The doctors never gave me any pain killer, not even aspirin, but there was no pain if I lay still. How long could I lie still, though? How long before I went crazy? Maybe they'll let me go outside again. Small things, like sunshine and fresh air, seemed so important. The big wedges of orange. My glass of hot sweet chai. Maybe the girls will come back for more Arabic lessons. I wonder if they have a gym in this place? I could start to rehabilitate. I could start slowly and work my way up, do a little weight training.

So the day passed: another trip to the bathroom, another meal, someone laying a blanket over me after darkness fell. I had been asleep for several hours when a sound woke me. The door opened, and a kerosene lantern filled the room with a flickering yellow light. I saw two armed soldiers. My attendant in the white robe, who looked like he, too, had been awakened from a sound sleep, was with them. He said to me, "You have to leave." Leave? I thought. Leave to where? I am perfectly comfortable here, and I'm not in the mood for another marathon bus ride. I had no choice in the matter, however. The attendant helped me stand and pushed my feet into a pair of clogs. Then he took the toothbrush and toothpaste from the nightstand next to the bed and pressed them into my hand until I could grip them. I smiled to thank him for the gift, and he shyly smiled back. I heard voices and movement from the other room, and I guessed they were also getting Stamaris ready to leave.

The older of the two girls came back to the room. She was sleepy-eyed, and must have been staying overnight in the hospital.

"Are you going home? Are you going home?" she asked me with a mixture of concern and excitement.

I looked at the two soldiers standing guard. They didn't look anything like home. "I don't think so," I said.

The nurse leaned over and carefully wrapped her arms around me. She squeezed me in a warm embrace and brushed her soft face against mine. I leaned into her, unable to hug her back because of my arms.

"Thank you very much," I told her. "Good luck."

"Goodbye," she said.

The soldiers motioned for me to leave, and they led me out of the hospital room for the last time.

10

The soldiers placed a surgical mask loosely over my eyes and led me outside to a bus waiting in the darkness. I still was wearing the green hospital gown that covered my arms and reached the ground. Stamaris was carried onto the bus on a stretcher. When we pulled away from the hospital it must have been around 3 A.M., and the streets of Baghdad were quiet. I didn't worry any more about being on the road at night, because now I felt sure the war had ended. We drove for about thirty minutes before we arrived in front of another building. No one ever told us where we were or where we were going, and I had no idea. I stared straight ahead, glancing occasionally under my mask but trying to be discreet. The guards marched us off the bus and led us inside the heavy cement building without a word. We were quiet, and I concentrated on not tripping over my robe. By then we had learned never to speak in front of the guards, because they yelled sharply at us. I did manage to quietly ask Stamaris how he was feeling. He said fine. Then we were separated.

Peering underneath my blindfold on the way inside the building, mostly so I wouldn't fall, I caught a glimpse of an Iraqi officer shouting at an older man in civilian clothes. I was pushed into a room, and in a few moments I heard someone enter behind me. I stood still, and the person reached out to remove the blindfold from my eyes. When I could see again, I recognized the man in front of me as the older civilian who had received the tongue-lashing from the officer. The two of us were standing inside a cement cell, which measured roughly ten feet by ten feet. I saw a pallet on the floor with a mat and blankets for a bed. The older man had brought a metal cot that was missing most of its springs. He gathered up the mat and blanket from the floor and set them on the cot, which promptly collapsed under the weight. I was standing there watching him wrestle with the cot, worrying that if I tried to sit down I would fall through. The officer, who was watching from the hall, started shouting again, and the old man hastily arranged the blankets and mat back on the floor. He scurried out the door and returned after a few minutes with another, sturdier, cot and made the bed again. This one did not collapse.

The man told me to get on the cot. I stiffly bent over and sat on the edge, my feet on the floor. He ordered me to lie down.

"I can't," I said.

The old man looked at me for a moment, decided not to argue, and left, pulling the steel door shut behind him.

After a time sitting there alone, I realized I had to use the bathroom. I struggled to my feet, walked to the door, and spoke through the little window: "Water closet."

The old man was outside the door and understood. He let me out of my cell and walked me down a long, dark row of cells. Apparently we were inside a prison of some kind, perhaps a military prison. The doors to the cells were closed, but I looked into the window on the door of the first cell and saw a Western-looking man. In the next cell, I saw another man. These must be other POWs. Each cell held a Western prisoner. This is great news, I thought. What a relief. I somehow felt safer being with other prisoners. I couldn't tell if they were Americans, but I thought that some of them must be. I looked for Troy, but didn't see him. I hoped nothing bad had happened to him. I didn't know what was going to happen to any of us, but it was better to be together. I knew they were moving us, and I hoped we were going home, but I half suspected we were going to make videos. They had been careful to keep us apart before, so I knew something big was in the works.

The older man, a gentleman, walked into the latrine first to make sure it was empty. It was a large, dirty room with peeling walls, apparently the only bathroom for the entire cell block. There was a trough on one side, and since I had not been in too many Iraqi prison bathrooms before, I wondered if the trough was for washing or urinating. Bracing myself against the stench of stale urine, I stepped into one of the stalls. With my arms set in stiff casts and supported by slings, I could move my fingers enough to carefully inch the surgical gown up to my hips. I was glad to be able to use the bathroom by myself again, even if it did take a long time.

When the guard led me back to the cell, I saw by the faint light coming in from the little window over my head that it was almost dawn. I sat down heavily on the creaky cot, hoping to rest. There seemed to be a lot of activity in the prison and I felt something was going to happen. I had only been there a few moments when another guard opened the door. He threw a plastic bag in front of me, and it skidded across the cement floor to my feet. I looked at the bag and saw it contained yellow clothing. I looked up at the guard, but I didn't move from my place on the cot. The guard pointed at the clothes and snapped at me in Arabic. He wore a green uniform and green sweater. He was in his late thirties and had a look so stern that all he needed was a riding crop to play in a Gestapo movie.

I presumed that he wanted me to get dressed. "I can't put them on," I told him.

He didn't understand, so he yelled louder.

"I have two broken arms," I said, nodding my head in the direction of the casts on my arms. My arms were covered by my green robe, however, and I realized he could not see them in the dim light of the cell.

Another burst of angry Arabic.

At that point, my Arabic included only a few words, and I didn't recognize any of them in his comments. Some things are easily understood, however, and I gathered this man was saying, more or less, "Put it on, you dumb bitch."

"I can't," I said again, more irritated than afraid.

When he finally understood that I wasn't going to move, he bent over and picked up the bag. He pulled out the yellow pants and shook them straight. They were enormous. The guard grabbed me from the side and proceeded to dress me. I wasn't wearing underwear beneath the hospital robe, but he didn't seem to care about anything except getting me into the yellow suit. He plunged my feet into the pants and hauled them up to my waist, shoving the long robe inside. The robe was as big as a tent, but the pants were huge and accommodating. The guard packed all the excess material inside the pants and wrapped a belt around the outside to hold everything together. Next came a yellow top, which he pulled over my shoulders and the casts, leaving the shirtsleeves hanging empty at my sides. The pants and top were made of a heavy yellow fabric, something between canvas and burlap. The back of the shirt was decorated in big letters: PW. The guard was not happy about any of this, and he jerked me around like a toy doll while shoving my body parts into the corresponding articles of clothing.

Once I was dressed in the suit, the guard threw another plastic bag containing two white sneakers on the floor in front of me. He yelled at me again, along the same lines as the first time.

I wearily sat back on the cot and said, ever polite and reasonable, "I can't put the shoes on myself."

Furious now, he kneeled in front of me and tried to jam my bare feet into the sneakers. The shoes were a size six and I wear an eight, so it was not going to happen. He called to someone in the hall, who handed the guard a larger pair of white sneakers, which he put on my feet and tied snugly. When he had finished and I was dressed, the guard opened the door and led me into the hallway. With the suit billowing around the middle, I looked like Humpty-Dumpty.

Other cell doors began opening at the same time, and soon a line of more than a dozen men dressed in identical yellow "PW" outfits was standing with me in the hallway. There was excitement in the air, and the guards bustled around us. Where's Troy? I scanned the faces of the men, but didn't recognize anyone. Most of them appeared European or American. I wasn't sure where they were from because we weren't allowed to speak. I wanted to find Troy. There was safety in numbers, and I wanted him to be with this larger group of prisoners. The guard blindfolded me, and someone ordered us to march out the door. I was looking at the ground, trying to follow the pair of yellow legs walking in front of me, when without warning I was hit by a blast of cheap cologne. I turned up my nose, held my breath and kept walking, but the smell was all over me. The guards must have decided that a woman should wear perfume when dressed in her finest prison-wear. I never wear perfume at home—it gives me a headache—and now I smelled like a cheap flower. Maybe the guards thought I smelled bad, and they were doing a favor for my fellow prisoners. All I know is that none of the male prisoners was hosed down with cologne.

We were led onto a bus, and I was put on a seat next to the window. The prisoners were silent as the guards ordered everyone to sit down. Someone sat next to me, and I could feel him looking at me under his blindfold. He whispered in English, "I know who you are."

That's bizarre, I thought. I certainly didn't know who he was. Perhaps he recognized my perfume. We were still blindfolded, but I knew there were guards everywhere so I kept my voice low: "What do you mean?"

"Sergeant Dunlap told us all about you," the other prisoner said.

Oh boy, I thought, what did Troy tell them? Where is that guy, anyway? He must be all right if he's telling stories about me.

"No talking!" a guard yelled, and we were quiet.

After a short journey the bus rolled to a stop, and the guards marched us blindfolded into another building. I knew it was Tuesday, March 5, the seventh day of my captivity, and from the light I guessed it was about 9 A.M. Once again, we were being moved to a new location. It seemed like every few hours I was being shoved on a bus to go from one cell to another. Maybe they were afraid of a rescue attempt. Whatever the strategy was, it was getting very tiresome. I was ready to stay put for a while. Someone removed my blindfold, and to my surprise I found myself standing in the lobby of a rather nice hotel. There were couches, a front desk, all very pleasant. I looked around and saw at least twenty other prisoners milling about in yellow suits just like mine. I was the only woman.

There also were a few Western civilians in the lobby, and one of them announced with a European accent, "You are safe. You are now in the custody of the International Committee of the Red Cross. It's over and you are going home."

The voices of the other prisoners grew louder as the news began to sink in and the men traded reactions. There were a few cheers and a couple of high fives among the other prisoners. I stayed quiet and to myself. I was not convinced. I felt relief, but not joy. I was glad to be out of those prisons, but I wasn't free yet. We were still in downtown Baghdad, a long way from home. And I hadn't found Troy.

Then I saw him. A few steps away, heading toward me, was Sgt. Troy Dunlap, U.S. Army. He was wearing a yellow POW costume, too, and was grubby and tired looking. I felt my smile stretch so wide that it hurt my face.

"Hey, Sergeant Dunlap," I called to him. "You made it." I didn't call him Troy because we were standing in a crowded lobby and instinctively reverted to military formality.

"Hi, Major Cornum. How're you doing?"

"I'm pretty good, considering." I felt another notch of tension loosen, like a weight I wasn't even aware of until it was gone. Troy was safe, and we were together. For the first few minutes we were both nervous, wondering how our relationship would be in new surroundings and with a group of strangers. Soon the others were forgotten, however. Troy and I were part of something special. We were members of the army, members of the 2-229th Attack Helicopter Battalion. We were crew members who had been shot down together and captured. More than that, we were members of the brotherhood of arms.

"Have you seen Dan?" Troy asked hopefully.

"He's okay," I said. "He was in the hospital with me. They operated on him, and he's doing pretty well."

"Let's go find him," Troy suggested.

We were talking fast, trying to make up for lost time. Now I felt much safer, more like we were on an adventure. Things were looking up. People gave me a wide berth as we walked through the lobby, I guess because I looked so pathetic with my casts, black eyes, and matted hair.

When we spotted Stamaris on a stretcher, I asked, "How're you doing, Dan?"

"I'm doing okay," he assured me, but he looked pale and drawn and couldn't talk much.

The three of us were talking when another prisoner, someone I had never seen before but who also was dressed in a yellow POW outfit and had a cast on one arm, approached with a smile. "You're the lady I heard," he told me.

"Pardon me?"

"I was in the same place you were, in the hospital."

"Really?"

"I heard you singing," he said, grinning.

"I didn't hear you," I replied, a bit embarrassed. I don't normally sing in front of strangers. I could imagine this poor man covering his head with a pillow.

"I didn't say anything, but I always knew you were there," the former prisoner said. "I could hear you real clear."

"Well, good, I guess. How do I sing?"

"You sounded real good."

Stamaris nodded in agreement. "I heard you, too. It sounded good."

I would have blushed, but I don't think I had enough blood. I was just relieved to have the three of us together again. At least we didn't lose anyone after the crash.

One of the Red Cross workers announced to the assembled prisoners: "The injured people will remain on the first floor. Everyone else may go to the fourth floor. We will have the hot water on shortly so you may take showers."

A doctor with the Red Cross team looked me over quickly and asked, "Is there anything you need?"

"These casts were put on yesterday," I said. "I'm fine, thank you. The best thing for me would be to go to the fourth floor with the others. I prefer to think of myself as a healthy person."

"The only problem is that there is no electricity in the hotel, so there is no elevator," the doctor explained. "Can you climb the stairs to the fourth floor?"

Troy, who was standing next to me, stepped in and said we could make it, no problem. After all, we had been through a lot worse together than four flights of stairs. Troy and I joined the line of people going up the stairs, and I felt good, safe, to be alongside him again. He was haggard-looking and thinner than I remembered, but he looked wonderful to me. Troy was serious and looked older. Maybe it was just the tiredness in his eyes, but he seemed to have aged. I could tell from the expression on his face that he had worried as much about me as I had about him.

"How was it where you were?" I asked him.

"The food was terrible, and there wasn't enough of it," Troy said, helping me step by step. "But I was so hungry, and I remembered what you said, so I even ate this bone with hair on it."

"I'm glad you remembered what I told you," I said, smiling.

"It was bad," he said quietly. "It was bad." But Troy did not want to say much more that day, even to me, about what he had experienced. I didn't want to press him. There would be time to talk later, if he wanted. We climbed the rest of the stairs in silence, glad to be together.

The Swiss Red Cross workers suggested that we clean up and rest, and they promised to bring us food shortly. The hotel had been closed since the war began, but the Iraqis had turned it over to the Red Cross to house the released prisoners. Years had passed since the American military had any experience with combat and POWs, but the International Red Cross people clearly knew what they were doing. They seemed to know just what we needed, and they provided it efficiently. They even had chocolates for us. The other prisoners looked to me—the doctor in residence—for advice on whether or not they should eat the candy. "You'll have the runs," I said, "but it's unquestionably worth it."

Even though the hotel had no other guests, and we had the entire fourth floor to ourselves, a dozen of us piled into two rooms. At that point our nerves were still raw, and no one wanted to be alone. The sound of voices, voices speaking English, was reassuring. I didn't care what anyone was saying, I just liked to hear the sounds again. There were men, all wearing yellow suits, sprawled on the bed, the couch, and the floor of the room. Troy stayed near me, watching over me like a mother hen. I still had not recovered from losing so much blood, and climbing the stairs had exhausted me. I told Troy I was tired, and he helped me lie down on the bed. I listened, quietly content, while the others talked.

When the hot water came on, the men took showers and baths in their rooms. When they were clean, they came back to the social room to be with everyone else. Because of my casts, I was the only person who couldn't take a bath. After Troy showered he volunteered to help me get clean. He was hovering anyway, and he seemed glad for something to do. He led me into the bathroom and placed a chair in front of the sink. By then he was used to moving me around without hurting me, and he expertly sat me down in the chair. He tipped my head back into the sink and gently washed my hair. I kept my eyes closed to keep out the soap, but I couldn't keep the smile off my face. We borrowed a brush from a woman with the Red Cross, but my hair was hopeless. Troy wouldn't make a good living as a beauty parlor attendant, but he made a valiant effort, and it was refreshing to be relatively clean.

There was a decent mirror in the bathroom, and I took stock. The rings around my eyes were lightening slightly from a purplish black to a purplish yellow with a hint of green. There were a few half-healed lacerations on my face, but no permanent damage. If my face was so bashed, I wondered what my helmet looked like.

Sitting around the room together, the prisoners talked more easily as the day progressed and people relaxed and opened up to each other. We felt a sudden bond, as if we knew each other better than we really did. Most were American, but there was one Italian and one Kuwaiti pilot, and a few British soldiers. The Brits entertained us with jokes, although one of them—a big curly-haired guy with a wide grin and terrific posture—told a sobering story. This was not the first time he had been captured, he said. He was in special operations and had been a prisoner in a previous conflict. He told us the name of the country where he was captured, but he wants it kept secret. That time the Red Cross took him from his captors, put him in a hotel, and gave him a shower and good food. He had just relaxed and started thinking about going home, when soldiers came to the hotel and took him prisoner again. So don't start celebrating too enthusiastically, he told us, because we're not out of here yet.

We exchanged stories about what had happened. The people who had been held the longest wanted to be caught up on the war and especially the news from their units. I was glad to hear that the fighting had ended with relatively few casualties for our side. I still didn't know about my battalion. One group who had been held together talked about horrible diarrhea from the bad food and about the night their prison was destroyed by our own planes. That was the last night they had been together. There was a target next to their cells, and when an allied bomb hit the target, the blast blew apart the prison. The walls crumbled and the men found themselves standing outside, but they couldn't escape because there was no place to go. The Iraqis had quickly rounded them up and taken them to different cells. It was a scary moment for them, and everyone feared being killed by one of our own bombs.

Troy and I were the only two prisoners from the army and the only Americans who were not pilots. Troy was the only infantryman and I was the only doctor. He was the only enlisted man and probably the youngest of all. The others were officers: navy, marine, and air force pilots who had been shot down by Iraqis using sophisticated air defenses. Some were American, others British. The oldest was probably Chief Warrant Officer Guy Hunter, a 46-year-old marine. There were thirty-five of us, and another group of ten prisoners had left Iraq the day before, driving from the hotel to Jordan and then flying to Saudi Arabia. One of them was Spec. Melissa Rathbun-Nealy, the only other woman captured during the war. On January 30 the truck she was riding in got lost, and she and another soldier were picked up by an Iraqi patrol.

A few of the prisoners talked about being tortured. Air force Maj. Jeffrey Tice, known as "Tico," told us about a device he ominously called the "Talk Man." Tico stood in the middle of the room, leaning against the dresser and sipping a soft drink. We would have been drinking beer if the Red Cross had found any for us. He told the story of his captivity like an entertainer, and we were enthralled. The atmosphere in the room was more like an officers' club than a hotel in enemy territory. The Iraqis had placed a wire over Tico's ears and around his jaw and connected it to a car battery. When he refused to talk, the interrogators gave him a jolt of electricity. One of the shocks was so strong it blew out a filling. I could be brave about some kinds of pain, but one of my great fears in life is going to the dentist. Thank God the Iraqis had not wired me with a Talk Man!

Other prisoners reported that they were beaten with fists, sticks, and rubber hoses. But even when talking about the torture they had endured, the men were very distant, almost clinical. No one broke down, and no one cried. It was as if we were talking about other people, not ourselves. I knew that I was doing this, too—I had had a detached view of myself from the moment I realized I was pinned under the fuselage of the helicopter. It was as if I were the doctor and my body was the patient. I remained free, but my body was a prisoner. I wanted my body to heal and be well, but I was detached from it, separate. I don't know if that is a healthy reaction, but it's a defense mechanism we all used to protect ourselves.

I told navy Lt. Jeffrey Zaun, the one whose battered face was on the cover of *Newsweek*, "You look a lot better than you did in your pictures."

"Everybody thinks the Iraqis did that," Zaun said, "but I ejected at five hundred knots, and you get beat up by the wind blast."

That made sense to me as a flight surgeon, but I also understood why Americans had been so upset when they first saw his face.

"How did you get here?" someone asked me.

"We were going to get Bill Andrews," I said, "and we got shot down." I was proud to be able to say that instead of saying we ran into an Iraqi sand dune. I considered it an honorable way to have been captured.

I found out that Andrews was downstairs with the other injured prisoners. Troy had already met him and explained that we were the ones who had tried to rescue him. I asked Troy to help me back down the stairs, and we found Andrews lying on a stretcher with his leg in a splint. I hadn't seen Andrews since that one time on the bus. I figured he would want to see us, to talk with us. If it had been me, I would have wanted to meet the people who had tried to rescue me, especially when five of them had been killed. I didn't want Andrews to feel any burden of guilt. We certainly didn't blame him for what happened. We were just glad he was safe.

"Captain Andrews," I said, "I just thought I'd come down and meet the guy we were trying to save."

He smiled. "Nice to meet you. Thanks for trying. How are you doing?"

"I'm fine," I said. "I saw you on the bus you know. Your nose is as big as mine, so I figured you had seen me under your blindfold, too." He laughed.

Now we really had completed our mission. The pilot we were supposed to rescue had medical care and he was with the doctor. We could go home with everything we came for.

Stamaris was down there, too, and we visited awhile with both men. Troy and I felt bad that they had to stay alone while the rest of us could be together. When we returned to the fourth floor, the mood was like a slumber party: people sat on the bed and the floor, and we talked all night. The Red Cross volunteers told us they were trying to get us back to Saudi Arabia as soon as possible. We assured them we weren't going anywhere without them. They served us soft drinks and spaghetti for dinner. Troy fed me and wolfed down his own dinner.

"This is great," he said, shoveling in the spaghetti. "This is great!"

During the night I hobbled to the bathroom and closed the door behind me. Noticing a stray towel on the floor, I stupidly tried to pick it up, using my one good leg. (I spent a lot of my time in the Persian Gulf fighting an uphill battle for neat and clean bathrooms.) I slipped and crashed into the tub in a broken heap. My good leg went inside the tub, and the cast on one arm was wedged in the sink. I balanced there, trying to figure out how to get up again. One of the pilots was standing outside the door waiting to use the bathroom. He heard the noise when I slipped, but he was too polite to interrupt a lady in the bathroom.

"Help! Help!" I yelled, hanging there above the floor.

My cry for help sent Troy jumping up from the bed and racing wild-eyed into the bathroom. He calmed down when he saw I had just slipped.

The pilot had finally come in and was fumbling to help me. "What can I do? I don't know what to do."

"You're going to have to put your arms under me and stand me back up," I explained. "That's what you've gotta do."

The pilot helped me to my feet, and Troy walked me back to the bed.

"What happened?" he asked, his voice full of concern.

"I fell," I said matter of factly.

"Ma'am, don't *ever* do that," Troy pleaded, shaking his head. "That was the scariest thing. Listening to you scream was the scariest thing. Major Cornum, please don't do it again. *Please* don't do that."

Back in bed I thought about what I had done. I felt guilty that I had tried to do something by myself and made a mess of it. I think right then Troy had a flashback that "Oh my God! They're doing it to her again." I promised to be more careful.

In the morning, the Red Cross people announced we were going to the airport, and told us to get ready. That didn't take long because all we had were the sets of yellow clothing we were wearing. Troy used a pair of scissors to turn my long, green hospital robe into a lighter and slightly more fashionable blouse. He cut off a strip of the extra material and used it to tie my hair in a ponytail. He tightened up my yellow pants, and they fit better this time without all the excess robe tucked inside. I stuck close to Troy that morning. I noticed that the air force pilots stayed together, too, and so did the navy pilots. We were told we were headed home, but none of us was taking any chances. The British soldiers asked for towels to wrap around their heads because they didn't want to be photographed by the reporters camped outside the hotel. Since the soldiers do special operations, they did not want their identities known.

We gathered in the lobby and then walked single file out to another bus. I saw a small crowd of photographers and heard the whir of cameras. We walked straight ahead and climbed on the bus quickly, without any comments to the reporters. Troy and I sat together. We left the curtains closed, partly because we were afraid of snipers—the Iraqis probably were not very happy to see Americans in Baghdad. Pulling aside a corner of the curtain, we peeked out the window and watched the faces of the people staring at our bus. I don't know where he found the materials, but Troy had managed to make a little cardboard sign to put in the window of the bus for our ride to the airport. He proudly showed me his handiwork, reading in thick letters: "USA #1."

"Sergeant Dunlap," I said in my most official voice, "I don't think we want to go down the streets of Baghdad with that in the window."

He was disappointed, but he knew I was serious. Reluctantly, Troy agreed to keep the sign hidden but put it up when we left the bus.

The bus rumbled out of the hotel parking lot. One more step completed. We looked out the window from behind the curtains. The streets of Baghdad were quiet. There were few people out, and they stared blankly at us or ignored us completely. I was next to the window, looking at Troy. I felt we were trying to make ourselves small on the bus.

As we settled in for the ride, Troy seemed to want to talk. "When they had me," he told me, "they wanted to know what I was doing in Iraq."

"What did you tell them?"

"I told them I came to kill Saddam Hussein."

"What happened?" I asked, sort of laughing but knowing from his expression that he was serious.

"They beat the shit out of me," he whispered.

A while later Troy showed me two Iraqi coins. He told me that before leaving the hotel, an Iraqi employee had given them to him as souvenirs. "One for you, and one for me," Troy said. We joked that we could use them like military coins. Every unit has its own coin, and if a soldier finds another soldier in a bar without his unit coin, the coinless one has to buy drinks. Laughing, we planned how we would use the Iraqi money to "coin" our friends when we got back to Fort Rucker.

"On the bus going to the hotel yesterday I sat next to this guy who knew all about me," I told Troy. "Do you know anything about that?"

"I told everybody about you," Troy stated without hesitation, obviously proud of himself, "so they'd know you were there in case something happened to me." That was a sobering thought, but I appreciated his good thinking and concern.

Arriving at the nearly empty airport, we drove up close to three civilian jetliners parked on the tarmac. We were told that the jets held the first three hundred returning Iraqi soldiers, men who had been captured by the allies and held in Saudi Arabia. I wondered if any of the soldiers I had helped capture were on board. We were part of a prisoner exchange supervised by the Red Cross. As soon as the Iraqis got off the planes, we were going to board and fly to Riyadh. We watched from the bus as the Iraqis, still in their green uniforms, stepped down to the tarmac. This was the first time they had touched their own soil since being captured, but none of them cheered, no one kissed the ground. They weren't smiling or talking, and no one was there to meet them, except more soldiers who quickly marched them off toward waiting buses. I remembered questioning the Iraqis we had captured during the war. Their political officers had told them that if they were captured, their families would be executed. It was a cruel way to discourage soldiers from surrendering or deserting. I wondered what fate awaited those men stepping off the plane.

When the Iraqis had boarded their buses, we walked across the tarmac and took their places on one of the planes. Troy and I found seats together again. The crew members, all of them volunteers, were excited to see us, and they presented us with little gifts: toys, cars, and model planes for our children. I hadn't been on a civilian jet in months and was impressed by how roomy and comfortable it was compared with military transports. The crew served sandwiches, but one of the flight attendants, Lorenz, said he wanted to do something "special" for me. He presented me with their last bowl of Frosted Flakes. I didn't care for anything, really, but he so wanted me to eat that cereal and enjoy it. So Troy fed me a bowl of Frosted Flakes, while Lorenz, beaming, looked on.

A few of the prisoners cheered when the plane left the ground, but none of us was really relaxed. We were about to fly through Iraqi air space in an unarmed plane, which made us feel extremely vulnerable. No one would say it, but I suspect we all were afraid of being shot down. During the war, we knew there were Iraqis at the front who had not talked with their headquarters in weeks. I was afraid there might still be a little nest of them, dug into bunkers in the middle of the desert, who didn't know the war had ended. They might see a big fat jetliner as an easy target.

Our pilot must have been thinking the same thing, because after a few minutes he announced, "Ladies and gentlemen, I want you to know we have now left Iraq and entered Saudi Arabian air space." Then we cheered: loud whoops and yells of joy and relief. A British Tornado jet roared up to escort us, flying so close that we could see the pilot's face. He peeled off, and an American F-15 took his place, carefully maneuvering so his stiff wing overlapped the long wing of the jetliner. At first I hoped he might be from Kory's squadron, but then I saw from the markings that the jet was from Langley Air Force Base. What a beautiful sight! We were almost home.

We taxied to a stop in Riyadh, and the door opened. I hadn't seen anything from the plane, and didn't expect a reception to be waiting for us. I didn't want to see anyone right then because I felt self-conscious. I was embarrassed to be injured and felt un-military. My injuries made me feel weak, and I didn't want people to feel sorry for me. I followed the others in the aisle and carefully climbed down the steep steps to the tarmac, going slowly because of my knee. Troy was right behind me, but the steps were so narrow he couldn't help me. I couldn't hold the railing with my arms in casts and slings, and I would've died of embarrassment if I had fallen out of the plane onto my face. Step by cautious step, I made it to the ground, and the first person to greet me was Gen. H. Norman Schwarzkopf. I had never met him before, but instinctively, I tried to snap off a salute. My arm was stopped short by the plaster cast.

"I'm sorry, sir," I said with a big smile. "I normally salute four-star generals."

Schwarzkopf laughed and reached out to touch my arm. He looked truly happy to see us. "That's okay," he said.

There were dozens of people on the tarmac, but we were told to just keep walking to the bus, following the person in front of us. A reporter yelled to me, "How do you feel?"

"Airborne!" I shouted back, giving the rallying cry of the airborne troops. The word just came out without me thinking about it. "Airborne" was the most positive, gung-ho way of saying I was glad to be home but ready to go back to war if necessary. The single word perfectly captured my feelings of joy and pride. As we say, it was a good day to be an American soldier. Some of the reporters misunderstood me, however, and at a briefing later that day one of them claimed I had said, "There are more." That touched off a flurry of questions to the Central Command about whether there were more prisoners still in Iraq. Luckily someone clarified the bad translation. My mother was home in Buffalo, watching the arrival ceremony on television, and she understood exactly what I meant. Later she told me that "airborne" had become her favorite word of all time, the single most important word ever spoken by any of her children. That was truly a "first word," she said, spoken by a child who had come back to life.

We were taken by bus to another plane, a C-141 transport that was not quite as comfortable as the civilian jet. The first person I saw on board was one of the crew chiefs who had flown me to Tabuk on one of my visits to see Kory. When he recognized me, he started jumping up and down and shouting. The chief crushed me in a big hug and began to cry. "We're so happy to see you," he said. "We thought the worst had happened." I hugged him back, as much as I could with two broken arms. The greeting of the chief, the familiar, cavernous air force transport with its smell of hot fuel—that was the moment when I finally said to myself: I really am safe; I'm going home.

The C-141 was headed for the little island nation of Bahrain in the Persian Gulf, where we were going to board the USS *Mercy*, a navy hospital ship. An army doctor was on board the plane, and he attached himself to me to see how I was doing. He wanted to talk about my injuries, and I sensed he also was feeling me out psychologically, asking me about my emotions and about my relationship with Kory. I assumed that was a normal precaution with returning prisoners, and I played along.

Once we were in the air, the first thing I wanted to do was get out
of my Iraqi POW clothes. I was not a prisoner any more, and I didn't
want to dress like one. I wanted to feel like an army officer again. I
didn't have a uniform with me, but one of the two flight nurses on
board kindly offered to let me wear one of her flight suits. The two
nurses crammed into the little bathroom with me and helped me dress.
They gave me a bra, and I borrowed a big brown t-shirt from someone. The nurses wrestled the t-shirt over my head and pushed the splints
through the sleeves. Changing my clothes in the tight confines of the
bathroom, I realized just how awful I smelled. The Iraqi perfume had
worn off, and I apologized to the nurses, explaining that I had not been
able to take a shower like the other prisoners. They told me not to worry
and helped me step into the flight suit and pull it up to my chest. There
was no way to get my arms in, so the nurses tied the sleeves around
my waist. I still had on my Iraqi sneakers, but I didn't mind. I felt
dressed again, getting stronger.

During the flight to Bahrain, my mind was racing ahead of my body.
My body was stuck in an airplane flying over Saudi Arabia, but I was
thinking about our farm and being home with Kory and Regan. I wasn't
sure when I would get to see them. I had talked with the other prisoners about what would happen to us, and whether we would be sent
back to our units. No one wanted to go back to Saudi Arabia, ever,
but we thought we should be with our units, even if the war had ended.
I was sure I would be sent home, though, because we had been evacuating
people with injuries much less severe than mine. I wouldn't be much
help to the pilots in the battalion, and I would actually make work for
the person who would have to take care of me. I wondered about Kory:
I didn't know where he was or what he had heard about me. Neither
I nor any of the other POWs had any idea of how much attention we
had received in the news media. Things were happening so fast, at that
point I was happy just to be carried along.

From the airport in Bahrain, we went by bus to the dock and walked
up the gangplank onto the *Mercy*. The ship was huge, white, and beautiful:
a well-equipped floating hospital. I was led into the triage area (where
the wounded were taken) and was told to sit down on a gurney. All I
wanted was to find out when I could go home, but that was the one
thing no one knew or could tell me. I was tired of seeing doctors and
wanted to be with the others. It turned out they were getting physicals, too. The doctor walked in, and I gave her a big smile of recognition. She was Brenda Alcovar, who had been a resident at Brooke

Army Medical Center in San Antonio when I was a third-year medical student there.

"Rhonda!" she said, greeting me warmly. "I can't believe you're here."

"I can't believe *you're* here, either, Brenda. The small-world theory is alive and well."

"So how are you feeling? Any problems?"

I told her about my injuries and the treatment I had received so far.

"That sounds fine. First of all, there's someone here who wants to see you." Alcovar excused herself and stepped out of the room.

Just then, walking around the corner and ducking to get in the door, came Kory. He looked so big and handsome in his flight suit.

"Hi Hubby," I said.

"Hi Wifelet," he answered, grinning ear to ear.

He came to me and wrapped his big arms around me, trying to figure out where he could hold me without hurting me. It was hard to hug me with the casts and slings holding me together, but he touched my face and kissed me gently. I looked at his face, and looked again. Surprise: he'd shaved off his "gnarly" mustache for me. I relaxed finally. With Kory there I didn't feel quite so obligated to act tough, and I felt safe to be emotional.

Alcovar came back, wanting to take blood and do more tests. There was no place to take my blood pressure because of the casts, but I told her it was normally 105 over 60, so that was what she put on my chart. She wanted more X-rays, my third set since I crashed. I quickly figured out that the ship was filled with orthopedic surgeons who hadn't done anything in months, and they were salivating to operate on me. Kory got me into a wheelchair and pushed me down to the X-ray room. A young corpsman expertly took the shots; it was such a treat to deal with someone who really cared about me. The last person to take my pictures had been the Iraqi technician who managed to turn his X-ray machine into a torture device. Kory sat happily with a covey of orthopedic surgeons, holding up my pictures and talking shop.

"Honey bear," I said to him, "I know you're a doctor, but right now I need you to be my hubby. You can look at my films later. Come sit with me." He did, and I felt better. I didn't care if we talked; I just wanted to be near him, to feel loved and appreciated. I leaned against him and was content to just sit there.

The doctors brought the films over to the two of us, and we all commented on the good job the Iraqi surgeon had done. The navy doctors cut off my casts and put on new ones. My smashed pinkie looked bad and would need more work, and my knee was going to take a long time to fully recover.

I looked up at one point and saw Dan Grant, a helicopter pilot from my unit. He had been sent by Lieutenant Colonel Bryan, my battalion commander from the 229th, to bring greetings from everyone and to brief me on what had happened in my absence. Each of the prisoners was greeted by a member of his unit, who then served as an escort. Grant told me the story of how he learned we had been shot down. After we crashed, the Apaches escorting us radioed back to the base camp. The signal was picked up by another helicopter, which was flying radio relay, and broadcast to the battalion. The message was that "Bengal one-five," which was our call sign, had crashed in Iraq. Then the message added, "The Doc was on board."

Grant said he was in the middle of landing his helicopter when he heard the news.

"How'd you do?" I asked him.

"I screwed up the landing," he admitted. "I jerked it back off the ground and tried to clear my thinking and finally put it back down."

"How did Lance do?" I asked.

Lance and the other Apache pilots escorting us made it back safely, Grant said, but Lance's aircraft had been badly shot up, and he was devastated about the wreck. The other Apache had been flying behind us, and the pilot reported that our aircraft had disintegrated when it hit the ground. He thought everyone on board had to be dead because no one could have survived that wreck. Lance hadn't seen the wreck with his own eyes, and he wanted to be sure, but it was too dangerous to loiter over the hot bunker complex. The Iraqis already had shot down Andrews's F-16 and our Black Hawk. The lead Apache pilot called in the coordinates where we had gone down, but he said there was nothing that could be done for us. Lieutenant Colonel Bryan wanted to work with the 24th Infantry Division (Mechanized), which was behind us, to recover the bodies and what was left of the aircraft. But the weather was too bad to fly the next day, February 28, and the recovery mission was grounded.

The following day, March 1, a team from our unit flew up in a Black Hawk. Lieutenant Colonel Bryan himself flew on the mission, and so did my friend Eric Pacheco, the pilot from Hawaii. They found five bodies amid the scattered wreckage, and Mike Pandol checked them to make sure no booby traps had been planted by the Iraqis. One of my medics, Sergeant Homan, officially declared the five men dead and prepared the bodies to put on the helicopter.

The crew searched everywhere, but couldn't find the other three bodies—Troy, Stamaris, and me. Outside the wreck they found my survival vest and helmet, which had a big crack. Widening the search, they eventually found my medical bag, which had been pawed through but still contained most of the supplies. Still no bodies. While the weather on February 28 had been too bad to fly, it had been good weather for tanks, and a fierce tank battle had taken place at the bunker complex. There were no Iraqis left in sight. The crew feared that we three had survived the crash and been taken to one of the bunkers by the Iraqis. They began searching all the abandoned bunkers, but with no luck. The other fear was that the Iraqis had buried us in a mass grave with their own dead. Lieutenant Colonel Bryan and the others would have to declare us missing, and there always would be uncertainty about what had happened to us. But why would the Iraqis bury three bodies and not the other five?

"We were prepared to find you dead, but it would have been horrible to never know what had happened to you," Grant told me.

"What did you think?" I asked him, after a long silence.

"I didn't think," he said, shaking his head. "I just hoped and prayed."

"Thanks for the prayers," I said, looking him straight in the eyes. "They worked." I felt bad hearing the story. The flight surgeon is partly responsible for the psychological well-being of the unit, and the one time they had a death and needed me, I wasn't there for them. "Well, how's everything else going?" I asked, trying to sound cheery.

"It's fine, everything's fine." He didn't elaborate. I knew there would be plenty of time to catch up at home.

"Are they still up in Iraq?" I was curious about the rest of the battalion. "Any idea when we're gonna go home?"

"They're still up there," Grant said glumly. "It looks like we're gonna be there forever."

11

Kory held the telephone to my ear, and I listened to the signal beep and bounce its way from the USS *Mercy* across the ocean to Fargo, North Dakota. The phone rang at the other end, and when a faint voice answered, I said, "May I speak to Regan?"

"This is Regan! Is this Mother?" she said, almost coming through the phone.

"Yes, this is Mother!"

"How are you?" she shouted across the telephone line.

"I'm fine," I told her, happy to finally hear her voice. "Well, I'm really not fine, fine." I giggled. "I have a few broken arms and things, but I'm going to be fine."

"When are you coming home?" Regan asked.

"Soon," I said, not really sure when I could leave, but smiling because I knew it would be soon. "I'll see you as soon as I get there."

Regan seemed very strong on the phone. She had already heard from my grandfather that I was safe, and Kory had called her from Saudi Arabia, but I know she was relieved to hear my voice for herself. She was astounded to be the center of attention at home and at school. Reporters had followed her on the way to school, asking her questions and recording her every move. She couldn't understand why she had become a celebrity.

"I love you, baby," I said.

"I love you, too, Mother."

The staff on the *Mercy* let us call anywhere we wanted, so I phoned my grandparents and Kory's parents. We called Peter Demitry, our friend from medical school. He had left Saudi before the war started and gone to school to be a test pilot. Despite our best efforts, though, it was not until the next day that I got through to the 101st Aviation Brigade.

I asked for Lieutenant Colonel Bryan or Lance, but neither was near the phone. "Tell them I'm going to call back at 1600 today and see if one of them can come to the phone," I told the staff officer who had answered. "This is Major Cornum."

"Major Cornum!" the brigade officer yelled. "How the hell are you?"

"I'm fine," I said. "How did the war go for the brigade?"

"We're all right, but you sure had us worried."

"Sorry," I replied. "I had myself worried for a little while."

We got through to Lance at 4 P.M., but the line was so scratchy I could barely hear him. I recognized the voice well enough to know who it was, but I could understand few of the words except for his shouted, "I love you!"

"I love you, too, Lance Man," I shouted back.

As the hours turned to days on the *Mercy*, the black rings around my eyes began to fade, and the dirt started to come off my hands with several hours of soaking. I must confess that the highlight of our stay on the ship was a hot-tub party in the physical therapy tank. Kory and a friend had gone out for lunch and come back with a few bottles of wine and their helmet bags filled with beer. Dale Storr, another ex-POW, joined Kory and me (with my casts covered with garbage bags) as we splashed and drank in a stainless steel tank that was as big as a horse tub. The navy staffers were not thrilled about us playing in their therapy tub, but what were they going to do, send us to Saudi Arabia and make me a POW? Anyway, sitting in a hot tub was a kind of therapy.

My twenty fellow American prisoners also were on board, and we kept the slumber party going. The only business we had to accomplish was debriefing military intelligence. Two men in civilian clothes interviewed me about what had happened and seemed most concerned about whether anyone was still being held in Iraq. I told them that I had not seen anyone else. We talked and talked among ourselves, and I learned that most of the pilots were terribly disappointed they had not been able to do more flying. Many of them had spent most of the war locked up in Iraqi prisons instead of in the air. Some of them adjusted to freedom less well than others and stayed in their pajamas instead of trying to get back into their uniforms, but overall everyone was in pretty good shape emotionally. I felt bad for Stamaris because he was stuck alone in an intensive care unit, so I visited him every day. Once again, he had to face an emotional strain—this time our new freedom—without the company and support of his comrades.

I met the other female ox prisoner, Spec. Melissa Rathbun-Nealy, on the *Mercy*. On the first day I arrived, she was sitting quietly in the corner, but then she came over to me and said, "Ma'am, I just wanted to say I'm happy to see you, and welcome home." We talked, and she volunteered to do my hair. She and I were the only two women POWs, and also two of only five people from the army on the ship. Rathbun-Nealy had been captured with another army soldier, Spec. David Lockett. The two of them, plus Troy and Stamaris, were the only enlisted soldiers, and they felt a little out of place among all those officers and pilots, even more so because they were from different services. Enlisted people normally live their lives somewhat segregated from officers, but suddenly these four young soldiers were surrounded by a bunch of loud, arrogant pilots—me included. To tell the truth, Troy was not terribly impressed with the officers.

"I can't believe some of the things they complain about," Troy said to me during a moment we had alone. Troy had eaten a lot of sand in Saudi Arabia, while people in the air force, especially the pilots, generally lived on comfortable Saudi bases.

"I know," I agreed. "It's just air force guys. They go to war expecting a hotel when they get there, and usually they get it. Forget about it; they're just a bunch of wimps, those air force guys." I laughed because I was married to one of those "wimps."

For entertainment, we drank beer and watched video tapes of the war, which had been filmed by cameras mounted in the aircraft. Some of the escorts had brought the tapes from their units. One of the tapes even showed one of the captured pilots being shot down. The video was shot by a camera in another plane, and the pilot doing the filming had watched in horror as his wingman was hit. He didn't see a parachute, so he thought the wingman was "gone." In fact, he had parachuted to the ground and been captured by the Iraqis. On some of the tapes, we could see the surface-to-air missiles and antiaircraft fire coming up. Our excitement at seeing these tapes sounds insensitive, I suppose, but I think it was healthy. After all, it was important to deal with what happened, since we all were planning to go back to doing the same thing for a living. Troy and I wanted the tape that the Apache escorts had taken of our wreck, but we were told there was little to see. That was disappointing, because we already had planned to put our tape on a music video to the Bon Jovi rock song, "Blaze of Glory."

We could joke about our wreck, but partly that was to bury the pain. During my second day on the ship, Dan Grant, the escort officer from my battalion, was scrubbing and polishing my boots, his head down and his mood reflective. He had collected my boots and a helmet bag full of my personal things from the last place I had camped with my medics in Iraq before being shot down. There was a hair brush, another set of dog tags, and some of my favorite letters from Kory, Regan, and Moshe, the Apache driver from Israel. My boots were not just unpolished, they were disastrous: scuffed and nicked and badly in need of repair. Grant, looking very serious, was fixing the divots in the leather and rubbing in layers of polish.

"Come over here and talk to me," I told him. Kory had gone off for lunch, and Grant and I were alone.

He put down the boots and sat next to me.

"How was it?" I asked.

"It was horrible," Grant said. "The whole battalion was devastated." He started to cry and we sat quietly for a moment. I looked at him and noticed the black shoe polish on his hands. Then he told me about the memorial.

The battalion had held a memorial service for the five crew members who were killed. The bodies were returned to the United States for burial, but the battalion gathered in the empty desert and stuck the barrels of five M-16 rifles in the ground. On the stock of each rifle, they placed a helmet. The carefully polished boots of each man were set on the ground in front of his rifle. The soldiers stood quietly, their heads bowed, while the chaplain said a final service for the five men who would not be going home to their families.

I listened intently as Grant told the story, and I could picture the scene so clearly. I felt proud of the men who had died, proud of the battalion. "Thanks, Dan," I whispered, and he went back to work on my boots.

My medical care continued on the *Mercy*, but there was little the doctors could do. I didn't want them to operate because I was afraid it would keep me from leaving with everyone else. So most of the healing was left up to me. The nurses were wonderful, and they spent hours helping me look like a girl again. The hardest part of my recovery was being so uncomfortable all the time. I could never find a comfortable position to sit or lie down, and every time I moved or shifted my weight, pain shot through my arms. I also felt dirty, and my teeth never got clean with someone else brushing them for me. I normally am terrified of dentists, but I felt so grubby that I asked to have my teeth cleaned by a professional. When I leaned back in the tilted dentist's chair, my arms fit perfectly, and I was comfortable for the first time. That night, tossing in my narrow bunk and unable to sleep, I remembered how comfortable I had been in the dentist's chair and I told Kory about it. He gathered up my blankets and took me back to the dentist's office to sleep for a few hours.

The ship's doctors also sent another psychiatrist to see me. I had spoken with a psychiatrist on the plane from Riyadh to the *Mercy,* but now it was time for another session with a different doctor. As a doctor myself, I had done my share of psychological interviews with patients, so I knew what he wanted to hear. The psychiatrist on the *Mercy* seemed pretty sure of my mental health, but he was following orders. His questions were perfunctory at best.

"How would you describe your emotional state?" he asked.

"I'm fine," I giggled, aware that we were playing out a charade.

"Yes, I know you're fine," he said, laughing with me. "But tell me how fine you are." The interview lasted only ten minutes, but it would not be the last one.

Kory also was interviewed by a brigade full of psychiatrists, to prepare him in case I was emotionally scarred by what had happened.

"Do you think I'm different?" I asked Kory when we were alone.

"No," he said sincerely. "I knew you'd be fine."

Kory never asked me what had happened, but I was dying to tell him in all the gritty details. Kory wanted to hear everything—not out of morbid curiosity, but to understand what I had been through and to empathize more. I volunteered that I had been molested but not raped, even though he never asked. None of the other prisoners ever asked me either; that just wasn't a major concern to military people. Sexual abuse was one form of torture, just like being beaten or wired with a Talk Man, and most of us were tortured in one way or another. Kory feels the way I do: arms and legs and eyesight are the most important things; everything else will get better.

"Kory, they stole my wedding ring," I said, recalling how incensed I had been. "I'm sorry. I thought about what we were supposed to do, that I was supposed to swallow it, but I had broken arms and couldn't get it off the chain."

"It's okay, Wifelet. It's okay. We'll get you another one."

He had guessed that I had lost the ring, and already had asked friends to call the goldsmith in Alexandria, Virginia, where the ring had been made, and order another one.

I also told Kory about Troy, and how much we had depended on each other. They had met before, the day that Kory was visiting the battalion and flew on a mission into Iraq. Troy was the nervous sergeant on the helicopter who had watched Kory playing with a captured rocket-propelled grenade launcher.

"Thank you for taking care of my wife," Kory told Troy, who looked embarrassed and mumbled something back. It was not an easy relationship for the two men. In one week as prisoners in Iraq, Troy and I had grown closer than most people will get in a lifetime. Abruptly returning to the way things were before the capture was hard for both of us. I felt a deep sense of loss, a nostalgia for the closeness we had developed so quickly under fire. We had been split up in Iraq after our interview in the Baath Party office—when I went to the hospital and he went to prison—but our relationship started right up again when we met in the Baghdad hotel. It was difficult for Troy to give up his role and hand me over to Kory. Making matters worse, he still had not been reunited with his wife, Bobbie, a specialist in the army who had stayed at Fort Rucker during the war. We never spoke of these things, however, because it was easier not to.

Kory also reintroduced himself to Andrews, the pilot we had tried to rescue. I say reintroduced because, as luck would have it, Kory and Andrews had both graduated from the Air Force Academy in 1980.

Kory had been in touch with my family. We still had not read a newspaper or seen the news on television, so I wasn't sure what my parents knew. I was mortified to learn that my father had sent telegrams to everyone from President Bush to General Schwarzkopf, saying, "You've lost my daughter. What are you going to do about it?" General Schwarzkopf was wonderful, though, and the day we landed safely in Riyadh, he called my father and left a message on his answering machine: "I couldn't have been happier if she were my own daughter, and the only thing that kept me from grabbing her and giving her a big hug were her injuries." Despite my embarrassment, I decided that there had been times when my father had been mortified by me and had survived. My grandfather didn't disappoint me: everything I had ever thought about him being the strong and silent type had proved true again.

Kory told me that he had learned I was safe on Tuesday, March 5, just two hours after he had spoken with my father again, trying to persuade him to be calm. Kory was sitting in the intelligence office at the air base in Tabuk when the Army Casualty Center called and announced, "The Red Cross has your wife in Baghdad."

Kory jumped up and down, yelling, "She's alive! She's a POW!" His friends hugged him and cheered. Three of them ran outside, shouting the news to the entire base. All the pilots gathered in Kory's room and packed his bag, drinking champagne and, as Kory says, "hooting and hollering." Kory and his roommate, Sly, decided to shave off their mustaches because they knew I didn't like them, even though the mustaches had become sort of famous. Lt. Gen. Charles Horner, the man who ran the air war for General Schwarzkopf, had been visiting the base just the day before and told Sly and Kory the mustaches looked "gnarly"—the ultimate compliment. Still, Kory had promised to be clean-shaven the next time he saw me.

Trying to arrange a flight to meet me in Bahrain, Kory ran into numerous bureaucratic obstacles, but he was not easily deterred. One of the obstacles was his first psychiatric exam, to determine if he was emotionally ready to see me. After the interview, the psychiatrist explained to Kory the reason for the meeting: "Everybody just thought you were acting too normal," he admitted. "I'm going to tell them you really are okay."

When Kory made it to the dock in Bahrain, he had to pass through a psychiatrist from the army and another one from the navy before seeing me. The psychiatrists tried to make the meetings appear to be casual conversation, but Kory realized he was on the examination couch. Kory understood the caution of his colleagues in the air force and the medical profession. They had never seen a case where the spouse of a POW was also in the military. Their experience had been with civilian wives who had no idea what to expect from their POW husbands. Kory is a pilot, an officer, and a doctor, and he did know what to expect. He saw my wounds as injuries that had occurred to a patient, and he knew the moment he saw me that the person inside the broken body, his wife, was fine.

The admiral in charge of the *Mercy* invited all the former prisoners to a reception, and I told Kory I wanted to go in uniform. There were only five of us in the army contingent, and we wanted to look sharp. Troy is a dedicated boot polisher, and he always looks impeccable. I couldn't fit into a uniform because of my arms, so Dan Grant took one of my flight suits to a tailor in Bahrain and had zippers installed from the wrists to the armpits and then down to the waist. Then Kory helped zip me into my customized uniform.

Kory wheeled me up to the reception, but I left the chair in the hall. I refused to be pushed around the party like an invalid. Standing uneasily and sipping beer from a straw, I tried to be friendly and sociable, but I was exhausted. After an hour at the party, I couldn't take any more. If there had been a road march to Bataan, I suppose I could have done it, but if I didn't have to endure a cocktail party, I was not going to. I still had not restored my blood level to normal, and with half as much blood as usual, I got twice as tired. I was taking iron and vitamin C to get my blood level back to normal. The doctors on the ship, just like the ones in Iraq, had tried to give me a transfusion. I preferred to make my own red cells, however, and by then I wasn't going to die from the lack of them.

On March 10, after four days on the *Mercy*, Kory and I and the other American prisoners boarded an airplane for Andrews Air Force Base outside of Washington, D.C. The crew promised us ham and eggs for breakfast, pizza for lunch, and filet mignon for dinner. Poor Stamaris, who had been left out of everything so far, also was left off this flight. He was sent home on a slower and less exciting medevac plane, but made it in time for the ceremony at Andrews. The most therapeutic part of our recovery was being together, and Stamaris had been cut out, ironically, because he was among the most badly injured.

On the way home I asked to listen to tapes of two of my favorite songs: one from the group Alabama about being southern born and bred (even though I'm neither), and Lee Greenwood's song, "God Bless America." I've loved the Greenwood song since I first heard it several years earlier, but this time I wanted to practice hearing it. The song always gives me goose bumps and makes me teary-eyed, and I was afraid that it might be played at the homecoming ceremony. I didn't want to cry in public since people might think it was because I was a girl and a wimp. I was excited about going home and proud to be an American soldier, but the song might push me over the edge. To be safe, I played the song four or five times on the way home, and then felt ready to face the public.

We stopped for fuel on the way home at the U.S. Navy base at Sigonella in Italy, and even though it was 1 A.M., the people there opened the Wendy's so we could have real burgers and fries. The families greeted us with cheers and flags and signs that read, "Welcome Home Troops."

Parents brought their children out to see the former POWs, and an 11-year-old boy came up to me and asked for my autograph. My hand was a little shaky, but he held the paper under my pen and I wrote my name for him. That was the first indication I had of how we were going to be received back home, of how big an item we had become. We also stopped for fuel at Shannon Airport in Ireland, where they opened the airport stores so we could shop, and gave us each a choice of presents. I picked a glass Aladdin's lamp because I had been granted my wish: I was going home.

There was much discussion on the flight home about how we should get off the plane, who would go first, who would be together, and how to handle the ceremony. The only thing that mattered to me was walking off with Troy. It was agreed that the senior officer of all the POWs, Air Force Col. David Eberly, would speak for us at the ceremony. Kory was told he couldn't get off the plane with us, even though the wives of the other POWs were all going to be at Andrews to meet us. He wasn't happy about the decision, but he agreed. When we landed, the steps leading to the tarmac were covered with red carpet, and as I walked out the door of the plane, I could see thousands of cheering people. Some carried signs that read, "Heroes" and "Red, White and Blue— Our Colors Don't Run." I saw Secretary of Defense Dick Cheney and several generals, whom I knew I should greet, but there was only one person I wanted to see right then, and I immediately spotted her in the crowd. Walking by the assembled brass as quickly as my bad leg would carry me, I headed straight for Regan. She put out her arms for me and I leaned into her, nestling into her body. I couldn't hug her with my arms in slings, but I pushed aside her hair with my face and nuzzled her smooth neck. Home at last. I had survived a week as a prisoner without shedding a tear, I had survived the joy of being released into freedom and the reunion with my husband. But seeing my daughter again broke the dam of my resistance, and I cried with my face hidden against her.

"I love you, baby," I whispered into her mane of blond hair. "I love you. I love you, baby."

"I love you, too, Mother," Regan cried.

Colonel Eberly spoke for us at the ceremony: "God saved us; our families' love and your prayers sustained us; and for many of us the camaraderie of our flying squadrons brought us home to fly again." Speaking of all the prisoners, Colonel Eberly said, "Their sense of honor to duty and country has been beyond reproach."

My parents, grandparents, brother, and sisters were there, and I was swept up in the crowd of hugging, crying relatives. We went to a hangar and the families exchanged teary greetings away from the reporters and cameras. Gen. Colin Powell recognized my mother and gave her a big, genuine hug. She said the general left tears on her black dress, and she comforted him with praise for the good job he had done during the war.

There was a bus to take us to Walter Reed Medical Center, and a police escort cleared the way. We all laughed that it was the fastest we had ever traveled in Washington. Working at Walter Reed during my internship, I had never even seen the hospital's VIP suite, but now I was going to be staying there. Troy and Stamaris and their wives were at the hospital, too, along with Lockett and his wife, and Melissa and her boyfriend, Michael Coleman, who later became her husband. Most of the relatives stayed at the guest house, but the doctors let Kory stay with me in my room, which quickly filled with flowers and visitors bearing beer and pizza. My mother was happy to feed me a bowl of chicken soup, which tasted so good that I made her try a spoonful. She was not impressed with the hospital soup, but then she had not spent seven months eating army food in the desert. Regan was disappointed with me: I had not brought back the bullet that had been removed from my shoulder. "That was the coolest thing that happened, and you didn't even save the bullet?" she asked, incredulous.

One of my first visitors was another psychiatrist, but I asked her to please come back another day.

My mother told me about receiving the dreaded knock on the door from the army major. A few days after being notified, she had spoken to a friend who claimed to have seen on television that I was not dead but had been taken prisoner. My mother called the local television station to see if they knew anything. They didn't, but they did want to come out with a news crew to film the grieving family. The news media had not heard anything about me, but now they smelled a hot story. My mother refused to go on camera, but she did give the reporter a picture of me from Saudi Arabia and one of Kory that I had sent to her at Christmas. In the photograph, I'm standing in the parking garage at King Fahd wearing a long t-shirt and my shoulder holster.

March 5 was my sister Eden's twenty-fifth birthday, and my mother had prepared a gooey cake with chocolate chips and marshmallows. She was ready to take the cake to Eden when Kory called to say that I was safe. The television crew arrived to film the happy family eating cake and celebrating the good news. Afterwards, my mother said she clipped out a story about another soldier in the Gulf, Maj. Marie Rossi, and posted it on the wall next to a picture of me. My mother was struck by the similarity of our lives: we had the same rank, we both flew helicopters, and both had husbands in the Gulf. The difference was that Major Rossi was killed in a helicopter crash and I survived. My mother stared at the two faces on the wall, and the faces seemed to change places in her mind. Thinking of Major Rossi made my mother cry, helpless and ashamed that she had been allowed to celebrate while other families still suffered.

A week after my mother learned I was safe, on March 12, we buried Billy Butts, one of our crew members. The day was cold at Arlington National Cemetery, and I froze in an army skirt. It was the first time I had worn a skirt in nearly a year. The white headstone read "William Thomas Butts, SFC, US Army, Persian Gulf, Dec 13 1960— Feb 27 1991, Grenada." Butts had also served in the 1983 invasion of Grenada. He was buried between a twenty-year-old marine and an army soldier whose life ended just a month before his twentieth birthday; both had been killed in the Persian Gulf. From the grassy cemetery, we could see the tall white obelisk of the Washington Monument and the dome of the Capitol across the Potomac River. Through the trees, I could see the brown stone walls of the Pentagon, and I thought it was good that the generals who send young people to war could see these graves.

I walked over to Butts's wife, Lisa, and she gave me a tearful hug standing on the grass.

"I'm so sorry," I told her. "He was brave, and he was proud to do what he was doing. I'm just real sorry." There was nothing I could say to make things better.

Before going to Saudi, Kory and I had talked about where we wanted to be buried, and neither of us had chosen Arlington, although for different reasons. Kory wanted to be buried at the Air Force Academy in Colorado Springs, but I chose our farm, where two of our horses and our old dog were buried. If he couldn't arrange that, I told Kory, then bury me in the little country cemetery just a mile from our house. I wanted to have deer grazing on me, and I wanted something a little different. At Arlington, every grave is exactly the same, and at the end of my life I wanted my one statement of individuality.

Billy Butts's casket was draped with an American flag, and the guns of the riflemen roared across the cemetery, filled with row after row of white headstones on the green grass. "Taps" sounded clear and clean in the crisp air, and I cried for Billy Butts and the four others who had died, and for all of those men and women who were not coming home from the Persian Gulf.

After the funeral, we stopped in Alexandria to check on my new wedding ring. The owner of the store, Mary Ehlers, remembered us from eight years earlier and said, "This ring is supposed to be bullet-proof, but in your line of work, I don't know."

That night we went to dinner at a Mexican restaurant in Washington. Sitting in the bar with Kory and some friends, I felt oddly uncomfortable. I couldn't put my finger on the cause of my unease. Maybe it was because I was wearing a sweat suit instead of the "yuppie" attire of the bar crowd. The sweatshirt was the only thing that would stretch over my bulky casts. Maybe I was uncomfortable because for the first time in months (aside from the week as a prisoner) I wasn't in uniform. Or maybe because this was the first bar I had been to in a long time. I decided that I just had not yet adjusted to being home. The bartender had put my drink on the table in front of me and I leaned forward to sip from a straw.

A man in the bar, drinking with a few friends, was watching me out of the corner of his eye. I tried to ignore him, until finally he turned to me and said in a quiet voice, "Are you a doctor?"

"Yes," I replied, startled.

"Were you recently in a helicopter wreck?"

"Yes," I said again, cautiously.

He looked at me and said simply, "Welcome home."

That was all he said. He didn't tell his friends or make a scene. He just told me, "Welcome home." It was a gesture that would be repeated many times in the coming days, but one that never failed to make me feel proud and warm inside. It also made me realize how far we had come from Vietnam. We learned that it is necessary to mobilize the nation as well as the military, and regardless of whether you agree with what is done, the soldiers who do it are heroes.

The next day, the army held an awards ceremony at Walter Reed for Troy, Melissa, Sergeant Lockett, Sergeant Stamaris, and me. We walked into the room and were told to take our seats with our families, so I sat directly in front of my mother, who was sitting between Stamaris's mother and Troy's stepfather. I was wearing my zipper-modified uniform. I had decided not to wear my leg brace that day, because I wanted to be able to march correctly to the stage with the others. Sitting there in my chair, waiting to go forward, my shoulders began to shake. After a moment, I felt my mother lean toward me and she whispered, "If you tremble, I'll goose you." I stopped shaking. When we went to the stage, I bit my lip against the pain and made a correct turn toward Gen. Carl Vuono, then the army chief of staff. I forced my arms to my sides to stand at attention, trying not to show how much it hurt. Vuono presented me with a Prisoner of War Medal and a Purple Heart. "You have paid a steep price in the name of freedom," Vuono told us.

When I finally was released from the hospital on March 14, an air force C-21 Lear jet was assigned to return us to Fort Rucker in style. Stamaris had to stay at Walter Reed a little longer, so Kory and I and Troy and his wife were the only passengers on the small jet. When we neared Fort Rucker, we stared eagerly out the windows, pointing out familiar sites on the ground below us. There was the Hanchey airfield and the one at Cairns. There was the range at Fort Rucker where we flew helicopters. It had been exciting to leave Baghdad, it had been great to arrive in Riyadh and Washington, but this was the best.

There were two open convertibles waiting for us. Kory and I got in one and the Dunlaps climbed in the other. Almost the entire population of Daleville, Alabama, the little town outside Fort Rucker, turned out to welcome us home. The signs in front of store after store read, "Welcome Home Maj. Cornum and Sgt. Dunlap." I knew someone on almost every corner, and I tried to wave with my broken arms. I felt strange being the center of attention, and Troy and I were not prepared for this reception. When we stopped, thousands of people filed by to shake our hands. Every time someone took my hand or tried to hug me, I felt deep pain in my arms, but we couldn't turn them away. There were former POWs from other wars and veterans from Vietnam and World War II. Some of them cried when they saw us, and one group of veterans gave Troy an old patch from the 509th Pathfinders, which was his unit. The military people could understand what we had gone through, but they often have a hard time expressing emotion. This was an exception, though, and the tears flowed freely.

I began to realize that these people, soldiers and civilians, were crying not only for me and Troy but for all of the soldiers of all of the wars. People came out and cheered not only for us as individuals, but for what we represented, which was every man and woman who went to the desert. We had done something remarkable: being shot down and living to tell about it is as close as a soldier can come to returning from the dead. All of the former POWs had become symbols of something greater—symbols of all the people who had served, and especially of those who had died. That made me feel proud, but I also felt an enormous responsibility.

After an hour of hugs and handshakes, I just had to leave, and we drove back to the airport to fly to Eglin Air Force Base, where Kory worked and where I was to be admitted for surgery. In the air, the pilot called the tower and requested clearance to fly over our house. "We've got an ex-POW and her husband on board and she wants to see their farm," the pilot explained over the radio.

The answer came back: "You are cleared for whatever you want to do."

That was how we always were received after we got home: Anything we needed, we received. I never heard anyone say "no" or "can't." We flew low circles over the farm, saw the house and our neighbor's fields. When we touched down at Eglin, again there was a welcoming crowd, mostly people from Kory's wing who had not gone to the war. More flowers, handshakes, and love. The homecoming truly was wonderful, but the only thing I really wanted to do was go home. Somehow I felt that this ordeal would finally be over if I just got home. We escaped for a while and stopped at the kennel to see my dog, Shemya, who is mostly wolf and all energy. Everyone was afraid she would be too excited and knock me down, but she knew right away that I was injured and threw herself on her back so I could scratch her stomach. My finger was wrapped in a bandage, and Shemya took it gently in her big mouth and just held it for a moment.

There were "Welcome Home" signs all over our town of DeFuniak Springs. When we arrived at the house, we found that our neighbors had cleaned everything, stocked the shelves with food, and cut the grass. I managed to slip away for a minute and go alone into our bedroom. I sat on the edge of our bed and stared at our wedding picture on the wall. My eyes got misty, but I felt stronger, recharged. I had to see the house, to sit there for a minute, to appreciate all I had risked losing.

There was a party that night for us at the home of Air Force Major Bill Cherry, my orthopedic surgeon at Eglin, and his wife, Kim. Our friend Opie Davis was there; I had called him at three in the morning from the *Mercy,* and I remember his voice as one of the happiest I'd ever heard. Bill showed everyone there, including the guy who was going to give me anesthesia, the steel rod he planned to install in my arm the next day. I urged them all to stay sober, but I think they ignored me.

On March 15 I had surgery to have the steel rod placed in my left arm. A screw was used to attach a chunk of bone in my finger. We had to put off fixing my knee until my arms were strong enough to use crutches, which was still several months away. I was released from the hospital after four days, and the phone did not stop ringing. There were calls from reporters and friends and one call from my boss, Col. David Karney, asking if I could come in to speak to a group of flight surgeons the very next day. I dreaded the idea of bending my broken body to fit into a car for several hours, but he said he would send a helicopter for me. The next day a Black Hawk, just like the one that had crashed, touched down in our field. I wrestled into my flight suit and boots and stiffly climbed aboard.

"Does this make you nervous?" one of the pilots asked me over the headset when we were flying.

"Getting in the aircraft doesn't make me nervous," I said, "but you're so high! I haven't flown this high in a helicopter in years." Most of the time in Saudi and always during the war, we had flown below fifty feet. Now we were at two thousand feet, and I thought my nose would bleed. The pilot laughed and went down lower, which made me feel better.

I enjoyed being with my colleagues at the lunch, although I had to be fed sitting at the head table. One of the people next to me told me, "Rhonda, I don't know what you did here. I mean the pilots just love you."

"I guess that's because I like pilots better than doctors and flying better than hospitals," I said. That was not a very politically astute remark to make in a room full of doctors, but it was true.

"I'm really lucky," I told the audience. "I'm lucky not just because of surviving this wreck, although I certainly was lucky there, but I'm really lucky because every job I've had in the army has gotten better and better and better, and I've always had what I thought was the best job in the army. When I worked in the Aeromedical Research Laboratory, I thought it was the best job available. Until I went to war with an attack battalion. That is really the best job in the army."

12

For several months after we got home, life never slowed down. I was amazed at the invitations we received to participate in all kinds of functions, from baseball games and parades to elegant dances. I also was asked to speak dozens of times about my experience. I had no illusions that I was any smarter than I had been before I got stuck in Iraq, and I was somewhat concerned that I would disappoint the people who invited us, but I did enjoy talking about my experiences.

One of the first parties we were invited to after returning home was hosted by Regan's bus driver, whose son, Sfc. Jody Foy, was a tank platoon sergeant during the war. Jody and I had exchanged Christmas cards and letters in Saudi Arabia, but we never lived on the same piece of desert and I had not been able to see him. At the party, as we were drinking iced tea and eating hamburgers, Jody told everyone about his final mission in Iraq. His orders were to take an Iraqi ammunition supply point where an American aircraft had been shot down. They were to blow up everything and everyone unless the Iraqis surrendered immediately. The Iraqis didn't surrender, however, and there was a tank battle. Jody and his men won, and afterward, searching through the battlefield, they came across the wreckage of a helicopter scattered across the desert floor.

I stood there listening to the story, a smile of recognition on my face as Jody described the scene. "You know," I told him, "that was my helicopter."

He had had no idea, but the news sweetened the victory for him.

Hearing the story also made me feel satisfied. I didn't want to seek revenge against an entire population, but I was happy to hear we'd gotten the guys who shot down my aircraft and killed five of my crew. "Glad you did it," I told Jody. "Great job."

The first Saturday after being released from the hospital, I was invited to the opening game of the Little League season in Freeport, Florida, which is even smaller than DeFuniak Springs. Kory and I rode in the parade, which consisted of the mayor in the town's one police car, the one fire engine, and all the Little League teams riding in pickup trucks. Since I couldn't bend my elbows, the parents let me place the ball on a ball stand instead of throwing out the first pitch. The town was incredibly supportive, and we were glad to feel a part of our local community again.

I also was invited to the opening game of the Oakland A's against the Minnesota Twins. I was asked to throw out the first pitch there, too, but at first I declined because my right arm was still in a brace and not working very well. The organizers told me stories of people who had thrown some pretty miserable pitches, and apparently they really wanted me to try. So I practiced and practiced with a tennis ball in our backyard. I had to throw underhanded for the game, but my pitch made it to the plate.

At a convention of newspaper editors, Kory and I spoke after CNN's Peter Arnett and Vice President Dan Quayle. Along with the Dunlaps and a group of other Desert Storm veterans, we flew to Los Angeles for the fiftieth anniversary of the USO with Bob Hope. There were military functions, too, and at the meeting of the Army Aviation Association of America, I saw Col. Tom Garrett, the commander of the 101st Aviation Brigade, the unit with which the 229th went to war. That continuity of seeing wartime friends and colleagues back home has been very important, as if I couldn't really believe people had made it back until I actually saw them one by one.

The mailbox along the dirt road to our farm filled up almost every day with cards and letters. People I knew well wrote me, but so did people I had not heard from in years and people I had never met. Every single letter included a heartfelt "Welcome Home." I tried to answer them all. One of my favorites was from Mike Pandol, the young lieutenant known as "Hammer" who had wanted my medics to load rockets on his helicopters. On March 9, he wrote from Saudi:

Dear Major Mom:

Just a quick note. I hope you're feeling well at this point in the "ball game." If not, I'm sure you can self-prescribe something to make your day. Whatever, I hope you're intact with all your parts functioning.

The information on this side of the lake is still sketchy about your downing . . . the scene was very hard for some of the troops to handle. I cleared the bodies for booby traps and Doc Homan checked for vitals. We found your flight vest and helmet. The sensitive items were collected. I then rigged the aircraft to blow in place.

Needless to say, I was relieved not to find you at the scene. It was my solemn intent that I would recover my men and you. Initially, Lt. Col. Bryan refused to let me go. I guess after attempting to stow away on board the aircraft, he decided I wouldn't be denied. Everyone cheered and cried when we found out about the "Three Amigos." Our worst fear was that you would remain an MIA.

I guess Lance said it best when he remarked about going off to pray alone. He said, "God, I never asked you for anything in Vietnam, but I'm asking you for something now. Please let her make it through this." At that point he said he knew God had answered his prayer, and that you were safe. I guess that kind of sums up how we all feel about you. You scared the hell out of us. Regardless, we love you and we're happy you made it out.

Just one question before I close. The boys and I were sitting around "shooting the bull" and we were wondering, how do you wipe your ass with two broken arms?

                                        Hammer

We also began to get letters from the news media asking for interviews. A supermarket tabloid even offered ten thousand dollars for my story. The letter said many people had a misconception of the tabloid, thinking it only covered UFOs and crazy things, when in fact it covered women's issues and was very supportive of the war. We declined the offer. We also got a letter from Jane Pauley, who was a little miffed that I had never heard of her. She came out to the farm and did an excellent interview. Every reporter wanted to be the first to interview me, and that caused a few problems. A writer for a well known magazine came down and stayed at a hotel the night before our interview was scheduled. We talked about the magazine donating the money to a scholarship fund for the children of the men killed in the crash. The night before the interview, I innocently took a call from *USA Today,* and their story ran the next day. The magazine reporter got mad, saying I was "no longer a cover," and never called again. Oh well. I got a crash course about competition in the news media.

At the end of April, I went back to work for about two weeks. My arms were healed enough to drive, but still weren't strong enough to allow me to use crutches, which I would need after knee surgery. I was relieved to be independent again, at least able to feed myself, brush my hair and teeth, dial a telephone, and perform the million activities of daily living that most of us take for granted. Returning to my cluttered, windowless office for the first time in nine months was strange, especially since everything was exactly as I had left it, down to the little yellow notes stuck on the door telling me to call this person or that. People asked me questions as if I had never been gone: "What do you want to do with the report for this meeting?" they would ask, but I had trouble even remembering what old experiment they were talking about. For my colleagues, life was continuing as we had left it. For me, everything felt new. Some of the old things were hard to take seriously. For example, we've always had a regulation that a pilot should have eight hours of uninterrupted sleep before flying a mission. Even before the war, I thought that was kind of silly, except as a way to keep commanders from abusing people, but now, after we had been grateful for a few hours' napping on the ground underneath the boom of a helicopter, the regulation seemed completely unrealistic.

The odd feelings I had at the office gave me an inkling that maybe I had changed. I attributed them to my being post-surgery or post-deployment. Maybe everyone feels different after being away for most of a year, no matter where they go or what they do. I didn't think much about it, but the feeling has persisted.

The sunny day in April when the 2-229th came back from Saudi Arabia was one of the most emotional days for me. Lieutenant Colonel Bryan had called from Saudi, so I knew everyone was safe, but I needed to see them all again. The homecoming was a big event at Fort

Rucker, and the entire post stood in formation on the grassy parade ground. All the families of the returning soldiers sat in the bleachers, fidgeting anxiously, waiting for their loved ones to be dismissed by Major General Ostovich. I had dressed in a flight suit and stood alongside the general with Troy, who was wearing chocolate-chip fatigues. I strained to recognize people as the three hundred men and women marched in front of us and stood at parade rest. When the ceremony finally finished, everyone fell out of formation and dashed across the grass to meet their families.

The scene reminded me of the day in August the year before, when the same families had gathered in the parking lot to say goodbye. This time the tears were not of fear and sadness, but of relief and joy, although all of us, soldiers and families, had aged in nine months. The significance of our being shot down was best stated by Rucie Moore, the young pilot I had danced with on our way to Saudi. His company had been executing an attack on a bridge over the Euphrates when he heard the radio message that "Bengal one-five" had been shot down and "Doc was on board." Rucie told me, "You know, it didn't seem real until then. It was like going to the range, or killing tanks in the simulator. All of a sudden it was real. There were enemy guys out there trying to kill us."

Troy and I wanted to hang back a little after the ceremony, to give people a chance to be alone with their families, but we were dying to join in the hugging and happy reunions. CW4 Bruce Miller, an Apache instructor, came up to me and said, "Hey Doc, there's someone here who really wants to see you." I thought maybe he was going to introduce me to his mother, but after following him about ten steps, there was Lance, a look of pure joy glowing on his face. Luckily my arms didn't hurt anymore, because I got the biggest, longest hug in the world. A friend took a picture of us, and it will always be one of my favorites. We were home.

Troy and I visited that day. He was back with his unit and was his old, gung-ho self. I was happy to learn that Troy's wife had gotten pregnant shortly after we returned home, as did the wife of Stamaris. Troy and I are still good friends, but our differences, which had been temporarily erased by our intense, shared experience, are more noticeable. I've gone back to being a medical corps officer, and he to being an infantryman. It's more obvious that I'm thirty-seven and he is still twenty-one. We stay in touch, but we don't seem to have as much to say to each other. For Christmas I gave Troy two eleven-by-fourteen-inch framed pictures that I knew he would like. One is a shot of the tail of our helicopter lying on the ground in Iraq and the other is of the entire crash site.

I had more surgery in May, this time for an anterior cruciate ligament graft in my right knee. Again, the surgery went well, and I was hobbling on crutches the next day. The only problem was being stuck in a knee brace for another six weeks, and once again needing help to get in and out of the car or the tub. After being injured for ten weeks, I had lost most of the muscle in both legs, and I struggled to build my strength. I will admit to being discouraged a few times, wondering if I would ever be my old self again. The frustrating thing was to be weak and not be able to do anything about it. I wasn't happy unless I could swim, go to the gym, do exercises, walk, or ride a bicycle. Almost a year after the wreck, I finally was able to start running again, beginning with a quarter of a mile and building up to longer distances. I felt pain, especially in my little finger, but only when I thought about it. There are two secrets to my relatively quick recovery. First, I have good genetics, which means I heal fast. Second, I was in good shape before the wreck and had been running four to six miles a day.

While I was recovering at home, we had many visits from friends who were concerned about me, but they also came to ask: "How's the airplane coming?" In the summer of 1989, a year before going to Saudi, Kory and I had bought a Glasair III kit, which is an all-composite, high-performance, two-seat aircraft. Before we left for Saudi, working on the airplane had been our entire social life, and we started work again when we returned home. Almost all of our friends are pilots, and many of them have put quite a few layers of fiberglass on the plane. While we were in Saudi waiting six months for the war to begin, Kory and I had both remarked that it was too bad we couldn't bring the airplane. With so much time and all those bored maintenance guys, we could have finished the plane and flown it home. The Glasair company sent us newsletters while we were in the desert, so we kept up on other plane builders.

Glasair owners from around the world gather at the annual meeting of the Experimental Aircraft Association, and Kory and I were asked to participate in the "fly-in" and air show in Oshkosh, Wisconsin. They had quite a "Desert Storm" representation, from General Horner to a stealth fighter pilot to our friends Lance and Dale Storr, a former POW who was our hot-tub pal on board the USS *Mercy*. Another aviator there was Bob Schumaker, who was shot down in Vietnam and held eight years, making him the second-longest-held prisoner in that war. The dinner was an emotional time for all of us, and we came to appreciate what a tight community has been formed by the people who build airplanes.

Actually the entire community of pilots is very close, and we were welcomed with open arms. Troy Dunlap, Dan Stamaris, and I received the rare "Citation of Honor" from the Daedalien Society, a fraternity of military pilots, named for the mythical craftsman who built wings for himself and his son, Icarus. I also was named a member of the "River Rats," a fraternity of fighter pilots, mostly from Vietnam. We went to their meeting in San Antonio in the spring and traded war stories, which got better and better over multiple margaritas. My pilot friends and I have had a lot of laughs about a "girl" having the best war stories and scars to show in the officers' club.

Within the pilot community, there is a tight fraternity of former POWs with both formal and informal networks to help each other. We all appreciate being able to talk with someone who has "been there." We new members of the fraternity are lucky to have been captives for only a short time. While the lessons and fears are essentially the same, we didn't have to spend years learning, and enduring, them, only days or weeks. I never realized how many former POWs there are, even right near our home. One man who works nearby in an auto parts store is a former POW from Vietnam, but that had never really registered with me before I was captured. Now I feel a bond with him and with the other Vietnam vets. For the first time, many of them are able to open up to me about their experiences, seeing me not as a voyeur but as a participant. My habit is to encourage people I care about, as a friend or as a doctor, to talk about bad things that have happened to them, but normally the doctor in me is looking for mental pathology. Now, when I talk with other veterans, we can share experiences and feelings.

While the spring and summer went by in a blur of surgeries, convalescent leave, and "functions," on August 1 I went back to work in earnest. A year before, I had been selected for Command and General Staff College, but I convinced the army (which in turn convinced the air force) to let me attend the air force equivalent Air Command and Staff College. The air force school was at Maxwell Air Force Base in Alabama, which would allow me to drive home on the weekends to be with Kory and Regan. Going to the army school would have meant moving to Fort Leavenworth, Kansas.

The courses at both schools are similar: military theory and practice, history, political science, and ethical issues, but the air force school was something of a culture shock for me and the other forty-four "exchange" officers from the army. I had an advantage being married to an air force officer, but the worlds still are different. I was the first medical corps officer they had ever had at the school, so it might have been a culture shock for them as well. There were times when the barriers between the services broke down, however. I remember one warm humid morning walking across the lawn to class. An air force major whom I had never met put out her hand and said, "I just wanted to say welcome home." She put her arms around me and cried.

I was not allowed to leave the school very often during the year, but I was permitted to attend a "Victory Award" ceremony chaired by President and Mrs. Bush for the National Rehabilitation Hospital in Washington, D.C. Each year, the awards are presented to "individuals who best exemplify exceptional strength and courage in the face of adversity." The awards that year were sponsored by the state of Kuwait, a country and society that itself was emerging after being held hostage for eight months, and doing so with dignity and courage. I think the Kuwaitis were using this opportunity to thank the United States. The other winners were baseball player Jim Abbott, who was born without a right hand; actor Billy Barty, who founded Little People of America; Rep. Charles Bennett of Florida, who despite having polio had not missed a House vote since June 4, 1951; Norm Crosby, whose hearing was damaged by depth charges on a submarine; actress Sandy Duncan, who had a brain tumor; and singer Gloria Estefan, who was injured in a bus crash. I accepted the award on behalf of all the disabled veterans of America, who must face each day with determination and the will to overcome adversity. The next day, Mrs. Bush invited us to the White House for tea and a pleasant chat.

December 7, 1991, was the fiftieth anniversary of the attack on Pearl Harbor, and also the date of the Army-Navy game. The military academy at West Point put on a commemorative half-time show, inviting a veteran from World War II, Korea, Vietnam, Grenada, Panama, and Desert Storm. I was asked to narrate the poem "A Soldier." Like "Taps" and the national anthem, the poem sends chills down my spine with its declaration: "I

am that which others did not want to be. I went where others feared
to go and did what others failed to do." I was doubly honored to recite the poem in a stadium filled with every cadet from West Point
and every midshipman from the Naval Academy. I have always taken
my responsibility as a role model for junior officers and enlisted troops
very seriously, but the duty seems greater now that so many more of
them know who I am.

Over Christmas vacation, Kory, Regan, and I were invited to visit
Kuwait as guests of the Ministry of Defense. It was one of the best
trips I've ever made, and the first family vacation we had taken in a
long time. We were able to meet people from all walks of life, from
princes to doctors in modern hospitals and enlisted soldiers serving
in the Kuwaiti army. One night, while returning to our hotel, our driver
pulled up to a building that reminded me of a nursing home. I could
see old men inside, talking and playing dominoes.

"Come, come," the driver insisted, using his only phrase of English.

The old men invited me to sit with them and explained in Arabic
how to play dominoes. Most people didn't know who I was, but being American was enough to make me an instant friend. Someone served
us hot, sweet tea, just like the "chai" I remembered from Iraq. I sipped
the tea and told Kory, "This stuff was the only good thing that happened to me as a POW."

I saw the reality of the brutal occupation of Kuwait, including the
"resistance house," where freedom fighters had died defending their
country. The walls are splashed with their blood, and the house has
been preserved as a memorial. I also noticed yellow flags flying throughout
the city, grim reminders that there are more than 2,000 Kuwaitis still
being held in Iraq or unaccounted for. Knowing the pain that "missing in action" caused my family, I grieve for the families of these men
and women, and can only hope we will not consider the war truly over
until their fate is known.

Despite the horror the Kuwaitis have endured, they were rapidly
rebuilding and apparently have discovered a new pride and feeling of
solidarity, much as we in the United States experienced. Like the Stars
and Stripes here, Kuwaiti flags were flying over most of the houses
that I saw; people assured me this was not true before the war. As I
did, the Kuwaitis learned to appreciate freedom more after having
temporarily lost it.

Part of my responsibility is to understand what happened to me and help others learn from my experience. This is similar to what we always do in the army after an exercise or an operation: an after-action report of "lessons learned." I have some lessons that I learned from my six months in Saudi Arabia and my week as a prisoner of war in Iraq. The lessons are personal, professional, and I suppose political. People have asked how I am different or how the experience changed me, and I have to say that I don't think I've had any profound changes. Some people, when they have a brush with death, vow to change their lives or do things differently. I was a prisoner for only eight days, and the experience already feels like a brief chapter in my life. Instead, the lessons I learned confirmed many of the ideas I had before the war. One positive outcome was the opportunity to appreciate what I have, both in the personal sense of my family and in the broader sense of being an American. I also appreciate living in a small town. Our neighbors, our friends, took care of everything for us while we were gone, and they have been wonderful since we returned. We had no right to expect that. I have been amazed and very grateful.

Being a patient for the first time taught me some important lessons about medicine and being a doctor. Never before had I paid sufficient attention to the nursing staff, but nurses provided some of my most important care in Iraq and after I was freed. I will never again underestimate the contribution of nurses, physical therapists, and other staff. Some people suggested that I might become more sensitive to my patients as a result of being a patient myself. Maybe. I do know that I was the best source of information about what was wrong with me, not just because I am a doctor, but because I was the one with the broken bones. I also am now acutely aware of the feeling of helplessness that patients must endure. On the other hand, I probably will be even less tolerant of a patient who feels sorry for himself. I have never liked whining (remember the sign in our aid station). Now I'm absolutely sure that whining does no good and might even slow the healing process.

My confidence level as a doctor received a boost from being in the desert, where I could not always rely on modern equipment or the second opinions of more senior doctors. If there was a problem, I was expected to solve it, and I did. I realize now that the training I have received in the army is excellent and truly prepared me for the real thing. I'm glad I went to the military medical school, where they stress the things we actually faced in the desert and the role of the "battalion surgeon" during war. I also saw many examples of truly selfless behavior among my colleagues. Teams of optometrists came to fit all our pilots who needed glasses with contact lenses so they could fly with the newest gas masks, and teams from Medical Research and Development Command taught refresher courses on treating chemical casualties. The teams lived and worked under very primitive conditions but never complained. Another example is a senior air force physician, the expert in night vision goggles, who gave classes all over the theater. He was tasked only with talking to air force pilots about the goggles, but he spoke to everyone from Riyadh to tents in the desert with the army's 82d Airborne Division, because he wanted all our pilots to have the best chance to make it back.

Were there problems? Of course. One night before the war a soldier ran up, breathless, to tell me a young man had fallen and was paralyzed. I ran down to the basement of the parking garage and found a group of people standing over a scared young soldier who said he could not feel or move his legs. One of my medics went to bring a pickup truck with a stretcher, and I knelt down to examine the soldier with another doctor who had arrived before me. We thought he might have fractured his lower spine when he fell on a large ridge of concrete. I held the soldier's hand and reassured him, but I knew he would have to be airlifted to a hospital.

We put him on a spine board and a stretcher, drove him out of the garage onto the flight line, and loaded him onto a waiting helicopter. The pilot asked me where to go, and I told him the Air Transportable Hospital in Dhahran. After a twenty-minute flight, the patient was in the emergency room, where he was X-rayed and seen by the orthopedic surgeon. He was terrified, afraid he would never walk again, and he asked me to stay with him at the hospital while he was evaluated. I spent the night and got a ride the next day back to King Fahd.

When I arrived, I learned the brigade surgeon was looking for me. He and the division surgeon were upset that we had taken the patient to an air force hospital instead of to the army's 28th Combat Support Hospital, which was undeniably closer. I explained that I had visited the army's hospital just hours before the soldier fell, and at that time there was no working generator, and thus no X-ray capability. Since the first thing this soldier needed was films, I couldn't see any reason to go there. Apparently that didn't matter. I received a letter shortly after from the division surgeon saying that I had done the wrong thing.

The officers in my chain of command defended my decision, but I was angry that some people seemed more concerned with procedure than with appropriate medical care.

Despite occasional irritation with the system, my experiences were overwhelmingly positive, and have made me more committed than ever to military medicine. As stated in the motto, the goal of military medicine is to "conserve the fighting strength" of the armed forces. Over the years, I have seen the positive impact "medics" can have on morale and readiness, but it was dramatic during the deployment to the Middle East. Maj. Jonathan Letterman, a surgeon in the Union Army, said it best more than a hundred years ago:

> A corps of medical officers was not established solely for the purpose of attending the wounded and the sick. . . . The labors of medical officers cover a more extended field. The leading idea, which should constantly be kept in view, is to strengthen the hand of the Commanding General.

With the daily pressure to provide care for a huge population of dependents and retirees, I am afraid that we sometimes lose sight of that goal. Another goal often forgotten is that military doctors also are soldiers who must be ready for combat. Some people think there is a contradiction between being a doctor and being a soldier, but I certainly don't. As a professional officer, I took an oath to defend the Constitution and to guide my actions with the principles of "duty, honor, country." As a physician, I took an oath to do what is best for my patients to the best of my ability. I haven't found any ethical dilemmas arising from adhering to both. I identify myself as a doctor and as a soldier, and I value both professions equally. Some people think the Hippocratic oath tells us, "Do no harm," but in fact we promise to do no harm to our patients. Nowhere does the oath say a doctor takes on the entire world as patients.

Military medicine does have its share of "Hawkeyes," folks who don't take the military seriously, although they are very serious about medicine. Apart from embarrassing other officers, they do fine in a peacetime environment. When we are not in the field, we basically practice medicine like civilians, especially in the big medical centers. During wartime, however, the commander must have confidence in the medical officer in his unit and on his staff. He needs to know that the physician has the same professional standards, ethics, and experiences as other officers. He needs to know the "Doc" will give him good advice based on the mission of the unit. If the physician is so ignorant of the military that he (or she) doesn't understand the mission, he can't possibly give good advice and will likely not have the plans, equipment, and supplies necessary to provide the best possible care for the soldiers. In my view, like the Union Army's Major Letterman's, that is the real reason for having military physicians.

Another lesson I brought home from the Gulf is that men and women can work well together. Saudi Arabia was a harsh reminder that America is not a Moslem society where women and men must be strictly segregated. Men and women like each other's company, both at home and in the workplace, so I think having men and women in the army actually is a plus. The war did not change the attitudes of the men I know, but then they already had worked with women and know it's possible, even desirable. The war might have changed the attitudes of some men who had never served with women for long periods under difficult circumstances. Part of the problem is generational: older people in the military have a harder time with men and women serving together. The young generations, like Regan and her friends, are used to playing soccer together, studying together, and being friends, not just boyfriends and girlfriends. For many young people, working together in the army is the natural order of things.

The war dramatized the fact that the role of women in the military already has changed. We are no longer nurses and typists serving in rear areas—there were nearly forty-one thousand women in the Gulf working as doctors, nurses, pilots, mechanics, truck drivers, cooks, clerks, intelligence officers, communication experts, and in a host of other specialties. There were women in every part of the theater, from the headquarters of General Schwarzkopf to a few women in the foxholes in Iraq and Kuwait. In my opinion, the war showed that America is ready for army women, all of whom volunteered, to serve throughout the army and not be excluded from combat jobs. Parents back home didn't miss their sons less than their daughters, and kids didn't miss their dads more or less than their moms.

Many people have asked if my opinion about "women in combat" has changed after my experience. In fact, I think exactly what I have always thought, that everyone should be allowed to compete for all available jobs, regardless of race or gender. There is no question that the "average" woman is not as tall, heavy, or strong as the "average" man; we don't need a congressional committee to tell us that. But what does that mean? I'd say it means that if the job requires someone to be tall, heavy, and strong, then fewer women will be competitive than men. But at least let them compete. Who cares what percentage qualifies?—just pick the best. On the other hand, there are many jobs for which height, weight, and strength are irrelevant. We should let all people compete for those jobs as well.

The qualities that are most important in all military jobs—things like integrity, moral courage, and determination—have nothing to do with gender. Everybody in the army—whether he or she enlisted, went to a military academy or ROTC, or received a direct commission— all volunteered to serve. No one has been drafted or otherwise coerced. I believe the military pays members for two things: the jobs they do daily and the willingness to risk their lives if called to war. Personally, I don't think "combat exclusion"—the rule that keeps women out of combat jobs—helps anyone. If I were a male soldier, I would resent women making the same money and holding the same rank but not being responsible for taking the same risks. On the other hand, combat experience is not only an important factor for advancement (as it should be) but ultimately is the reason for having the military. As a female soldier, I would resent being excluded. We preach "equal opportunity" everywhere. I believe we should also be preaching "equal responsibility."

One area of responsibility for everyone, including military people, is having children. Like joining the military, having children is a decision people make, not something that occurs randomly like lightning or cancer. If an individual, male or female, feels that being a parent is not compatible with a military profession, that person certainly has the option of postponing children or changing careers. But I don't believe that the people who feel that parenting and a military life are incompatible should determine everyone else's career or parenting decisions. I am extremely happy with my family and both my professions, the military and medicine. Neither my family nor I feel that my career and family life have been at all incompatible. I am inspired by the fact that Regan and Kory love me and are proud of me not only as a mother and a wife, but also as a doctor and a soldier.

What about all that famous male bonding? Well, when a unit contains only men, you certainly get male bonding. When there are women present, you get male and female bonding. I just call it unit bonding, and it does occur. Whether a unit "bonds" or not is based on many things: the circumstances, the leadership, the threat, and the makeup of the unit's members. When we were in the desert, people got along well and bonded just fine. I've been to war with a combat unit, and the men in our unit did not try to protect the women any more or less than the rest of their comrades. On a personal note, I suspect Troy Dunlap felt no more "protective" of me than I felt of him.

My commanders agreed that the presence of a woman did not hurt our unit's performance. In my Officer Evaluation Report for the period from August 13, 1990, through February 27, 1991, the day we were shot down, Lieutenant Colonel Bryan wrote about me:

> Outstanding performance in combat. Rhonda Cornum is the finest aviation medical officer in the Army. She is a tough, no-nonsense officer who has demonstrated magnificent technical skill combined with outstanding leadership. Rhonda had the most profound impact on the combat effectiveness of my battalion. Rhonda Cornum makes things happen. People follow her anywhere. She goes where the soldiers need her. A true ultimate warrior.

Colonel Garrett, the commander of the 101st Aviation Brigade and my senior rater, added: "Rhonda Cornum is chock full of the right stuff."

My life might have been different if the army didn't have restrictions on women. For one thing, I probably would have gone to flight school had I been allowed to fly attack helicopters instead of just transports. Looking back cynically, I think that might actually have *saved* me from being captured. During the war, we didn't have any Apache or Cobra attack pilots captured, but the Iraqis did get my lightly armed Black Hawk. As a medical officer, my career has not been much different because I am a woman. I have, however, been denied certain assignments—the 82d Airborne, Special Forces, and a Ranger battalion—because women were not allowed.

Being a woman also prevented me from going to the Persian Gulf on a deployment a few years before the war with Iraq. That time the army asked for flight surgeons to serve on a navy barge where our OH-58D helicopters were based. Because I was the flight surgeon for the 58D instructor company at Fort Rucker, I knew many of the pilots and a fair amount about the mission and their aircraft. I volunteered and was recommended by the commander of the hospital at Fort Rucker. We were told no, that there were no facilities for women on the barge. I complained to the army's legal office, the Judge Advocate General, and then the decision was blamed on the navy admiral who "owned" the barge. Eventually, everyone agreed I could go but would have to stay in a hotel in Bahrain instead of on the barge. That would have made it too difficult to do my job, however, and I would have been a burden on the pilots who would have had to chauffeur me every day. Later, the pilots who lived on the barge told me that a group of women did spend the night: the Dallas Cowboy cheerleaders. Hmmm. Would that happen today? Who knows.

Less than a year after returning from the war, I listened to a very senior officer tell a room full of soldiers why women could not serve in some special operations units. Comparing the "elite" troops and their missions to the Kentucky Derby, the officer said you could probably take a mule and beat it around the course, but it would never win. During the question time, I pointed out that fillies occasionally win the Kentucky Derby and asked about the role of women in special operations. He replied that there were women in special operations—lawyers and support personnel—but he had never met a woman who could be a Navy SEAL. We fly incredible missions behind enemy lines, he said, going fifteen feet above the ground completely blacked out with night vision goggles. I wondered what he thought the rest of us did; he obviously did not know who I was. That kind of talk not only makes us "fillies" mad, but also all the plain old army "mules" who supposedly can't handle special operations.

The role of women in the military has been changing fast. My husband Kory was in the first class at the Air Force Academy, the class of 1980, that had women cadets. A few of his classmates were bitter about women being there. He saw how the women were singled out and measured by a tougher standard than the men, but they still did well. Kory thinks women ought to be able to do any job they are qualified for in the military, as long as there are no quotas for the number of women and no lowering of standards to help them. He is especially adamant about quotas, after seeing how they worked, or didn't work, in the air force. Under one policy, the wing staff had to have 1.8 women, whatever that means, even though the women were not necessarily qualified. I agree with him that it would be better to have no quotas and simply accept the fact that sometimes three or four women will be on the staff and sometimes there won't be any. Kory and I firmly believe that the standards should not be lowered for weaker or less qualified people, regardless of gender or anything else.

Although I like to say that my own life has hardly changed because of the war, there have been new feelings and sensations. The first time I realized something was different was while riding in a parade in San Antonio. Kory and I were in an open car waving and smiling at the crowd. We drove past tall buildings and parking garages filled with people watching the parade. I turned to Kory and commented wryly, "You know, this would be a great place for a sniper to get us." I never would have thought of that before being captured. I am frequently asked if I have flashbacks of being a prisoner. The story would be better if I said yes, but it isn't true. Only once, while walking the six-mile loop around the flight line at Maxwell Air Force Base, did I have an overwhelming sense of being back. The white moon, the smell of the moist air, the runway lights and chain link fence along the quiet road—everything seemed the same as walking the flight line in Saudi Arabia. I sat down with my back to the fence for a few minutes and relived some of our deployment. Rather than being frightening, the experience was comforting.

My family has recovered, and if anything, we are closer now after what happened. I worried a little about Regan, but she already is tougher than I was at that age. She has suffered more loss than I had as a girl, and that has made her stronger. If Regan had been captured instead of me, she would have tried to reason her way out, and she certainly would never have cried either. She always has felt the importance of being strong. When she was eight or nine years old, she fell when she was jumping one of our horses, Granny. Granny stepped on Regan's foot, and Kory wanted to take her to the hospital because he thought the foot might be broken. Regan had a soccer tournament that afternoon and was afraid she would miss the game. "If my foot's broken," she said, "it'll still be broken after the game, and I can see the doctor then."

My relationship with Kory picked right up again. It would have been much harder for him to deal with the situation if he had not been in Saudi Arabia. Being there made him better able to understand what I had gone through, and made it less scary for him. When we returned home, he hovered at first, trying to make me more of an invalid than I wanted to be. While I tried to push myself to the limit, to exercise more to heal faster, he wanted to calm me down, open all the doors for me, and make me wear a brace even if I was going across the room.

Our future is untold. My plans were not really changed by the war, although my confidence level is higher. I admire people who can turn a disadvantage into an advantage: that's what I hope to do. I remember being a little girl and reading about a husband and wife tending a garden. She tells him, "If I can do anything a woman can do, and you can do anything a man can do, then together we can do anything." The next step for me is to find another challenge, something demanding and worthwhile.

The entire experience of the war was a challenge that will be tough to match: deploying to the desert, caring for so many soldiers, fighting a war, and surviving as a prisoner. When I was a girl, I remember fantasizing about being lost in the wild and having to survive. Walking through the woods with my dog, I imagined what it would be like if I were five hundred miles from civilization and not just three miles from my house. I'd debate the survival tools I'd need in the woods, comparing how heavy they were with their value to me in the wild. Or I imagined being on a plane that crashed in the arctic or being shipwrecked on a desert island. In my imagination I was like Robinson Crusoe, and being stranded alone was not horrible; it was fun, a challenge. I wanted the ultimate challenge, something where the stakes were higher than a game of cards. I don't know that I ever really expected to be faced with it, but at least it wasn't a foreign idea when it occurred.

One night in Iraq, after an exhilarating day of clearing bunkers and taking prisoners, Mike Pandol and I talked about this notion of challenge. He told me about his many years in the army, first in the military police, later as a warrant officer instructor pilot, and most recently as a lieutenant platoon leader. He said that that day clearing Iraqi bunkers was the best day of his career. He already knew he was a good pilot and officer, now he felt like a good soldier. I know exactly what he meant: I knew I was a good doctor, scientist, and athlete. Now I feel like a real member of the brotherhood. I don't think of myself as a combatant—those are the people who physically engage the enemy with weaponry—but I feel confident now that I could have been.

The greatest challenge of all was being forced into a situation where I had lost control. My life has been a series of efforts to gain control, to dominate a situation and move on to something else. I don't even like to be a passenger in a car; I like to be the driver. That's why I want to be a surgeon; that's why I like riding horses; and that's probably why I didn't get along with my parents when I was a teen-ager. When I joined the army, I gave up some of my control, but the decision was voluntary and helped me reach a greater goal.

I had always wondered what it would be like to lose that control, to have it taken away. Now I know. Being a prisoner of war is the ultimate loss of control, especially for a POW with two broken arms. The best analogy I can think of is rape, and both experiences have the potential to be devastating. Being a POW is the rape of your entire life. But what I learned in those Iraqi bunkers and prison cells is that the experience doesn't have to be devastating, that it depends on you. Other POWs, and most recently the hostages released from Lebanon, have found the same thing: you can *give* up control of your mind, but no one can take it away from you. Your captors can torture you and even kill you, but you still have control as long as you can think. I remember wondering if my body would ever be strong again, if my arms would ever heal, if I would ever be able to run again. I wasn't sure how I would adjust to being slower or permanently disabled, but I convinced myself that as long as my brain was working, I would be fine. I think the idea was best expressed by David Jacobsen, who was held hostage in Lebanon: "As long as you have your brain, your mind, you are free."

I am very, very blessed to be here, free, today.